P9-CQR-835

Praise for Nikolai Grozni's *Turtle Feet*

"Having quit music school, Grozni takes vows of celibacy, memorizes texts and strives not to kill the bugs that carry malaria. For a time, his renunciation of art, sex, and empiricism seem worth the sacrifice. His is not the romantic Buddhism of five-star tourists and college freshmen. Subsisting in filth near the Dalai Lama's compound, he begins to question his 'giving up piano after fifteen years of practice, ending friendships, destroying my parents' hopes . . . to be humiliated by some belligerent old monk who hated Westerners and couldn't talk to people unless he was debating.' The descriptions of India's daily grind . . . are intimate and precise."   —*The New York Times Book Review*

"[A] thoughtful, sharply funny memoir . . . Though Grozni's quest ends short of nirvana, his elegant story makes it clear that the ride and not the destination is the source of joy."   —*People*

"The book is hilarious, a phrase not often associated with the memoirs of monks."   —*Wisconsin State Journal*

"This is a rare and wonderful book, unlike anything I've ever read before. Rich in detail and humor, with a quirky and exotic cast of characters, it's an exquisitely written journey through life in a Tibetan monastery and village, where a brilliant young Western monk encounters discipline, freedom, Buddhism, and himself."   —Anne Lamott, author of *Grace (Eventually)*

"Funny, insightful, musical, and poetic. One wouldn't expect anything less than that from a Bulgarian, jazz-playing Buddhist Tibetan monk."

—Etgar Keret, author of *The Nimrod Flip Out*

"Readers who take a Zen approach to the text will probably get sucked into monastic simplicity and Buddhist philosophy . . . something original and special. Zen and the art of writing a pretty cool book."   —*Kirkus Reviews*

"*Turtle Feet* is a remarkable book. . . . Yes, it's a spiritual journey filled with beautiful insights—but it's also a funny and gritty tale of dysentery, stoner roommates, cranky monks, and flirty nuns. I felt enlightened for having read it."   —A. J. Jacobs, author of *The Year of Living Biblically*

"There are passages of beauty about the nature of the mind and existence that few books about Buddhism can rival."   —*Publishers Weekly*

Turtle Feet

THE MAKING AND UNMAKING
OF A BUDDHIST MONK

Nikolai Grozni

RIVERHEAD BOOKS

NEW YORK

RIVERHEAD BOOKS
Published by the Penguin Group
Penguin Group (USA) Inc.
375 Hudson Street, New York, New York 10014, USA
Penguin Group (Canada), 90 Eglinton Avenue East, Suite 700, Toronto, Ontario M4P 2Y3, Canada
(a division of Pearson Penguin Canada Inc.)
Penguin Books Ltd., 80 Strand, London WC2R 0RL, England
Penguin Group Ireland, 25 St. Stephen's Green, Dublin 2, Ireland
(a division of Penguin Books Ltd.)
Penguin Group (Australia), 250 Camberwell Road, Camberwell, Victoria 3124, Australia
(a division of Pearson Australia Group Pty. Ltd.)
Penguin Books India Pvt. Ltd., 11 Community Centre, Panchsheel Park, New Delhi—110 017, India
Penguin Group (NZ), 67 Apollo Drive, Rosedale, North Shore 0632, New Zealand
(a division of Pearson New Zealand Ltd.)
Penguin Books (South Africa) (Pty.) Ltd., 24 Sturdee Avenue, Rosebank, Johannesburg 2196,
South Africa

Penguin Books Ltd., Registered Offices: 80 Strand, London WC2R 0RL, England

The publisher does not have any control over and does not assume any responsibility for author
or third-party websites or their content.

Some things pertaining to time and space have been changed. Some names and identifying
details have been changed. It is important to bear in mind, however, that most Buddhists regard
time, space, names and identifying details as nonexistent.

Copyright © 2008 by Nikolay Grozdinski
Cover design and imaging by Honi Werner
Cover photograph © Jerry Redfern/OnAsia.com/Jupiterimages
Book design by Gretchen Achilles

All rights reserved.
No part of this book may be reproduced, scanned, or distributed in any printed or electronic
form without permission. Please do not participate in or encourage piracy of copyrighted
materials in violation of the author's rights. Purchase only authorized editions.
RIVERHEAD® is a registered trademark of Penguin Group (USA) Inc.
The RIVERHEAD logo is a trademark of Penguin Group (USA) Inc.

First Riverhead hardcover edition: May 2008
First Riverhead trade paperback edition: May 2009
Riverhead trade paperback ISBN: 978-1-59448-376-9

The Library of Congress has catalogued the Riverhead hardcover edition as follows:

Grozni, Nikolai.
  Turtle feet : the making and unmaking of a Buddhist monk / Nikolai Grozni.
    p.   cm.
    ISBN 978-1-59448-984-6
  1. Grozni, Nikolai.   2. Buddhists—Biography.   3. Spiritual biography—
India—Dharamsala.   I. Title.
    BQ960.R645A3   2008   2008006836
    294.3'657092—dc22
    [B]

PRINTED IN THE UNITED STATES OF AMERICA

10 9 8 7 6 5 4 3 2 1

For Tsar

He has chakra wheels engraved on the palms
of his hands and on the soles of his feet; he has
perfectly aligned nails and turtle feet . . .

—From the eighth chapter of Maitreya's *Abhisamaya Alankara*,
describing the body of the Buddha,
translated from the Tibetan by the author

Prologue

We tiptoed to the edge of the giant, kidney-shaped volcanic rock and looked down the vertiginous abyss. From up here the Himalayas appeared subdued, almost shy: their razor-sharp pinnacles were below us; their arms and vertebrae stretched to the horizon, exposed. Shimmering in the reddened six o'clock sun, the cluster of mud houses on the bottom of the valley looked like a reflection on a still lake.

"I have to jump *now*," Tsar announced, unbuckling the paraglider backpack. "As soon as the sun disappears behind the mountains, the temperature will drop, and I'll never get past the border."

I knelt on the ground and helped Tsar unpack the red-and-white-striped paraglider. Studying his face for what I imagined could be the last time, it occurred to me that if he were to die today, he would at least look romantic and adventurous—with a gray three-day beard, long sideburns, and an incongruous patch of white hair twisted over his forehead.

"Here," Tsar said, pulling the very top of the paraglider. "Hold this end and wait until the chute fills up with air. Then let go."

I stood up and stretched out my hands.

"If you don't hear from me in a month, send the letter that I gave you to the Netherlands," Tsar instructed me as he came closer. We held tight. He smelled of nicotine and cheap deodorant.

Looking quickly away to hide his glossy eyes, Tsar pulled a packet of India Kings out of his front pocket and stuck a cigarette in the corner of his mouth.

"My last one," he said, smiling cynically. "Before I step in front of the . . . what do you call it?"

"Firing squad," I offered.

"Right."

Tsar took a few rushed drags, flicked the cigarette into the abyss, and, with his hands in his pockets, sauntered to the edge of the rock.

"I don't know why people are so afraid of dying," he said, dangling one foot over the void. "It only takes a moment."

"A moment for you, and a lifetime of nightmares for me," I countered, feeling like I was going to throw up.

I understood how Tsar felt, though. At this height the world seemed fixed and unreal, without the complications of before and after. Even the string of eagles and few daring crows tracing the slow-moving air currents high up in the mercurial blue seemed strangely stuck in time, their long ellipses suggesting a state of being in which things always *were*, again and again, from past into present, and from present back into past.

"Muzaffarabad must be somewhere in that direction," Tsar observed, studying his compass. "I'll have to veer to the right and glide between those hills over there."

"Do you think you could do that?"

Tsar dismissed my question and put the backpack over his shoulders, pulling down the straps. "I'm ready when you are," he said, looking straight ahead with fierce determination.

I stepped over the deflated chute and put my hand on his shoulder. "Tsar, please think this over one more time. I know how badly you want to escape from India, but this is almost equivalent to suicide. The Indian-Pakistani border is the most heavily guarded in the world. On top of that, we are in Kashmir. There are thousands of soldiers on both sides waiting for an opportunity to fire their guns."

"Come on, Nikola," Tsar said. "Don't ruin my mood. Let me at least enjoy the flight."

I picked up the center of the chute with both hands and walked backwards, allowing the chilly breeze to ruffle inside it. And then Tsar snapped away. It was so unexpected that I almost screamed *Where are you going?* For a second he seemed to fall straight down and I thought that the strings must've gotten tangled up, but the paraglider quickly filled with air and bounced up, veering west, in the direction of the setting sun.

I watched as Tsar entered the canyon that opened up onto what, according to our map, was the Pakistani-controlled part of Kashmir, then walked back to the mountain trail and started running down the hill. It was getting dark and I didn't want to stand there, above the world, when the crackling of the first gunshots echoed throughout the valley.

One

It was eight o'clock in the morning and I was wearing a long cotton skirt, or *shanthab*, a buttonless vest with two bizarre rags hanging under the shoulders like a pair of elephant ears—courtesy of the sixteenth-century Tibetan saint and fashion enthusiast Tsongkhapa—and a fifteen-foot-long prayer shawl, or *zen*, that wrapped around the upper body like a sari. Ani Dawa, a tiny Tibetan nun in her forties, walked ahead of me, leading the way.

"Are you sure you want to do this?" she asked when we reached the ramparts of the Main Temple, where Jogibara Road opened out into a large square, covered with plastic bags and cow dung. "This is your last chance to go back."

I felt the patch of unshaved hair on top of my head with my fingers and nodded.

We entered the monastery compound and started walking upstairs, past Tibetan monks who were pacing up and down the hallways, reciting their textbooks. The overpowering ammonia stench from the lavatories and the smell of insipid cauliflower curry wafting from the kitchen nauseated me, and for a second I caught a glimpse of what it must be like to spend your life in a monastery, waking at five, chanting prayers until seven, going to classes and rushing to lunch, metal plate in hand, followed by more chanting, dinner, an evening debate session in the courtyard, and then your little cell and bedbug-infested sheets.

The abbot's main attendant, a bulky, middle-aged man with an intense expression, greeted us at the top of the staircase.

"Kirti Rinpoche is expecting you," he said and gestured at the open door.

Ani Dawa and I removed our shoes and entered the room. Kirti Rinpoche, the abbot of the monastery who, as his title *Rinpoche* indicated, was believed to be the reincarnation of an important Buddhist figure, sat on a throne made of stacked Tibetan rugs, drinking butter tea from a wooden cup and reading a *pecha*—a traditional Tibetan book consisting of long, loose sheets of paper. Ani Dawa bowed down. I followed her lead. Kirti Rinpoche leaned over and whispered something in his attendant's ear.

"Rinpoche would like to know whether your parents object to your decision to become a monk," the attendant announced solemnly.

"Well, they're not happy, but they aren't going to stop me," I answered. Receiving your parents' consent was one of the prerequisites for becoming a Buddhist monk. When I had called my parents to ask them, formally, if they approved of my decision to lead a celibate life, they had thought that I was being derisive. "If you want to spend your life like a freak, that's your problem," my mom had said.

The attendant relayed my response to the abbot, speaking cordially into his ear, pointing at me, and then pointing to the large world atlas on the wall next to the door.

Kirti Rinpoche tilted back and smiled. He was a frail seventy-year-old man with a gentle expression and a slight tremor in his fingers. When he spoke he lowered his head and looked over the rim of his glasses, as if they were an obstacle and not an aid.

"When did you arrive in India?" he asked me in Tibetan, enunciating carefully.

"Four months ago," I replied.

"You are very lucky to have her as your Tibetan teacher," Rinpoche continued, pointing at Ani Dawa with an open palm. "She is one of the best language instructors in town."

"It's true," I agreed. "She is a great teacher."

Ani Dawa wasn't just my Tibetan language teacher, she was the closest thing that I had to family in India. I practically lived with her and her mother. I went to my room—which was about fifty feet away from hers—only to sleep. When I first started taking lessons with her a week after I had arrived in Dharamsala, she had been reserved and somewhat suspicious, testing me to see if I was really serious or just another Westerner for whom studying Buddhism and Tibetan language was part of a vacation package that also included mountain climbing, spending a night in a cave, and spotting members of the Beastie Boys in local chai shops. After a month of lessons, when Ani Dawa was finally convinced that I was reliable (I hadn't slept with any of her younger girlfriends and cousins, I never got drunk, I meditated, and I spent four or five hours a day memorizing new words) and that I wasn't going to change my mind overnight and go camel riding in Rajasthan, she embraced me as her own son and began to prepare me for my ordination. She gave me a Tibetan booklet explaining the thirty-six vows of a novice monk, took me to a tailor who made two sets of robes suitable for my height, asked Kirti Rinpoche to set a date for the ordination, and, on the morning of the ceremony, shaved most of my hair and cooked a large bowl of rice, cashews, and raisins, which I was supposed to bring to the monastery as an offering.

"Now we start," Kirti Rinpoche announced, placing his wooden cup on the table in front of him.

The abbot's attendant pulled a razor blade out of a secret pocket in his *tonka* and, before I could react, scalped the remaining hair from my skull. Now I was bleeding, which I guess was fine because I was wearing all red anyway.

"Use this," Ani Dawa offered, handing me a scrunched-up handkerchief.

Kirti Rinpoche pulled another voluminous *pecha* from a bookshelf next to his bed, unwrapped the saffron-colored cloth that bound the loose pages, and began reading aloud. My knowledge of written Tibetan (which is archaic) was quite limited at that point, and so I turned to Ani Dawa for help.

"What are they doing?" I asked her.

"They are listing the circumstances that may prevent you from becoming a monk," Ani Dawa replied, hiding her mouth with one hand.

"Can you please name some of these circumstances?"

Ani Dawa was hesitant. "Well, for instance, it is said that you can't become a monk if you have green hair. Or yellow hair."

"What else?"

"You can't be bald, toothless, or have an elephant head. You can't have two heads, pig ears, elephant trunk, one nostril, one tooth, or donkey teeth."

Ani Dawa smiled at Kirti Rinpoche, as a way of apologizing for talking during the ceremony, and then lowered her head, signaling that she was done interpreting for me.

After spending nearly an hour discussing the different physical and mental flaws that barred one's entrance into the monastic community (something I found quite shocking, since the divide ran clearly along caste lines: an untouchable stood a far greater chance of missing his teeth, a finger, or an eye than a Brahmin did), Kirti Rinpoche stopped reading and asked his attendant something that I couldn't decipher. They spoke to each other in Amdo dialect, which was very different from the other two main Tibetan dialects— U-Tsang and Kham—that I had been used to hearing.

"What's the matter?" I whispered.

"They are upset because they've lost their sieve," Ani Dawa explained. "At the time of the Buddha, monks always carried a sieve to purify the water they were drinking. You need to have a sieve during the ordination."

The attendant walked out of the room and returned with a metal colander in hand. "You have to bow down to Rinpoche now," he ordered, out of breath.

I did as I was told, struggling with my *zen*, which spilled on the floor and nearly covered the entire room. The attendant helped me straighten my sagging *shanthab*, annoyed with my clumsiness, and pressed my back, indicating that I should assume a praying mantis position. Kirti Rinpoche took a silver plate from the bookshelf behind him and began tossing handfuls of saffron-colored rice in the air.

"Rinpoche does this to appease the millions of angry goddesses present in the room at the moment," Ani Dawa explained, lowering her voice. "They are angry that you are renouncing the world of desire."

"How vengeful are these goddesses?" I asked Ani Dawa. "Should I expect a mob of naked girls breaking into my room tonight?"

Ani Dawa ignored my question and offered to refill Kirti Rinpoche's cup with warm butter tea.

With that, the ceremony was over. Smiling mysteriously, Rinpoche's attendant produced a miniature copper sundial, showed it to Ani Dawa and me, and stepped out onto the balcony.

"It is very important to record the time of your ordination," Ani Dawa told me. "It's like a birth date. Tomorrow at this time you will be exactly one day old."

Kirti Rinpoche got off his throne, went outside, and bent down to take a closer look at what was happening. The attendant rotated the sundial, trying to catch a shadow, but the Tibetan numbers engraved on the copper disk remained uniformly dark. The sun was a gray halo wrapped in a thick monsoon cloud.

"Why do they have to establish the time using a sundial?" I asked Ani Dawa. "They're both wearing wristwatches!"

"You have to do things the right way," Ani Dawa replied.

Finally, Kirti Rinpoche looked at his watch and inscribed the date and time on a small yellow card: July 11, 11:07 a.m. He paused for a moment, thinking something over, and entered my new name: Lodro Chosang.

"You are now officially a monk," Ani Dawa announced and bowed down to Kirti Rinpoche.

I thanked Kirti Rinpoche and his attendant and exited the room backwards—the proper Tibetan way.

Since it was July, the Himalayas looked like a collapsing mud cake: roads gave way to uprooted crags, fortifications yielded to sinking houses, electricity poles pointed to the horizon, water pipes burst and dug gullies. At the top of the hill, Ani Dawa and I paused to catch our breath. Dharamsala's main street was right below us—a narrow dirt road lined with rows of shops and restaurants stacked upon one another like towers made from a mishmash of incompatible construction sets. A web of telephone wires, dilapidated awnings, and dirty plastic sheets wrapped the street and all the buildings, giving the impression of a village seized by a monster spider. Homeless cows wandered between the vegetable stands, gnawing at cardboard boxes and rotten potatoes. Street dogs, pink and furless, lay about on the ground like bits of tattered rags. Crates of milk, packaged in small, square plastic bags, blocked the entrances to the chai shops and attracted clouds of flies and wasps.

Approaching the housing complex where Ani Dawa and I lived, I saw Purba, one of my closest friends in town, standing in the middle of the road, arms akimbo. Purba was a twenty-seven-year-old Tibetan from Tibet's Amdo region, a tough-talking, swaggering ex-monk with a skeptical smile, glasses, and smooth, chubby hands. Ani Dawa said good-bye to me and went into her house.

"So, you did it," Purba said with a big grin.

"That's right," I answered proudly.

He fell on his knees and bowed down to me, pressing his forehead against the street's mossy surface.

"What the hell are you doing?" I yelled at him, embarrassed.

"This is the first and last time I am showing respect to you," he replied, as he got up and wiped his hands on his jeans. "So, what's your new name?"

"Lodro Chosang."

"Don't tuck it in," Purba said and pulled my vest out of my *shanthab*.

"Why did you do this to yourself? I told you that taking vows is a stupid thing to do."

"Well, maybe I'm stupid, but I had to do it. Life is short. I want to study the Tibetan texts, I want to take classes in the big monasteries. That's why I came here."

Purba walked over to the tiny chai shop owned by my landlord and sat on the front steps.

"Why are you holding yourself like that?" he asked, pointing at my crotch.

"You are not going to believe it but I've had a hard-on ever since I left the monastery. And it really shows through the skirt. It's my own fault, though. I didn't put any underwear on."

Purba chuckled and opened a bag of betel and tobacco mix. "You better get used to it. It's not going to go away for the rest of your life. And now you can't do anything about it."

Purba stuffed the mix in his lower lip and looked at his watch. "Today is Tuesday, isn't it?"

"It is."

"And they shaved your hair?"

"The abbot's attendant did. Just a small patch. I had shaved most of it last night."

"Still." Purba spat between his legs and covered the dark red splotch with his shoes. "It's bad luck to cut your hair on Tuesday. Haven't you noticed? None of the Indian barbers work on Tuesday."

"It seems like I'm starting off on the wrong foot, aren't I?"

Purba disappeared into the chai shop and returned with two cups of milk tea. He blew into his cup, pushing the dark brown layer of cream to the side, and his glasses fogged up.

"Did you know that if you go into a dark room with the intention to have sex with a woman named, say, Ani Dawa, but end up in the wrong bed and have sex with her girlfriend instead, you wouldn't be breaking your vows, technically speaking?"

"Purba, where the hell do you get your information?"

"I've read it in the texts. In your mind you think you are having sex with Ani Dawa, but in reality, you are sleeping with a Tibetan girl named Pemo. You have no intention of having sex with Pemo. So, technically speaking, you are not breaking your monastic vows."

"Okay, Purba, but what if I never find out that I've had sex with the wrong person? Am I still going to be a monk or not?"

"See? This is what you are getting into! The whole thing is a mess. You could have twelve judges and hundreds of witnesses, and you still wouldn't be able to say who is breaking the rules and who isn't. Technically speaking."

Mrs. Lakshmi, my landlady, and her daughter Reena came out of the chai shop to witness my metamorphosis. After a thorough examination of my new outfit, each performed an affirmative head wobble (a sideways nod) and sauntered down the road, followed by the family cat, an emaciated gray creature covered with bloated ticks. Next came my landlord, Mr. Chandradas, a seventy-year-old man wearing ragged ashen *shalwar* pajamas and a traditional Indian linen cap. He stood in front of me, hands clasped behind his back, and stared hard into my eyes. He had never spoken to me before (perhaps because he had fought the British, or maybe because he just didn't like Westerners) and I was surprised to see him suddenly animated, groping for words, eager to communicate his feelings to me.

"Look at them," Mr. Chandradas shouted, pointing at his wife and daughter receding into the distance. "It's nothing but trouble. If I was young like you . . ."

Unable to think of the right words in English, my landlord pretended to cut his penis and throw it across the street in the bushes.

"To the donkeys!" he cried, and Purba and I burst out laughing, only to realize seconds later that my landlord wasn't joking.

"To the donkeys," Mr. Chandradas repeated quietly, and just before he walked back into his chai shop, I noticed that his eyes were filled with tears.

I should've felt inspired by my landlord's display of contempt for the world of desire, but instead I felt embarrassed, like a thief who has been mistaken for a savior.

Purba and I walked into the chai shop, ordered parathas, and sat at a table by the window. Outside, the sky was rippled by a magnificent formation of heavy rain clouds advancing towards the Himalayan ridges like a fleet of battleships loaded with ammunition. The trees had flipped their leaves upside down, changing their color to match the monochrome grayness of the monsoon sky. The air was steeped with an intoxicating sweet scent, a weather warning signal released by millions of anguished Himalayan flowers. More often than not, July rains started off with a devastating barrage of hail.

I turned around and looked at the newspaper clippings, empty liquor bottles, and jars of spices crowding the shelves of the large cupboard on my left. An old photograph of Mr. Chandradas showed him as a young soldier dressed in full military attire, a bayonet-topped rifle in his arms. I caught a glimpse of my own reflection in the windowpane, and the reality of what I'd done—the robes, the shaved head—hit me for the first time. Who was I now? An Eastern European kid who spent his childhood playing piano eight hours a day? A worn-out Berklee College of Music student getting stoned in Harvard Square and jamming with other musicians in the practice rooms? Or was I Lodro Chosang, a twenty-two-year-old monk who spoke Tibetan, memorized cryptic Buddhist texts, bathed in the muddy river, and made perfectly round chapati?

I wished I could see what was in store for me. I could sense the future reconfiguring, events taking form and gathering momentum. It was all there, in my landlord's flour-covered hands, in the steady rumble of the kerosene stove, in the smell of fried chilies, and the cold kiss of the monsoon fog streaming into the chai shop. Everything leading to my encounter with Tsar and the fantastic events that took place at the house on Jogibara Road had already been woven into the present.

Two

My journey from Boston to New Delhi took almost ten days. In addition to layovers in Prague, Athens, and Rome I also spent a few days in Sofia, my birthplace, where I was dragged by a mob of aging and increasingly demented relatives to a series of ritualistic family dinners, during the course of which I was informed that I had wasted my life and talent (I had won my first international piano competition, in Italy, at the age of nine) and that I would be wise to prepare for a premature and very painful death.

"People in India drop like flies," my grandmother Mila, of Slavic origin, told me, after consuming half of the baklava she'd made in my honor. "You're going to die there for sure. And we'll never see you playing the piano again!"

"What are you going to India for?" shouted my grandfather Dimitar, of Tatar origin, between shots of ouzo, his fingers still greasy from cutting up a baby lamb, which he'd baked whole. "If you want to see India so bad, go to Istanbul! It's the same thing, and it's only a few hours away by bus."

Dimitar, a sworn pacifist (he'd fought in the Second World War, first on the side of the Germans against the Serbs, and then, after deserting, with the

Serbs against the Germans, without firing a single bullet), was famous for, among other things, experiencing timelessness when, at the age of twelve, he'd met the Devil face-to-face in the small village near the Black Sea where he'd grown up.

My uncle Yurai—a Czech—seemed more upset with me than anyone else. Yurai was a philosopher and eccentric, and was known for harboring strange hobbies. When I was a teenager, for example, he'd memorized the entire Chinese-Russian dictionary—two large volumes—despite the fact that he had no interest in reading Chinese literature. Yurai seldom spoke, but when he did, usually after sufficient alcohol, his words rushed out like a hurricane and his persona—a cross between a mad Nietzsche and a despondent Samuel Beckett character—suddenly filled up the entire room, as he knocked glasses and dishes to the floor. "Nikolai, you cannot, you will not, I repeat—and I apologize, forget everything I've said, I've said nothing!—you have something extraordinary, you owe it to the world and no matter what you do—forget everything I've said, it's all an unbearable drivel, bullshit, I'm an idiot—you'll always regret giving up the only thing you're good at, the piano, that is. . . . I remember attending your concerts, a little kid—ten, eleven maybe—playing Debussy. . . . Damn it! You have to go back to playing or I don't know what's going to happen!"

The only one of my older relatives who had a somewhat positive reaction to the news of my going to India to become a Buddhist monk was my grandmother of Jewish heritage—a retired cardiologist and religious hypochondriac who, for the past twenty years, had never failed to remind her visitors that she was dying.

"So tell me, my dear, do the Tibetans have some mantra that can cure the tingling sensation in the lower parts of my torso? Ask them about an ointment of some sort, or maybe a visualization. My legs are atrophying, I can barely move my toes—see, watch. Did you say something?"

"I said nothing, Grandmother."

"What did I tell you? I can't even hear. And I'm losing my vision in my right eye."

On my third day in Bulgaria, after countless servings of baklava, stuffed grape leaves, oily Turkish casseroles, moussaka, buffalo yogurt, deep-fried animal organs, and endless lectures on the unfathomable intellectual powers of the average Eastern European (even our taxi drivers can talk about quantum physics and Dostoyevsky!), I found myself kissing my airplane ticket to New Delhi and swearing that I would never again return to the land where Orpheus allegedly descended into the Underworld.

The day before I left, as I was walking through downtown Sofia, during one of the rare occasions when I wasn't surrounded by relatives, I bumped into an old girlfriend of mine, also a piano player, whom I hadn't seen in five years. Though it was March and quite cold, she was already wearing a summer outfit—miniskirt, tights, blouse, high heels. She told the man accompanying her to take a walk and then peered hungrily into my eyes.

"So," she began with a lascivious smile, "you're back. How was Boston?"

"It was nice," I said. "But I'm leaving again. Going to India."

"India!" she repeated, shaking her head in pity. "I always knew you were going to end up in India—with the Hare Krishnas."

"It's not the Hare Krishnas," I said, angered by her condescending tone. "I'm going to study Tibetan at a monastery. I'm also going to become a Buddhist monk. Buddhists don't believe in God, by the way."

"Poor Niki!" she sighed, pouting. "He is angry at the world again!"

"Of course I'm angry at the world! The world is fucked up. And I'm getting out."

"What you need," she said quietly, checking to see if her boyfriend was looking at us, "is a week of really hard sex. Are you staying at your parents' apartment?"

"I'm leaving tomorrow," I told her apologetically. "But I'll keep in touch."

. . .

THOUGH THEY WERE severely disappointed by my decision to drop out of
college shortly before graduating and abandon a promising career as a jazz
pianist and composer, my parents made heroic efforts to rein in their scien-
tific misgivings about organized religion and remain somewhat upbeat during
my visit.

"At least you'll get to climb a tall mountain," said my dad, a heart doctor
and science fiction writer, who had published a novel in which Jesus traveled
to ancient Greece in a time machine and had sex with the beautiful Helen of
Troy while the Greeks scurried around in a giant wooden horse.

"And you're going to see live elephants," my mom, a dentist, added.

My sister, fourteen, giggled from some far corner in the apartment.
Growing up in a family of total lunatics hardly makes for a dull adolescence.

After leaving Sofia, I spent a night in Athens, roaming the streets confused and disoriented until one o'clock in the morning. I suddenly found it
hard to remember any of the compelling reasons why I'd decided to go live in
India in the first place. It was too late to go back to playing piano now, and
yet my future as a would-be monk seemed completely sealed, impenetrable.
The only things that propelled me forward were a gut feeling that India was
the place where I needed to be and a memory of the hundreds of Tibetan
words I had memorized while living in Boston.

At the Indira Gandhi International Airport in New Delhi, the passport
control officer pulled me aside and called his superintendent.

"Who is this man?" bellowed the superintendent, dressed in full military
attire, pointing at the photograph of a stern eighteen-year-old boy with
shoulder-length hair and bangs covering a large part of his face.

"Well, it's me," I replied, realizing how absurd this assertion must seem in
light of my new haircut, which had left an inch of hair sticking out in every
direction.

"This passport is fake," the superintendent concluded, putting it in his coat pocket. "Give me your real passport."

"But I can prove that this is me," I said, dropping my backpack on the ground. "Look at my lips—very full lips, right? Then look at the protruding Adam's apple."

The superintendent and the officer examined my Adam's apple and the fullness of my lips and shook their heads, unimpressed.

"Do you see the tiny black dot on my lower lip?" I continued. "And what about the small scar on my chin—do you see that?"

The scar and the black dot caught their attention. They called another passport officer and the three of them began dissecting the photograph, arguing loudly, and then pausing to stare at my face.

"Go," the superintendent said in the end and waved me away. "But you need to get a new passport. Next time we might not let you through."

Later that night, on the bus to Dharamsala, my final destination, I recalled the passport incident and tried to excavate its deeper meaning. Being hopelessly superstitious, I couldn't help but invest my first experience on Indian soil with the power to foretell my future in the Himalayas. What did all this mean—the discrepancy between my photograph and me, the three pairs of eyes studying my scar, my moles, and the shape of my lips and eyebrows? Did it symbolize a battle of identities? Did it suggest that in my future life as a monk I was going to pretend to be someone that I wasn't? That I would never be able to change my personality? Or was this a sign that in order to become someone new, I had to first completely erase my past?

At five o'clock in the morning, as we entered the Himalayan foothills and the air became significantly colder, the bus briefly skidded off the road. Catching a glimpse of the open gorge below my window, I was quickly reminded that this was all real: I was in India, the air smelled of kerosene, the bus driver was smoking *biddies*, the windows closed only halfway, my luggage was tied to the roof with a rope, my mouth was dry and full of dust, the metal frame of the bus squeaked and bent as if it was about to crack open. Time itself seemed to be made out of rubber, stretching and retracting without reason, as minutes turned into hours and hours flickered by like trance-induced images. I remembered my grandmother Mila wearing an apron, sitting behind a large plate with stacked baklava pieces, and looking at me with a mixture of anger and disappointment. She had warned me. She'd seen how it ends. *We'll never hear him playing the piano again!*

Three

I don't know if it had to do with shaving my head on a Tuesday, but when I woke up the morning after my ordination I felt so depressed and disoriented, I couldn't get out of bed until the afternoon. I looked at the *zen*, *tonka*, and *shanthab* folded neatly on the chair next to my bed. I touched the smooth surface of my head and tried to determine the precise moment when the jazz pianist had ceased to exist and the Buddhist monk had taken over. The feeling of euphoria that had motivated me in the weeks and days leading to my ordination had evaporated overnight, and even the thought of venturing out the door in my new outfit made me cringe. Was I shy? Insecure? I recalled the time when my mother used to beg me to go outside and play with the other kids in the courtyard. I must've been no older than three, but I remembered perfectly how scared I had felt to face the world.

At exactly eight-thirty, Ani Dawa knocked on my door and glued her face to the window.

"Lodro? Are you coming for breakfast?"

"No, thank you," I yelled, sitting up and grabbing a book.

"Are you okay?"

"Yes. I am just in the middle of memorizing *Sherab Nyingpo*."

Ani Dawa remained by the window for another minute or so, and then walked back to her room.

I am going to be fine, I told myself as I stared at the crack in the long wooden beam that ran across the ceiling above my bed. I tried to calculate how long it would take me to jump out of the way should the beam snap under the weight of my three-hundred-pound landlady, Mrs. Lakshmi. Upstairs, Reena was playing the latest Bollywood hit single, *Tujhe Dekha To*. The only time Reena was not blasting Bollywood music was when she was asleep, and that didn't usually last more than four hours.

At noon, Ani Dawa knocked at my door again and offered to bring me lunch. I thanked her and told her that I was fasting. At two o'clock it started raining and I thought that this was a good opportunity for me to leave my room and go to Upper Dharamsala, since I'd be hiding my face under my umbrella and no one would know whether I was a Westerner or Tibetan. I tied my *shanthab* with the saffron-colored monastic belt, flung the *zen* over my shoulders, and walked out the door.

The first thing that I usually did when I got to town was run into the post office. I didn't have to go through the towering pile of new letters—the postal worker, a sari-wrapped Indian woman dwarfed behind an enormous wooden counter, was always kind enough to let me know if I had any mail as soon as I walked through the door. She responded to any question or challenge from the outside world with a head wobble. She performed two kinds of head wobbles: with a smile (*Yes, a new letter arrived for you today*) and without (*There are no letters for you with this morning's mail, sir*). Conversely, to the common question "Do you have any stamps?" she responded with a head wobble and a blank expression, meaning, *We've been out of stamps for a month, what do you expect from a post office?*

Today the post office was deserted. There was no pile of newly arrived letters on the counter. It appeared that the postal truck had never made it to town. I sat on the front steps, a foot away from the open sewer that ran alongside the street, and weighed my options. I could buy a bar of soap and take a shower for ten rupees at the Green Hotel, or I could wander around inspecting all the chai shops and restaurants in the hope of bumping into some friends. There wasn't much to do back then, in those listless months before Tsar came along.

At the end I decided to go to Smiley's chai shop and wait for Damien—a twenty-two-year-old guy from L.A. who talked about Eastern philosophy the way rappers talk about the 'hood: *I dig the dharma, bro, dig that shit, you know what I'm saying, emptiness, reincarnation—you can't mess with that. These Indian motherfuckers finished off existence two thousand five hundred years ago, you know what I mean? They fucking killed it. They killed the self, bro, the atman. No one can do that now, people are fucking pussies.*

Walking past the small Buddhist temple opposite the whorehouse, I was nearly knocked over by Hans, a German monk, who jumped—his hands spread out, karate-style—from the top of a giant prayer wheel and landed on my toes, his monastic garment getting wrapped up around my head. Hans was not really a friend of mine. You could befriend Hans no more than you could befriend the homeless cow with the broken ankle who camped out in front of the post office. Hans was just an integral part of the local scene, and despite his karate performances and his claim to possess knowledge of Tantric spells that could dry up the Ganges or flood the Rajasthan desert, he was really a benevolent soul who never tired of offering practical advice and helping others along their path to spiritual awakening. Hans was in his late thirties, with heavy glasses, a protruding jaw, a crooked nose (perhaps broken), and monastic robes that were too big for him.

"Hans, man, you almost killed me!" I complained, massaging my toes.

"It vas a good jump, vasn't it?" Hans said, smiling in self-congratulation. "I can show you a different move, if you vont."

"Thanks, Hans, really. That was enough for today."

"How is your Enlightenment coming along?" Hans asked with fatherly interest. "Are you vorking hard?"

"Oh, well, you know how it is. I've been experiencing some difficulties."

"Like vot?"

"Well, I'm just a little confused about what it means to be a monk. Maybe I am having an identity crisis of sorts."

Hans winked at me and pointed at his shaved head. "Zeh key is in zeh brain, my friend. In zeh brain."

"Yeah."

"Do you see zeh big gray cloud crawling over zeh sharp Himalayan ridges?"

"I see it."

"Very good. Now votch carefully."

Hans squatted in the middle of the street, teeth clenched, and started pumping his fists as if he were milking a cow.

"Is it moving?" he said, wiping the sweat off his forehead.

"What?"

"Zeh cloud!"

"No."

"Votch carefully."

I stood and watched obediently as Hans unleashed his telekinetic powers. Ten minutes later, the cloud was above our heads, curled up and heavy with water. Hans got up and wiped his foggy glasses on his *zen*.

"You did it, Hans." I congratulated him.

"I know," he said, looking up. "I am zeh master."

AFTER AN HOUR OF WANDERING around town and drinking chai, I suddenly realized what I had to do. I rushed to the taxi stand, hopped in a beat-up white minivan, and told the driver to take me to Mr. Chandradas's paratha shop on Jogibara Road. When I got out, Mrs. Lakshmi peeked out of the paratha shop and pointed at the courtyard surrounding Shiva's sanctuary. "Ani Dawa was looking for you," she told me.

Climbing Ani Dawa's doorsteps in a rush, I forgot to duck at the entrance and smashed my head in the door's upper threshold, which had been designed for people under four feet tall.

"*Kugpa!*"—Idiot!—Ani Dawa's mother, Ama-la, cried as I knelt on the floor, seized with pain.

"Are you okay?" Ani Dawa asked, squatting beside me. "Let me see."

"I'm going to live, for now," I assured her, showing her my fingers: there was no blood.

"He can't even fit through the door," Ama-la mumbled, dipping her pinky in her cup of butter tea to check the temperature. "When he sleeps, his feet stick out of the bed."

Despite her cranky personality, raging superstition, and inherent contempt for Westerners, Ama-la was a good-natured woman, never too stingy to offer her guests a piece of desiccated, rock-solid yak cheese, considered by most Tibetans a priceless delicacy.

"Tell him to have some," Ama-la said, placing a slab of yak cheese at the center of the table.

Ama-la never spoke to me directly, though I understood everything she said. She had two teeth, gray-blue eyes, and waist-long white hair, interlaced with colorful threads and knitted in braids. When she laughed, she stuck her tongue in the space between her two upper teeth and threw herself backwards, onto her pillow. Although she never missed a chance to ridicule me, I'd come to love her the way one loves an eccentric. I saw her as an artifact from a world that no longer existed, a world where Buddhist monks flew in the sky, riding on top of Tibetan yaks, where thunder was the sound of burping dragons, where the earth was a square copper plate carried by four elephants, and where people prepared to exit their bodies by opening a crack in their craniums.

"Ani Dawa," I said, out of breath, "I need you to take me to the Mo Lama, now. Please."

"Why?" Ani Dawa asked, rinsing her hands over a bucket of water. "What's wrong?"

"I need someone to do a *mo* divination for me. It's going to make me feel much better."

"Have you changed your mind about being a monk?"

"No, that's not it. I just have a lot of anxieties about the future."

"He is going to go crazy, just like the rest of the *Engies*"—Westerners—Ama-la snickered. "Give him a month."

Ani Dawa looked at me intensely, and grabbed her *zen*. "Okay. If that's what you want to do, let's go."

Terchen Migme Rinpoche, the Mo Lama, lived in a pink four-story mansion that functioned as a guesthouse, monastery, and private residence. When Ani Dawa and I arrived on the third floor, we were intercepted by a beautiful Tibetan woman in her twenties, who gestured at us to be quiet.

"My father is seeing someone at the moment," the Tibetan woman said. "Maybe you should come some other day."

"Please," Ani Dawa pleaded. "It will only take a minute. Rinpoche knows me."

The woman shrugged and ran downstairs.

"She knows who I am," Ani Dawa said with a smug smile. "When Mother was sick, I used to come here every day."

I leaned against the yellow balcony railing and tried to make out the familiar buildings and streets of Lower Dharamsala, which was spread out like a satellite map six thousand feet below. Enclosed by the arching horizon, the Kangra Valley looked like a slum city crammed in a crystal ball, with tiny feather clouds swimming, spinning, and then landing on houses, Hanuman temples, and black Shiva lingams.

The door to Rinpoche's room opened and out rushed two sobbing Tibetan women, each with a white *katak*—a traditional Tibetan silk scarf—slung from her neck.

"Ready?" Ani Dawa whispered, holding the door open.

The audience room was dim and for the most part empty. Terchen Migme Rinpoche, a sixty-something man with noble features and a weary

gaze, sat cross-legged on a throne of stacked-up Kashmiri rugs, facing a lacquered cabinet that served as an altar and a library. The grainy, mustard-
colored walls were decorated with traditional Tibetan paintings depicting
historic Tibetan figures sitting on clouds and centipedic Tantric monsters
dancing on top of choked-up Hindu gods.

Ani Dawa and I offered Rinpoche our *kataks* and sat on the cold, glazed
cement floor, preparing our introductory speeches. Rinpoche was in no hurry
to find out why we had come to see him. Smiling like a little kid posing for a
camera, he put on a pair of thick-lensed glasses and inspected the objects
placed on the low table in front of him: a tall, leather-sheathed cup, an
astrological booklet, a second pair of glasses, a bowl filled with chunks of
yak cheese the consistency of limestone, a mahogany butter tea cup, a few
chewed-up pieces of yak jerky, a tiger-eye rosary, a dozen tiny plastic bags of
Tibetan medicine, an ancient radio with a missing antenna, and a long metal
stick with a white plastic hand affixed to its tip. Noticing that the silver
parasol-shaped lid on top of his butter tea cup had tipped to one side, Rinpoche chuckled, and held the lid in the light.

"*Ale-e-eh!*" he exclaimed with sudden clarity as he examined the lid's
intricate design closely.

He returned the lid to the butter tea cup, and after spending a whole
minute trying to make it stay level, he leaned back on his pillow and held his
index finger in front of his nose.

"*Ale-e-eh!*" Rinpoche repeated, this time with a self-reproachful tone.

He took off his glasses and grabbed the second pair from the table.

"Oh!" he shouted as if he had just seen us for the first time. "The weather
is really nice, isn't it? Especially the sun."

"It is most wonderful," I agreed, nodding respectfully.

"Rinpoche . . ." Ani Dawa began, pointing at me with an open palm.

"Especially the Indian sun," Rinpoche interrupted her, unable to contain
his excitement. "Every year, it gets hotter and hotter!"

"I wonder why," I said, shrugging my shoulders.

"They say it's getting bigger," Rinpoche informed me, wiping his forehead with a white handkerchief. "When I was a child growing up in Tibet, the sun was very small. We didn't need a bathroom or toilet paper: everything turned into ice. It was very clean."

"Rinpoche," Ani Dawa intercepted cautiously, "this boy here, his name is Lodro Chosang."

"*Ale-e-eh!*" Rinpoche intoned. "Would you like some butter tea?"

Before I could answer, Rinpoche took the plastic hand from the table, reached out, and started scratching the mosquito net covering the window, to attract the attention of his daughter. A minute later the door opened, and in came Rinpoche's daughter, carrying a two-gallon thermos and two porcelain teacups.

"That's better," Rinpoche commended me as I filled Ani Dawa's cup with butter tea.

"Would Rinpoche like some more?" I asked, approaching the table.

"Just a little," Rinpoche answered, smiling, and then, suddenly, smacked me on the head with the plastic hand. "Oh! I am sorry. So many flies! I need my reading glasses."

I topped off Rinpoche's mahogany cup with tea, screwed the cap back on the thermos, and looked on and around the table for the second pair of glasses.

"They were right here a minute ago," I noted, pointing at the center of the table.

Rinpoche grew somber and started fumbling in the folds of his maroon robe.

"*Ale-e-eh!*" Rinpoche sighed, pulling a box of cookies from under his legs. "Very surprising! Do you like butterscotch cookies? We should have some."

"Rinpoche," Ani Dawa began for the third time. "We came to ask you to perform a *mo*. Lodro Chosang became a monk yesterday and he'd like to know what his life is going to be like from now on. If there are going to be obstacles and so forth."

"I see," Rinpoche said with a grave expression. "This is a very important question. Perhaps we should have some butter tea."

"I am afraid I can't find the lid for your teacup," I informed Rinpoche with a sorrowful smile.

"Very surprising," Rinpoche murmured, looking under the table. "Sometimes things start rolling around, especially round things—they fall on the floor and then disappear, rolling."

Absorbed in thought, Rinpoche took the plastic hand and began scratching his back. When he was done, he opened his astrological booklet and, pretending to read, gestured for Ani Dawa to move closer.

"Is he Tibetan?" Rinpoche asked her, whispering. "I can't see very well."

"No," Ani Dawa answered in a low voice.

"Is his mother Japanese?"

"No, he is an *Engie*."

"*Ale-e-eh!*"

Rinpoche adjusted his robe and upper garment and reached for the leather-sheathed cup on the table. With a distant look in his eye, intended to announce the beginning of the *mo* ceremony, he pulled three dice out of the cup, held them above his head, and mumbled a long mantra. After a moment of silent contemplation, he dropped the dice back into the cup, shook it violently, and slammed it upside down on the table.

"Very strange," Rinpoche mumbled, as he lifted the cup. "There is only one dice here."

He leaned back on his pillow and held the cup in the light, to see if the missing dice weren't somehow stuck to the bottom.

"They must be in the room somewhere," I said, crawling about on the floor.

"Now," Rinpoche began, looking up at the ceiling fan, "there are some signs that seem to suggest that your monk path is free of obstacles. However, staying in Dharamsala for some time might lead to a lot of unfavorable circumstances, and even disaster."

"What kind of disaster?" I asked.

"You might come under the influence of a hungry ghost who will lead you astray and shorten your life span."

"Where will I find a hungry ghost?"

"He will come to you," Rinpoche assured me, nodding.

"So what should I do?" I wondered.

Rinpoche smiled and pushed the bowl of yak cheese to the end of the table.

"Have some *chura*," he encouraged me, while he himself went for a stick of yak jerky. "I will tell you a story, if you are not in a hurry."

"We are not," Ani Dawa and I answered in unison.

"In my home village back in Tibet," Rinpoche reminisced with a blissful smile, "lived a man by the name of Tenzin. He was famous for making the best *chura* in the entire Kham region. One day another famous *chura* maker, from Amdo, passed through our village and tried Tenzin's yak cheese. Now, the man from Amdo was also a *ngagpa*—a magician—and when he realized that Tenzin's *chura* was much better than his, he secretly cast an evil spell on Tenzin and then disappeared, never to be seen again. Soon Tenzin began experiencing strange things. One time he bought a cucumber from the market and came home with a snake. Another time he was followed by a hungry ghost. Finally he went to the abbot of a nearby monastery and asked him to do a *mo*. As long as you stay in your house and don't go out, the abbot told him, the spell is not going to hurt you. Tenzin stayed at home for three years. On the fourth year, a yak dropped on top of his house and killed him on the spot."

I looked at Ani Dawa and she nodded: it was time for us to leave. I thanked Rinpoche for the *mo*, placed an envelope with fifty rupees on the table, and edged toward the door. It had stopped raining and the pale pink sky was dotted with countless black clouds, burning coals ignited by the setting sun. The nunnery gong, a soft but insistent A-flat, reverberated across the valley. It was only fitting, I thought, that a sound so lonely should come from a place where solitude was the goal.

I filled my lungs with the crisp, ozone-scented air and looked at the cluster of shanties and mud-brick houses that composed my landlord's family compound. It was stupid of me to expect that the Mo Lama would tell me why I had experienced a panic attack on my second day as a monk. Clairvoyant people, as it happened, spoke only in indecipherable parables.

I wasn't disappointed, though. Seeing the Mo Lama had helped me realize something very important. As I had sat on the cement floor, listening to him talk about hungry ghosts and yaks falling from the sky, it had occurred to me that trying to identify completely with my new self and my new way of life would only drive me insane. What was the use of replacing one painful identity with another? It made a lot more sense to step back and allow things to happen. It was wiser to be an observer, an anthropologist stranded on a virgin island.

They say that a Buddhist monk has to change three things: his clothes, his name, and his thoughts. I had changed my clothes and my name. My thoughts I wasn't giving up yet.

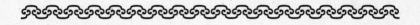

Four

When people talked about Dharamsala, they usually referred to a general area that included about a dozen or so localities. Lower Dharamsala, situated in the foothills of the Himalayas, was an Indian village with two year-round bazaars, a bus station, government offices, banks, and a cricket ground. Above it was Gangchen Kyishong, a quiet and well-kept Tibetan neighborhood built around two small monasteries, the Library of Tibetan Works and Archives, a Tibetan-run hospital, and the many offices of the Tibetan government in exile—one of them wishfully called the Tibetan Parliament. Climbing up the road above Gangchen Kyishong, one passed through Gamru village (where I lived for the bigger part of my stay in India), then the Dalai Lama's residence—which was connected to Namgyal Monastery and the Institute of Buddhist Dialectics—and finally arrived in McLeod Ganj, a former British hill station and at present a gathering place of backpackers, junkies, and dharma tourists.

Despite the presence of a Tibetan parliament filled with ministers, many of them monks and lamas, the existence of a Tibetan government was largely an illusion. Since the Dalai Lama's escape from Lhasa to Dharamsala in 1959,

and the annexation of Tibet's territory by the communist Chinese government, the Tibetans living in India have been struggling to find their identity:
they didn't want to go back to their home country because it was part of communist China; the Indian government refused to grant citizenship even to
the children of Tibetan refugees born in India; and the so-called Tibetan government in exile lacked the legislative power and wherewithal to protect and
provide basic services to its constituents.

On the surface, the relationship between Indians and Tibetans seemed
congenial, but in reality both sides harbored a great deal of resentment. All
the Tibetans I met were unanimous in their disdain for the customs and
lifestyle of their Indian neighbors—despite the fact that a large part of Tibet's
cultural heritage, from its alphabet to its philosophy, scholarship, and art, had
been imported from India in the seventh century A.D., when the Tibetan king
Songtsen Gampo made Buddhism the official religion of his kingdom. Not
many Tibetans would look at an Indian holy man, or saddhu—barefoot,
soiled, dressed in rags, with a Rastafarian hairdo and a wild look in his eyes—
and think, hey, this is what the Buddha probably looked like when he emerged
from the jungles of Bihar twenty-five hundred years ago and postulated the
four principles encapsulating the Buddhist worldview: that all compounds are
impermanent; that all physical and mental states, born out of a misconception
about the ultimate way of things, are in the nature of suffering; that all
phenomena are devoid of objective reality; and that Nirvana is peace.

The Indians, for their part, found many Tibetans to be hypocritical and
opportunistic. They couldn't understand how the Tibetans, who had arrived
in the late fifties in India with nothing and had presented themselves as the
last survivors of a dying culture that needed to be saved, now controlled large
portions of land, ran hundreds of guesthouses and restaurants, employed
lower-caste Indian boys and teenagers as slaves, sold jewelry and antiques,
and refused to do any labor-intensive jobs, such as working construction or
plowing the fields.

Lobsang—one of the hundreds of Tibetan refugees who crossed the Chinese-Indian border every year—lived near the Library of Tibetan Works and Archives, in a detached, flat-roofed stone room cracked in half by an earthquake, one part of the building apparently on its way down the slope. Barely sixteen, he was a chain-smoker, the tips of his fingers browned by filterless cigarettes. His long, curly hair, pale pink lips, and cute boyish face were a bit deceiving: Lobsang was an old soul, one that didn't get too hung up on things like food, or tomorrow, or dying.

Even though he was six years younger, I had come to look up to him as a mentor. He had taught me how to drink water from a leaking pipe sticking out in the middle of a road. He had taught me how to fix my kerosene stove: working on his knees and elbows, kerosene tar smudged across his forehead, he had taken the whole stove apart and showed me how it worked. This is the valve: it gets clogged. This is the piston: when the insulation rubs out, the pressurized air escapes.

He had taught me how to eat at the cheapest, and invariably dirtiest, chai shops in the vicinity, using my fingers instead of utensils (as Indians do) and swallowing chilies by the pound—to protect myself against the amoebas.

Lobsang was the first person to point out that my habit of extracting the cooked flies and stones from my food, and arranging them in a long row on the table, could be interpreted as a sign of disrespect. "The cook is going to get offended," Lobsang explained, nodding at the chai shop owner, a fierce man presiding over an array of roaring kerosene stoves, stirring a pot of *aloo gobi* with one hand and massaging his testicles with the other.

Aside from teaching me basic survival skills, such as handling snakes and scorpions, Lobsang was also my ultimate guide into the workings of Tibetan society. He didn't withhold any information. He told me that the stray dogs around town were believed to be the reincarnated souls of former monks who had broken their vows. He told me that in Tibet people wiped their asses with stones. He told me of a matriarchal Tibetan tribe where women apprehended occasional male wanderers and raped them. He said that he knew a Tibetan girl from that region and proposed to introduce me to her.

When I visited Lobsang one Sunday afternoon, I found him stooped over a pile of books, memorizing a list of irregular English verbs. The room was filled with a pungent odor.

"It's tiger oil," Lobsang explained. "When I rub it on my temples, it increases my memory."

Unlike most people I met, Lobsang never made me feel self-conscious about wearing robes. He understood that being a monk was just another job, like driving a rickshaw or squeezing sugarcane juice in front of the post office for three rupees a glass.

"Yesterday I saw your teacher, Ani Dawa," Lobsang informed me, as he pumped the kerosene stove to make tea. "She thinks that you are trying to pick up some of the young nuns that she is friends with."

"No!"

"*Kun chog!*" Lobsang shouted and burst out laughing.

Kun chog is part of the Tibetan expression *kun chog sum*, which means "three precious ones." The three precious ones are the Buddha, his teaching, and his enlightened followers. In conversation, *kun chog* is used to mean *I swear!* whereas *kun chog sum* has the connotation of *Jesus Christ!* or *Goddamn it!* Tibetans love to overdramatize every bit of news they present or receive, interchanging *Really?* with *Kun chog!* the way gospel singers trade phrases at the culmination of a song.

"I am not trying to pick up anybody," I told him. "She introduced me to her nun friends."

Lobsang sat on his bed, one leg over the other, lit a tattered cigarette, and pointed at me, scrunching his eyebrows.

"What's your friend's name?"

"Which one?"

"The one from Los Angeles, with all the tattoos."

"Oh, you mean Damien."

"Damien," Lobsang repeated with pleasure. "He's got a nun girlfriend."

"No!"

"*Kun chog!*"

"How do you know?"

"A friend of mine told me. He saw a nun go into Damien's house and stay overnight."

"I don't believe it."

Lobsang stubbed his cigarette in a tin can and produced chewed-up bubble gum from behind his ear.

"I have a new girlfriend," he told me, squatting by the stove to pour the tea.

"Another American, ten years older than you?" I suggested.

"No, a Tibetan. An ex-nun."

"What's with you and nuns, man?"

"You know the song," Lobsang replied with a wicked smile. "All the pretty girls are in the nunnery."

There was, in fact, a popular Tibetan song that went "All the pretty girls are in the nunnery," and I happened to know it quite well—it was one of the first things I ever memorized in Tibetan. The frustration of adolescent Tibetans was understandable. According to one figure, prior to 1959, the monastic community in Tibet had comprised almost sixty percent of the population.

"So how does it feel, dating an ex-nun?" I asked.

"She tells me stories you wouldn't believe."

"Like what?"

"Like how nuns do it together."

Lobsang looked at me intensely, gauging my reaction, and then exploded with laughter.

"You are full of shit," I told him, adjusting my *zen*. My stomach was aflame, my heart fluttered. "Tibetan nuns would never brake their chastity vows."

"*Kun chog!*" Lobsang jumped, suddenly dead serious. "She tells me everything."

I knew I shouldn't ask any questions but it was already too late. "And how do they do it?"

"With an egg," Lobsang confided, thrilled that he got me begging for more information.

I was completely baffled. Of all things at their disposal, an egg!

"What kind of egg?" I wondered, realizing that I must sound like an idiot.

"What do you mean?"

"I don't know—a raw egg, or a hard-boiled one?"

"A raw one," Lobsang declared with authority.

I felt anxious. My hands were sweaty. I finished my tea and looked out the window. At one time, before the last major earthquake split it in half, Lobsang's room had been a government office. Now the windows were broken and the rain poured through the crack in the ceiling and disappeared into a crack in the floor.

"Lobsang, man, you are going to kill me," I said, conceding defeat. "How can they possibly do it with an egg, and a raw one at that?"

"You know: two nuns and an egg. Think about it."

"I am thinking about it," I replied. "I will probably stay awake thinking about it for the next five years."

"Maybe you should ask Ani Dawa to explain it to you," Lobsang proposed, giggling.

"Actually, I will," I said. "I will tell her how I got the information, too. Then she will lead a delegation of elderly Tibetan women and whip you to death with bundles of poison ivy."

"She will," Lobsang agreed.

Laughing, we exited the room and headed downhill, to catch a bus to Upper Dharamsala. I needed to buy kerosene for my stove and Lobsang assured me that he knew a man who might be able to sell me a few gallons on a Sunday. Passing near the Library of Tibetan Works and Archives, we saw a

Western man in his sixties, sitting cross-legged on the glazed cement floor of the spacious portico, an open book in his lap. He had long, curly, reddish-blond hair, a prominent mustache, and wore a discolored T-shirt and a pair of gray-and-blue-striped linen pants.

"*Ni hao*," Lobsang greeted him in Chinese.

The man responded in Chinese with a thunderous whisper, and my attention was immediately drawn to the pink scar on his neck.

"This is Vinnie," Lobsang explained. "He is fluent in Chinese."

"That's amazing," I said, clearly impressed. "Where did you study it?"

"In Singapore," Vinnie replied. "I was married to a Chinese woman."

"What happened?" I asked shamelessly.

Vinnie took a deep breath, closed his book, and stared at me with a grave expression. "Her mother chased me out of the house with a knife."

The second he said "knife," Vinnie jumped to his feet and exploded with wheezing laughter, stomping his feet and throwing his fists in the air. Lobsang and I quickly followed suit.

A tall Western Buddhist monk, carrying an umbrella and a suede duffel bag slung over one shoulder, came out of the Tibetan Library and walked up to an Indian man selling chickpea masala. "Tsar!" Vinnie called out after him. The monk turned around and smiled. He was in his late thirties, good-looking, with a prominent forehead, piercing black eyes, sensual lips, a small, straight nose, and clawlike laugh lines around his eyes. He didn't fit the Western Buddhist monk stereotype: he had broad, muscular shoulders, a smug Mickey Rourke smile, and the swagger of a boxer who was about to jump in the ring.

"I figured out how you could've won the game that we played last Sunday," Tsar said to Vinnie, by way of greeting. "Remember, I played King Indian."

Vinnie snorted and sat back on the cement floor. "I don't even remember the face of my mother, and you're talking to me about some stupid chess game from a week ago."

"Give me the chessboard," Tsar demanded as he reached for Vinnie's rucksack and pulled out a chessboard and bag of pieces. In less than thirty seconds he had managed to set up a typical end-game position and was holding the white queen to demonstrate his point.

"Remember now?" Tsar asked. "You take my rook with the queen, and I can't take back with my knight because you advance your pawn, uncovering a check by the bishop, and then you get a second queen, checkmate."

Vinnie held his head, all red with rage, and swept the pieces off the board with a violent gesture.

Tsar laughed and pointed the tip of his umbrella at Vinnie's heart. "So are we going to play chess or are you going to go kill yourself?"

"By the end of the day, you're going to be begging for forgiveness," Vinnie replied, putting the chess pieces and the board back into the rucksack.

"Hey," Tsar turned to Lobsang. "Can I borrow a cigarette from you? I know you smoke."

Lobsang looked confused for a second (smoking in the Tibetan monastic tradition is absolutely verboten) but then quickly pulled a pack out of his pocket.

"And don't tell the Dalai Lama," Tsar said as he took four cigarettes.

Lobsang laughed. Had he been even slightly religious, the Western monk's comment would've triggered a fistfight.

"You're going straight to hell," Vinnie remarked, as the two headed off.

"Hell's got the best sunsets, my friend," Tsar replied. "And Nirvana is a place for pussies."

"Is Tsar his real name?" I asked Lobsang after Vinnie and the monk had disappeared under the crown of the magnificent oak tree shading the gate of Nechung Monastery.

"I have no idea," Lobsang answered. "All I know is that he and Vinnie sit in the chai shop behind my room and play chess all day long."

As Lobsang and I began walking toward the bus stand, I wondered why the monk had avoided making eye contact with me. Was it because he had perceived me as a rival, or had he thought that I was going to be just another rigid and insufferably boring Western Buddhist monk on a mission to reach Enlightenment before everybody else? I wished I had been bolder and had told Vinnie and the monk that I was coming with them, and I was going to play the winner. I really craved talking to someone other than Ani Dawa and the Tibetan teachers I visited daily, someone who defied the wall of dogma and insurmountable Buddhist logic that I felt closing around me with each memorized definition of reality.

The bus looked like a severely abused primeval creature, its engine coughing, its body slumped to one side, threatening to tip over. Its face was decorated like that of a second-rate deity: heavy garlands made of strung-up dandelions outlined the front window; temple flags, *rudraksha* bead rosaries, and plastic jewelry hung from the mirrors and the windshield wipers; white *om* and *om-Shiva-om* tattoos adorned the rusted tin. The carved head of a red-faced monster with horns and a giant black tongue was placed right at the center, above the window, to scare away drunk drivers, telegraph poles, and potholes. A pair of kids' shoes dangled under the axle for good luck. Lobsang and I passed the open doors, crammed with people, baskets, and the occasional yellow-eyed goat, and went for the ladder on the back of the bus. There is no such thing as an Indian government bus that is filled to capacity—there just isn't. The ticket master, a surprisingly pliable guy with a comb-over, knew this well and was eager to help everyone get on board, no matter what. Armed with a professional referee's whistle, a stack of tickets, and a hole puncher, he walked around directing passengers to the available spots. His reasoning went like this: if I can cram eighty people in a fifty-seat bus, why not cram a hundred and sixty? He hocked a loogie, spat, and whistled the crowd into submission—"The lady with the chickens, you can get on, but you have to hold the chickens out the window. Sir, I told you that you can't bring the metal rods inside. Put them on the roof."

Lobsang and I didn't need to be told what to do: we were experienced bus passengers. We could ride sitting down and standing up. We could ride with up to seven elderly Indian women plus one goat in our laps, and we could ride horizontally, stretched between the two handrails. We could ride on the roof or under the bus, hanging on to the muffler. We could ride under the front seat, helping the driver hold the steering wheel and keep the gas pedal pressed to the floor while he looked for matches or kicked the car stereo or screamed at the ticket master or dipped his pakoras in a jar of mango chutney. We could ride on the steering wheel, and in more challenging circumstances, we could even ride on top of the driver's cabin, serving as manually operated windshield wipers. Lobsang really did this once: it was raining, the windshield wipers weren't working, and the driver announced that he needed someone to go on top and keep the window clear for the next hour or two. Lobsang volunteered. No one seemed too bothered by the sight of the new hybrid wiper (part human hand, part metal and rubber) drawing half-circles across the wet window.

Riding on the roof of an Indian government bus is a lot more than a head rush; it is a metaphysical experience. This time, Lobsang and I sat at the very rear, cramped between a metal trunk and an Indian soldier who held his enormous World War I rifle sideways, with the potential of putting a bullet through my thigh. I looked at him, nodded at the rifle, and he responded with a head wobble, as if to say, *I know, it's a very good rifle. It's the best rifle to get shot with.*

The bus jumped forward and all the passengers on the roof lowered their heads to avoid electrocution and possible decapitation by the high-voltage wires strung low across the road and sometimes hidden between tree branches. The driver put on a tape of *ghazals*, traditional Indian songs, and suddenly we were part of an epic Bollywood picture.

Wriggling out through a passenger's window, the ticket master pulled himself to the roof and demonstrated his professional skill. Jumping over people and often balancing on one leg, he handed out tickets, shouted prices, deposited bills in a small purse, and engaged in casual conversation about the weather, all the while dodging high-voltage wires and taming his comb-over, which fluttered in the wind like a flag.

"*Kana jaiga?*" the ticket master asked me, and I said, "Upper Dharamsala," pointing casually at the sky.

Hypnotized by the syncopated tabla groove pumping from the driver's cabin, the Indian soldier next to me had dozed off, his fingers coiled around the rifle trigger, his head banging loudly against the railing. I moved the barrel away from my stomach and paid for his ticket. "A friend?" the ticket master suggested, raising an eyebrow. "A friend," I confirmed.

As the bus driver worked himself into a frenzy, making sharper and sharper turns and swerving violently into the opposite lane for no reason other than to see how well the passengers were holding on to the roof, we passed a Shiva temple busy with saffron-colored saddhus and lay worshippers admiring a giant black Shiva lingam standing erect in the middle of the front yard. I couldn't help but wonder how the actual god Shiva would have reacted to this three-story-high replica of his penis towering autonomously above the Kangra Valley, making love to the low-flying clouds, and getting caressed by little girls in blue uniforms and white stockings returning home from school.

Beyond the temple we were greeted by an immense billboard that read:

FREE CONSULTATION! GUARANTEED PRIVACY!
VD, STD, hemorrhoids! Best treatment in the world!
You have something venereal, come to me. Don't give it to others!
Dr. Singh, VD specialist. 21 Kangra Road,
Dharamsala, Himalchal Pradesh

A head shot of a fearless and deeply concerned Dr. Singh on the upper left corner of the billboard urged the infected masses to come forth without hesitation.

Next we passed a cremation ceremony. The deceased, wrapped in a white blanket like a mummy, laid on a freshly erected pyre, a few steps away from a brook. The relatives stood around, despondent. A drunken and completely out-of-synch trio (one guy on tuba, one on trumpet, and one banging a tabla) added to the somber mood with wild screeches, chaotic tabla grooves, and unexpected, low-pitch explosions.

In some strange way, these three images—the cosmic phallus, the poster about sexually transmitted diseases, and the body on the pyre—made perfect sense to me now. In the beginning, there was Shiva's enormous penis. In the end, your life was reduced to a handful of ashes and then thrown down the river. In the middle, Dr. Singh took care of your hemorrhoids.

"What is it?" Lobsang asked, noticing that I was smiling.

"Nothing. I just feel like I have finally come home."

"What do you mean?" Lobsang asked confused.

Home was not a word that young Tibetans—especially those born outside India—used lightly. Lobsang had been away from Lhasa, his hometown, for almost three years. He had hitchhiked to the Indian-Chinese border and then crossed illegally into Sikkim, India, dodging bullets and almost freezing to death. In the note that he'd written to his parents, he had said simply, "I'll be right back."

"I mean India," I said, pointing at another road sign that read "Slow down! The life that you save might or might not be your own!" "I've never been to a country where nonsense is the norm. It's like a big joke—life, death, rebirth, Enlightenment—it all amounts to nothing, a play on words, a crazy puzzle that can never be solved. No wonder they came up with the idea of maya, or illusion, you know. In the West things are taken seriously. Life is a serious matter. Eating is a serious matter. Tomorrow is a serious matter. Here I can finally breathe: there is no pressure to stay alive! Whatever happens is okay. Dying is okay, begging is okay. I don't have to plot my life. I can sit back and actually enjoy it."

"Really?" Lobsang asked in disbelief.

"*Kun chog!*" I answered, imitating him.

Ah, it was so beautiful: the wind, the tiny raindrops, the colossal fence of glistening pinnacles, women tossing rice and beating their laundry with sticks to chase the dirt away. Every house was full of music and here I was, on the roof of a suicidal bus, owning one pair of clothes and one pair of shoes, savoring the honey-on-a-razor-blade taste of relinquishing all control and walking on, come what might.

A black baby goat jumped over passengers, trunks, and wicker baskets and crawled in my lap, shaking its butt like a playful puppy. I rubbed the little bumps on his head that were going to grow into horns and petted his back. In return, he peed on me. He peed for a long time, too, and when I picked him up to move him away, the pee got on my face and in my undershirt, and then trickled down into my underwear. Lobsang thought this was very funny—me holding the peeing goat over my head.

The Indian soldier next to me woke up just in time to witness the whole ordeal. He said, "You are wet!" and, after repositioning his rifle so that it pointed again at my stomach, fell back asleep, his head still banging against the railing, one finger coiled around the trigger.

Five

One of the key events that marked my quiet period in India—before things went out of control and my life's trajectory altered dramatically—was witnessing the apparent nervous breakdown of a well-known and respected American Buddhist nun.

It happened on an August afternoon, as I met Damien for lunch. Damien was a postmodern tourist. He never tried to hide his Westernness. On the contrary, he walked the streets of Dharamsala with the swagger of a gangster, addressing shop owners and passersby with a thunderous *What's up, dude?* and *Yo, keep on rolling that chapati, bro!*, doing complicated handshakes with fingerless beggars, and pausing to show his tattoos to shocked elderly Indian ladies.

His entire body was covered with tattoos: his shoulders were dragon heads spouting flames, his hands were reptilian tails, his chest was a dragon wing.

When I saw him that day, he was wearing a white wife-beater, silver-rimmed glasses, a pair of loafers, and jeans that hung below his navel, exposing his underwear. He was sitting on the curb opposite Shangrila Restaurant, admiring the human and animal traffic moving up and down the street.

"Check out this cow, bro," he said to me as I drew closer.

"What about it?" I asked.

"It's tripping, man. I gave her a page of my Tibetan book of sutras, and she ate it."

"Why would you give her a page of your book?" I inquired, sitting on the curb next to Damien.

"Well, if that fly got to be reborn as a human because it circled a stupa on a piece of shit, then this cow's definitely going places, you know what I'm saying?"

Damien was referring to the famous Indian story about the fly who had earned the privilege of being reborn as one of Buddha's disciples by inadvertently floating around a half-submerged Buddhist shrine atop a buoyant turd.

We watched as Dekyi, the prettiest Tibetan prostitute in town, strolled past fruit and vegetable stalls, lifting one side of her immaculate indigo *chuba*, the traditional Tibetan dress, above her ankle as she climbed the stairs that led to the entrance of Shangrila Guest House. Holding the door curtain with one hand, she looked at me and said cheerfully, "Kushu-la, *ku sug de bo yin pe?*" How are you, Reverend?

"I am fine," I answered, rewrapping the *zen* around my shoulders. "How about you?"

Dekyi didn't reply—just waved good-bye and disappeared into the guesthouse.

I was in love with her. Every time I saw her, the Tibetan term for prostitute, *shang tsong ma*—literally, "she who sells her ass"—rang in my ears for hours. Oftentimes I would sit in Shangrila Restaurant and imagine Dekyi upstairs in a darkened room with a cold cement floor, a ceiling fan spinning slowly, mixing the smell of sweat, sex, and incense, mixing up memories and minutes, stranger's faces and gestures, things people said and things that were left unspoken.

"Dude, your face is red," Damien informed me. "What's going on here? Why the fuck is she saying hi to you?"

"I don't know. She's seen me around, I guess."

"That's bullshit!" Damien shouted, scaring off a bronze-painted saddhu carrying a huge, drugged snake.

"Well, believe it or not, ever since I became a monk, I've developed a special bond with all the nuns and prostitutes in town. I am not sure why that is—maybe it's because we've all decided that sex means nothing."

Damien thought about it, pushed his glasses, and looked at me boldly. "Do you jack off?"

"No!" I answered, taken aback.

"You know, you are not allowed to masturbate," Damien said instructively.

"Duh! I am the one who took vows!"

"Just checking, bro," Damien assured me, raising his hands ghetto-style, as in *We're cool, no need to draw guns*.

"For one thing, *I'm* not dating a nun," I noted casually.

"What do you mean?"

I giggled.

"That's harsh, man," Damien said, suddenly depressed. "What exactly did you hear?"

"Well, rumor has it that a young Tibetan nun stayed overnight at your place."

Damien spat on the ground and shook his head. "I am glad you're telling me this. I know where it's coming from."

"Where?"

"It's this Indian guy who works at the German bakery. I always catch him snooping around. He lives next door to me and pretends we are great friends and bullshit. Man, back in L.A., before I became a pacifist, I would walk up to him with a samosa in my hand and put a bullet through his head, no questions asked, you know what I'm saying; just *bang*, end of story."

"Why would you walk up to him with a samosa in hand?"

"For distraction," Damien explained. "It'd be like saying, hey, look what I have here and then *bang*, see you later and have a nice trip."

"I didn't know you used to shoot people before you came to India."

Damien seemed flattered. "Well, it's not like that's what I *did*, but in a situation like this, man . . . that poor girl could be expelled from the nunnery if any of the senior nuns found out. She'd be on the street. She's got no family in India, no home."

"So what happened when she stayed over at your place?"

"Nothing! She just helped me get through a short Tibetan text, and then it was too late for her to walk back to the nunnery. She slept on my bed, I slept on the floor."

"And you didn't think it's weird that a young nun would rather sleep in your bed than return to her nunnery?"

"I know what you mean," Damien said in a humble voice. "She wants me really bad—I could tell—but I ain't going down that road. I am not going to be the one to get her disrobed."

"You are a stud, man."

"Shut up."

Half an hour later, the door curtain at the entrance of Shangrila Guest House lifted and out came Dekyi, poised and confident, her hair tied back in a loose ponytail. Walking past us, she gave a perfunctory nod, dropped a few coins in the tin cup of the leper who always camped out across from Samosa Shop No. 13, and stopped at a vegetable stall to buy some okra. A dust devil rose from the ground, at first slow and shapeless, then suddenly wild and tight as a rod, scooping up plastic bags, leaves, and newspapers from the ground and hurling them high in the air, above guesthouses and electric poles. The street dogs, many of them blinded, scarred, or bitten by leopards, woke up from their perpetual nap, ate a few fleas, and dashed after the dust devil, barking at the floating rags and papers to get back down on the ground.

It was the end of a long, rainy summer and the Himalayas were undergoing a metamorphosis: the towering pinnacles had shed their granite somberness and looked phosphorescent and intangible, like an extension of the feathery clouds sliding through the sky. The smell of burning leaves and

pine needles—a precursor of the three-month fall season, marked by immaculate indigo skies and temperatures set at 75—spread through the village like
a purifying agent, erasing memories of damp, unlightable matches, rotten
clothes that ripped upon stretching, soft, fungus-coated wood, moldy books,
mushrooms growing on every wall, scorpions and crabs crawling under the
bed. In the distance, a string of goats traced the mountain trail leading up to
the goatherd's village, abandoned during the monsoons and the winter. The
nunnery gong signaled lunchtime and all the dogs began howling, replicating
the gong's soft ring. For some reason, Dharamsala's street dogs were very
musical. ·

"Here comes Ani Lamo," Damien announced, pointing at the American
nun who had just appeared from behind Smiley's chai shop. "I have to go,
bro. Last time I met Ani Lamo on the street, she talked to me for three hours
about whether or not the Dalai Lama walks through walls when nobody's
around. I don't think I can take that today."

Nodding good-bye, Damien got up and quickly disappeared down the
narrow passageway separating the two restaurants behind us.

"I thought you were going to start classes at the Institute of Buddhist
Dialectics," Ani Lamo said by way of greeting. Ani Lamo, originally from
Brooklyn, was in her late forties, a heavyset woman with a mournful expression, slow stride, and even slower manner of speaking. She had been in India
for four years and was considered by all standards an old-timer.

"I am," I said, nodding eagerly. "Soon."

"So what are you doing now?" Ani Lamo pressed on.

"Watching the prettiest prostitute pick vegetables from the market,"
I answered, suddenly deciding that it was better to tell the truth.

"Oh, I'm sure," she said dismissively. "And how are things going with
Ani Dawa?"

"I honestly don't know what it is," I replied. "She has decided to adopt
me—she calls me her son, and wants me to get a *Geshe* degree"—the Tibetan
equivalent of a Ph.D.—"so that I can get a tenure position in the big monaster-

ies in the South. And that's just not going to happen. First of all, I didn't quit playing piano to pursue a theological career in Buddhist logic. And second of all, the Tibetans are never going to let a Westerner tell them what to do."

"I wonder who I can ask," Ani Lamo said, looking around distractedly. "All morning I've been trying to find this American nun, Tashi Nyimo, and at this point I think I'm just going to go home. Have you heard about her? She meditated for three years in a cave. She's supposed to be enlightened by now."

"Maybe you should ask Hans," I suggested. The German monk had just turned the corner of the McLeod Ganj temple and was spinning the prayer wheels mounted on the temple's fence with all his might. "He knows everything. He's out all day and night. I don't think he ever sleeps."

"Yeah, right," Ani Lamo scoffed, rolling her eyes. "The guy is a total lunatic."

"Hans," I shouted. "Come here for a second."

"Vot can I do for you?" Hans asked in an even, metallic voice as he approached us.

"Have you seen an American nun walking around this morning?"

"I have seen many zings," Hans replied smugly. "In particular I've vitnessed a tall Vestern nun performing a strange dance on zeh roof of Kamal's two-story phone booth, on zeh next street."

As much as we wanted to dismiss Hans's testimony, something about the image of a Western nun dancing on the roof of a phone booth compelled us to remain silent. *It was possible.* Stranger things have happened in the Himalayas.

"Follow me," Hans commanded, jumping lightly over the open sewer separating the temple from Samosa Shop No. 13.

There was something epic about the scene that followed—the Indians shaking their heads, the Tibetans clicking their tongues, and then high above, Tashi Nyimo, looking intensely into the distance, as if waiting for the right moment to jump into the Absolute.

Kamal, the owner of the phone booth, appeared on the second-floor balcony, climbed on a chair, and extended his hand, inviting Tashi Nyimo to come down.

"I am the Buddha and no one can fucking touch me," she shouted and walked to the opposite corner of the roof.

"Shouldn't we try to bring her down?" I asked.

"She's not going to jump," Ani Lamo said with disdain. "I know her. She just wants some attention."

At this point three Indian police officers arrived on the scene, dressed in thick beige pants and sweaters, polished bamboo bats dangling from their belts. The senior police officer, a man of courage and mustache, walked straight to Ani Lamo and pointed at the roof of Kamal's phone booth.

"May I inquire what this proper woman is doing up there?" he barked, standing on tiptoe for greater effect.

"You may," Ani Lamo answered nonchalantly.

"Then I must!" the senior officer ordered, clasping his hands behind his back.

Ani Lamo and I looked at each other and it was understood: we had to bail out before the situation turned sour. Taking advantage of the heated exchange that had arisen between the officers and Kamal, Ani Lamo began edging out toward a dark alley between the nearby buildings. I took a few steps sideways toward a mobile omelet stall and bent down, pretending to root for something very important in my bag.

"May I inquire after the proper name of the woman standing on the roof?" the senior officer demanded, catching up with Ani Lamo.

"I do not know that proper woman properly," Ani Lamo responded, suppressing a smile.

Clearly confused about the meaning of this answer, the senior officer shouted at the other two policemen to bring him a glass of chai, then pulled a notepad and a pencil out of his back pocket. "May I take madam's personal information—name, address, country of origin."

"My information?" Ani Lamo asked, pointing at herself. "Tomorrow."

Fortuitously, at this moment the crowd was dispersed by the appearance of a giant Tata Motors truck, which brushed a string of tables exhibiting plastic paraphernalia and cheap gadgetry—sending the sellers running for their lives—and then got jammed between a telephone pole and a taxicab parked under a balcony. Severed electric cables dangled ominously above the truck driver's cabin, where a small Indian man kept revving the engine, convinced, against the odds, that he could destroy every obstacle standing in his way and squeeze through the narrow street.

With the situation descending into chaos and the senior officer blowing his police whistle and screaming at the truck driver to get out, Ani Lamo and I fled the scene, each taking a different route.

I decided to walk home through the forest to clear my thoughts and get some perspective on the events of this afternoon, but soon discovered that I was being followed. I sped up, jumping from one volcanic rock to the next without considering the distance or the texture of the surface on which I was going to land. After I slipped and nearly killed myself on a surprisingly slimy and mossy stone, I turned around and saw Hans, jumping incautiously, his *zen* wrapped around his waist.

"What's wrong with you, Hans," I said, exasperated. "I thought I was being followed by the police!"

"Your nun friend," Hans said with a big grin.

"Ani Lamo? What about her?"

"She has zeh balls," Hans announced, as if he were revealing a secret.

"What balls?"

"Zeh balls."

I looked around in desperation and tried to think of ways to end the conversation as quickly as possible. Ani Dawa's mother was right: Westerners were insane. Their search for truth was just another delusion of grandeur, their Enlightenment nothing more than a nervous breakdown.

"Hans," I said in a cold I've-had-enough-bullshit voice, "I've no idea what you are talking about."

"Zeh. Balls," Hans repeated, this time with a fierce expression.

We stood and looked at each other for about a minute, and I realized that I had taken the wrong approach.

"Why don't you use your supernatural powers and make some rain," I suggested casually. "Look at this weather. It's too perfect."

"Okay," he consented.

Then I turned around and walked home. It rained all night.

Six

I met Om Giridi for the first time in October, while I was still living on Jogibara Road. Om Giridi was a forty-four-year-old Indian Shiva priest with long, knotted hair, a thin beard, incredibly delicate fingers, and a serene, handsome face at odds with the stunned and disoriented look in his eyes. When I found him sitting cross-legged on my doorstep, smoking a *biddie* and molding a Play-Doh-like mixture of herbs and incense, I had no other option but to invite him in. He didn't say much, except that he could spend three days and three nights buried underground without any air. It was a ritual that he performed at least twice a month a sacred spot on one of the hills above Dharamsala. As he got up to leave, he stood for a minute or two by the window in a trance, his eyes fixed on my small table loaded with Tibetan books, and then decided to consecrate the room by placing lucky charms in all the strategic spots: one above the door, one tied to the leg of my bed, and one in each of the room's four corners. Walking out onto the patio, he summoned my landlord, Mr. Chandradas, and his wife, Mrs. Lakshmi, and gave them a long talk, interspersed with fiery, rhetorical questions and finger-pointing at the sky. It all ended with Mrs. Lakshmi placing a glass of chai and a bowl of *suji* on my doorstep—a sign that my status had been suddenly raised to that of a saddhu, or holy man. Slightly embarrassed, I took the chai and the *suji*, nodding at Mrs. Lakshmi, and in reply, both Mr. Chandradas and Mrs. Lakshmi got off the ground and, palms clasped in prayer, bowed down with such vigor that I thought they might keel over and fall at my feet. I never found out what Om Giridi had told them.

A few days later, I was walking back home from Sherig Parkhang, the Tibetan printing press, with a dozen looseleaf books tied together in a bundle, when I noticed that the metal gate of the recently built roadside Shiva temple was ajar and someone had placed a lit butter lamp and a stick of incense at the entrance. Curious to see what the new temple's interior looked like, I climbed the stone stairway and came face-to-face with Om Giridi, who was smiling, a *kusa*-grass broom in his hand.

"*Namaste*, Gi," he greeted me, tipping his head to one side. "You came to see me?"

"I actually didn't know this was your temple," I confessed.

"Let me finish, and we will go inside," Om Giridi said. With a few quick strokes of the broom, he scooped the leaves scattered around the temple into a small heap.

Keeping a constant *om-shiva-om, om-shiva-om* drone under his nose, he walked over to a squat yellow room at the far end of the courtyard and ushered me in.

"This is my new home," Om Giridi informed me, propping the broom in a corner. "I will sleep here every Tuesday."

"Why only Tuesday?" I wondered.

Om Giridi kneeled next to a kerosene stove and fumbled in his bag for matches.

"On Monday I sleep in Dharmkot; there is a temple near the waterfall. Wednesdays and Thursdays I sleep outside in the forest."

I sat on the floor and watched him start the stove. He moved slowly and gracefully, almost as if he were afraid to stir up the air. When he got the flame to the size that he wanted, he tore the corner of a plastic bag of milk with his nails and dumped its contents into a blackened brass pot. Next, he grabbed a rusted tin can from behind the stove and pulled out a dozen newspaper rolls twisted on both ends like bow ties. The first one that he opened contained a slice of hash the size of a cigar. He smelled it, tested its firmness with his fingers, and set it aside. In the rest of the newspaper bow ties he found unprocessed black tea leaves, cardamom shells, cinnamon sticks, cloves, sugar, nuts, raisins, and masala spices. He cracked a few cardamom shells, crushed the microscopic seeds that spilled onto the cement floor with a spoon, and added the powder to the milk.

While we waited for the chai to cool down, Om Giridi grabbed a pitcher of water and two glasses and went outside to rinse them out. I studied the bare walls, the paneless window, the rope of dandelions outlining the door frame, the bell and the rusty metal trident placed on the floor next to a calendar-size painting of an Indian yogi, and tried to imagine what it must feel like to live the life of Om Giridi, looking after remote Shiva shrines, sleeping alone under the stars, and collecting donations from the local villagers.

Grinning, Om Giridi tiptoed across the room and filled the clean glasses with chai.

"I am very happy that you are my friend," Om Giridi confided, pulling a packet of cigarette papers out of his bag. "I saw you and thought, he and I are the same."

"Well, for one thing, if I were buried alive, I wouldn't last more than a minute."

"Oh, that's easy," Om Giridi laughed modestly. "I can teach you."

"Really?"

"Yes. You just need to know *dhayani*." Om Giridi pronounced the Sanskrit word for "absorption" with extra breath, turning the *h* into a long, eerie sigh.

"So how does it work?" I asked.

"First I go very, very deep," Om Giridi explained, raising his hand as if he were addressing a large gathering of people. "Then I think *om-shiva-om*, *om-shiva-om* until everything is Shiva. My hand is Shiva, and my leg is Shiva, and time is Shiva."

"That's incredible!" I said, trying to look impressed.

"It takes some practice."

"What about flying?" I said. "Do you think people can learn how to fly?" "Flying is nice," Om Giridi said, with an approving head wobble. "My teacher who lives on the other side of the mountain—he used to fly all the time."

"Why doesn't he fly anymore?"

"He broke his leg," Om Giridi said, massaging his knee with a pained expression to demonstrate how much it must have hurt. "He doesn't like flying anymore."

I looked at Om Giridi, puzzled. He was so humble and unpretentious that I felt compelled to give him the benefit of the doubt. Perhaps when Shiva priests got really, really stoned, they became lighter and started floating about like helium-filled balloons. Maybe Shiva priests only appeared to have a physical body, but in reality they resided in a black hole filled with Shiva essence. Maybe Himalayan cows were representatives of an advanced bipedal civilization that safeguarded the doors to other dimensions.

Om Giridi rolled a joint made of crushed *biddies* and four fat balls of hash and licked it sealed. Palms clasped together, he nodded in the direction of the Shiva temple, and then lit the joint, sucking at it with the ferociousness of someone who had been denied air for a long time.

We fell silent, and I watched him slip into a reverie, breathing slower and slower, his wide open eyes staring right through me. With his disheveled hair, blistered feet, cheeks hardened by sun and wind, and ragged saffron robe that smelled of moss and underwood, he was a true child of the mountains, a friendly Himalayan leopard that could go near humans but would never betray its nature.

Sitting diagonally from the door, I could see an Indian man with a basketful of lychees on his head squatting on one of the white-painted metal

barrels delineating the outer edge of the road curve. The remaining white
barrels were occupied by monkeys, who didn't seem at all concerned by the
proximity of the man or the basket of lychees and watched poignantly as each
passing car went around the curve and disappeared down the slope, raising a
cloud of dust. It was fall, the wedding season, and I could hear the distant
thunder of tablas, now overlapping, now going out of synch, their echo
bouncing from hill to hill and then blending with the relentless roar of river.
Perched on cedars, pines, and rhododendrons, local Indian women dressed in
salwar kameez outfits and armed with tiny curved blades lopped off twigs and
whole branches, turning every tree into an armless trunk with a crown of
shrubs at its top. Shimmering in the soft, amber hue of the late afternoon sun,
the Himalayan pinnacles looked like a sundae that was about to melt away.

Om Giridi snapped out of his trance, smiled at me, and quickly relit his
joint.

"Did you see what I have?" he asked, pointing at the rectangular box
behind me. "You said you like to play music."

My heart jumped. I turned around, removed the maroon scarf that the
box was wrapped in, and discovered a beautifully lacquered harmonium with
seven knobs and a range of three and a half octaves. An inscription on a
small metal plate read "Pakrashi & Co, 82 Rashbehari Avenue, Calcutta."

"Do you play?" I asked him, caressing the keys.

"I only know a few Shiva songs," he replied. "Please, try it."

After tinkering with the knobs for some time, I realized that four of them
controlled the volume, while the other three were drones. Pushing the bel-
lows with my left hand, I struck a few seventh chords, but they sounded
horrible, so I resorted to running Indian scales with an A-sharp drone on the
bottom. Om Giridi was very pleased.

The feel of the keys under my fingers and the hashish smoke billowing
around me triggered a rush of memories: I saw Boston's rooftops and Mass.
Ave. with all the beggars collecting change in Store 24 paper cups in front of
Berklee College of Music; I remembered the dizzying effect that the sun,

setting over the red-and-white arteries of the Mass. Turnpike, had on me as I waited for the bus outside Tower Records, a current of hot air infused with sweat and machine oil gushing out of the T entrance behind me; I remembered smoking pot in the Berklee practice rooms, and jamming with whoever was around—a saxophonist, a bass player, a drummer; I remembered going to the nine-o'clock Jazz History class on Monday, still drunk and stoned from Saturday and Sunday, and sleeping through Miles Davis's quintets or Coltrane's *Giant Steps,* occasionally waking up to the voice of the professor sitting at a small table on the unlit stage of Berklee Performance Center, who would announce the year and the name of the track that he was about to play: "Here is a piece called *The Believer* from December of 1957, recorded in Hackensack, New Jersey, with recording engineer Rudy Van Gelder." For some reason, it was always Hackensack, New Jersey, and always Rudy Van Gelder.

I wondered what I'd be doing now if I hadn't left Boston. Would I still be in school or would I be out in the real world, looking for gigs in Cambridge and Jamaica Plain? Now there was the insurmountable question: what life-altering circumstances had brought me to India? Lots of people smoke pot and break up with their girlfriends. Something else had happened, a sudden convergence of separate narrative lines, of different life cycles. When I had woken up early that morning, two summers before, when the course of my life had changed completely, I'd had no way of knowing that in just a few hours I would travel farther than any airplane could've taken me; that I would end up in a place I'd never conceived of before. I wish I could say that there had been some dramatic event—maybe lightning striking my piano, or an apparition of the Buddha floating out of my closet—that could explain my sudden loss of interest in the path I'd been pursuing up to that point in my life. But there'd been nothing dramatic: no visions, no brain-shattering spiritual insights, no guiding voices, no thunder and lightning. I woke up just as on any other day—preoccupied with thoughts about classes, deadlines, bills, work, and girls. I went to the bathroom to brush my teeth and see if the previous night's drinking and smoking had left any visible traces on my face. Feeling too lazy to take a shower, I combed my shoulder-length hair and tied it in a ponytail. Then, somewhere between the bathroom and the living room, I lost my sense of purpose. I sat on the floor by the window, staring at the daycare playground next door. I lived on Harvard Street in Cambridge, across from a very old and now abandoned factory at the back of a baseball field. Moving my attention from the chatter of the kids running around the playground to the chatter in my mind, it occurred to me that I had absolutely no control over my reactions and my emotions. A paranoid thought made me paranoid; a happy thought made me happy; a sad thought made me sad. I was a puppet pulled by strings, strings that extended beyond my control and the confines of my being. All the anxieties about dying and surviving and achieving the things that I was supposed to achieve—where had they come from? Who was in control of my life? And what did I really want to do with my life? I had never asked myself this question before, not in an honest way. What would I learn after four years of going to classes, working, and partying? What would I learn after a hundred years of piano playing? Wasn't life a secret, a primordial code waiting to be cracked? Wasn't there a higher truth that explained everything, an ultimate truth? I had always been convinced that such a truth existed, even though I had no idea what it could have been about. Staring out the window at the tall chimney of the old factory defining the skyline of Central Square, I toyed with the idea of dropping everything and embarking on an epic journey to discover the ultimate truth. If I really wanted to be honest with myself—for once—I would follow my heart and do what I thought was really important. But how did one go about finding the ultimate truth? Which religion or philosophy professed to know about it? Having grown up in a communist utopian society whose penchant for initiations, rituals, burial ceremonies, and mummy worship had rivaled the necromantic fanaticism of the ancient Egyptians, I had learned very little about world religions. At school I had been forced to study *Das Capital*, *The Communist Manifesto*, and the dogma of historical materialism. I had never opened a bible or taken a religion class. I hadn't even read Hermann Hesse's *Siddhartha*, on the grounds that all my friends had read it before me. What I had read was the Russians: Bulgakov, Dostoyevsky, Goncharov, Chekhov, Ilf and Petrov—especially Ilf and Petrov, obsessively. My awareness of the East, as a mythological construct, had been purely tangential—a vague idea of the existence of a strange dimension that provided the larger context for the Bulgarian subculture of black magic, divination, and witchcraft. Growing up in Sofia, the Bulgarian capital, I had heard and witnessed things that had defied all common sense and logic. I'd had my share of the supernatural—from the hundreds of Gypsy women who had stopped me near the old mosque in downtown Sofia, told me the future, and then prepared magical bullets; to my mother's clairvoyant powers (on one occasion in the early eighties, she'd saved the life of her first cousin by not letting him get on an airplane that he'd bought a ticket for. I had witnessed how my mom had held his hand on that eerie morning and begged him to unpack his suitcase and stay over at our house another night, repeating again and again that she'd had a bad dream. I had also seen the cousin's expression upon hearing the news of the plane crash—his plane—a few hours later); to the surreal stories of my grandparents, great-grandparents, and relatives communicating with the dead and knowing the time of their death. And whenever I had talked to my parents about all this—both of them doctors, and sworn atheists—we'd come to the inescapable conclusion that these things had come from the East—from the Gypsies, the Thracians, and the original Asian tribes who had invaded the Balkans in the sixth century.

Determined to find out right away what had been written on the subject of the ultimate truth, I walked to the Harvard bookstore and returned with a little book on meditation. Sitting cross-legged, I counted my breath—one, two, three . . . twenty—and then watched my thoughts arise magically, from nowhere, like dust devils transporting leaves and debris from one place to another with a great amount of energy and determination, but ultimately with absolutely no purpose. Why hadn't I been taught how to do this before?

I was twenty years old and had never looked around the space where I'd lived. My whole life, I had assumed that I'd lived in a room within a house within a city. I had never thought of looking into the room within the room, the inner space of shadows and winds and strange clouds gliding over the surface of an alien, uncharted landscape. It seemed to me that the very posture of meditation—legs tied in a knot, arms forming a loop—shifted the axis of perception, making the self something external and observable, a wild horse that had been hobbled and forced to lie quietly on the ground. When I finally decided to make my morning coffee, it was ten o'clock. My roommates were still in bed, and I'd already begun making plans to quit school and go to India.

THE SOUNDS OF INSISTENT HONKING and a minivan door sliding shut caught my attention, and I immediately sensed trouble.

"Lodro Chosang?"

Ani Dawa's voice sounded crisp and resolute. Om Giridi's eyes widened, and he quickly stubbed his joint on the cement floor.

"Hi," Ani Dawa said as she peeked into the smoky room.

"Have some chai, Ani Dawa," Om Giridi offered, pointing at the kerosene stove. "Please, sit down."

Ani Dawa looked at him sternly and took a step backward. "The taxi is waiting for me. I have to go."

"Do you need any help with something?" I asked, getting up.

"No, no, you should stay," Ani Dawa said, walking away. "Bye!"

How did Ani Dawa find out that I was at the Shiva temple? I knew that she hated Om Giridi. She thought that in addition to being a follower of a crazy, non-Buddhist religion, he was a fake saddhu and his real job was selling drugs to Westerners. To her, that I would choose to befriend such a man was most certainly a sign of betrayal.

I thanked Om Giridi for the chai, promised to return, and ran after Ani Dawa. By the time I reached the road, the taxi had already left and so I cut across a precipitous hill and managed to intercept the cab just as it emerged from the sharp curve at the bottom. The driver hit the brakes and pushed the sliding door open, releasing a deafening accretion of violin screeches, tabla thunder, and piercing female voices.

Ani Dawa was clearly mad at me: she was sitting next to the driver, hugging her bag, and staring out the window.

"Is Ama-la okay?" I shouted over the music. "I noticed that she wasn't feeling well this morning."

"She is fine," Ani Dawa shouted back.

"What's wrong, then?"

Ani Dawa turned around and pulled a *katak* out of her bag.

"Oh, Jesus," I said, breaking into a sweat.

"You should say, 'oh, Shiva,'" Ani Dawa suggested.

"'Oh, Shiva' is much better," the taxi driver agreed, turning down the volume.

"I waited for you all afternoon," Ani Dawa said. "And my aunt is coming over tonight. I haven't had a chance to buy groceries yet."

"I am really sorry, Ani-la, what can I say? I thought we were meeting Geshe Yama Tseten tomorrow."

"People told me you were smoking *tamak nagpo* and playing music at Om Giridi's temple, and I didn't believe them."

"I didn't smoke hashish with Om Giridi!"

Ani Dawa shook her head and handed me a piece of paper folded into a perfect square.

"What's this?" I asked, unraveling what appeared to be a note in Tibetan, scribbled indecipherably.

"It's the name of the textbook that you have to bring on Friday at eight o'clock in the morning," Ani Dawa announced smugly.

"So Geshe Yama Tseten agreed to take me on as a personal student?"

"Yes, even though he hasn't met you. I had to lie to him and tell him you didn't come to introduce yourself because you weren't feeling well."

"I am so sorry, Ani-la!"

"I am not doing this for you anymore. I am a nun and I lied to one of the highest teachers in Namgyal Monastery. I will probably be reborn as a hungry ghost."

"That's great! I am planning to come back as a hungry ghost myself."

Though I joked and went out of my way to apologize for being an absent-minded *Engie*, there was no denying that Ani Dawa's controlling personality had started to worry me. I knew that she meant well, but I didn't want her to lie for me, and I certainly didn't want her to tell me what to do and who my friends could be.

We entered the Katwali bazaar and the driver pulled over next to a juice stand that smelled of wine and was coated with a veil of flies. Within seconds, we were surrounded by a dozen beggar kids, whining *Guru-ji, chapati dedo! Chapati dedo, Guru-ji!*, tapping their stomachs, and stuffing their mouths with imaginary food. I started searching my bag for coins, but Ani Dawa scolded the kids and pushed them away.

"Ani-la!" someone shouted across the street. I turned around and saw the Western monk with the smug smile and suede duffel bag who had made the comment about Nirvana being a place for pussies.

"*Tashi Delek*," Ani Dawa greeted him. "Have you met my student, Lodro?"

The monk glanced at me briefly and extended his hand. "I think I've seen you before. What's your real name?"

"Nikolai," I said. "We met briefly in front of the Tibetan Library a month ago."

"Nikola," he repeated slowly, dropping the *i* and placing the accent on the *o*. "It's a Serbian name. They call me Tsar. How long have you been a monk?"

"Three months. How about you?"

"The same."

"And how has it been for you so far?"

"Oh, it's been great," Tsar answered, putting on a grave, almost religious expression. "I wake up at five o'clock in the morning and meditate all day. I never thought I'd be able to quit smoking—but here I am, haven't touched a cigarette in three months."

How strange, I thought to myself, remembering the four cigarettes he bummed off Lobsang the last time I saw him.

"Lodro is from Bulgaria," Ani Dawa informed Tsar. "That's close to Bosnia, right?"

"You are Bosnian?" I asked incredulous. I'd never expected to meet someone from that part of the world, let alone another monk.

"I was born in Bosnia, but I've lived everywhere," Tsar explained and then turned to Ani Dawa. "How is your mother, Ama-la? I stopped by your house a few times but you weren't home."

"She is doing well—she is out all day, walking around. Would you like to come over for dinner tonight?"

"I don't think I can come tonight," Tsar said, glancing nervously at the tailor shop across the street. "Maybe next week."

"We should get together sometime," I suggested.

Tsar looked uninterested. "Yeah. I am sure I'll see you around. I have to go now. Good-bye Ani-la, and say hi to your mother for me."

"Maybe we can play a game of chess," I called after him.

Tsar immediately turned around. "I live in Durga Nivas, in a family compound. Just ask anyone and they will tell you which room I'm in."

He nodded good-bye and made his way through traffic, pushing a homeless cow with his umbrella and forcing an incoming rickshaw to swerve frantically around him, almost hitting one of the beggar kids standing outside the bank.

"It's really funny that he tells people to call him Tsar," I observed.

Ani Dawa shrugged her shoulders. She didn't know what "Tsar" meant.

Seven

Twice a month the monks and nuns in Dharamsala gathered in the Main Temple to attend *so jong,* a purification ceremony where they confessed their minor transgressions, such as singing, dancing, touching money, eating at night, walking alone with members of the opposite sex, and masturbating. There were two prevailing classes of Buddhist monks: novices, or *getsul,* and fully ordained monks, or *gelong.* Being a novice monk, I was responsible for keeping thirty-six vows, of which I could remember only eight or nine at any given time. *Gelong* monks, in turn, had to keep two hundred and fifty-three vows. The only person I knew who was capable of enumerating all of these vows was Josh, a British monk with a Sex Pistols tattoo on his arm. Legend had it that he had arrived in Dharamsala with a green Mohawk, ragged jeans, and a taste for hash parties. In his manifestation as a Buddhist monk it was nearly impossible for me to imagine him singing in chorus with Johnny Rotten or holding a joint. To say that he was zealous would be an understatement. If he had lived during the Spanish Inquisition, he would've surely been appointed to the Supreme Council. Josh, incidentally, was also the only monk in Dharamsala who observed the vow of not touching money. He had unordained Tibetans withdraw money from his bank account and buy his groceries. In the first days following my ordination, Josh lent me a thousand-page book (an English translation of a Thai monastic manual) that offered a detailed analysis of the scriptural basis and interpretation of Buddhist monastic laws. In it I found the stories of the so-called first-timers, those disciples of the Buddha who had set the precedents for the two hundred and fifty-three monastic transgressions. I learned that the no-sex rule had been originally established after a seemingly devout and diligent monk named Sudinna had taken his former wife to the forest and had sex with her three times, apparently in an effort to please his mother, who had gone hysterical about having grandkids. I learned that a monk who commits any of the four downfalls destroys the physical basis for holding monastic vows and automatically becomes a layperson. The four downfalls were: having sex with a human being or an animal, killing a human, stealing an object worth more than 1/24 troy ounce of gold (roughly twenty dollars), and lying to others that one had supernatural power. How one could destroy the physical basis of the monastic vows, I could not figure out. What kind of substance were the vows made of? Say I stole an umbrella that had originally cost fifty dollars and that could be resold for anywhere from one to forty dollars. How would my monastic substance know if I had committed the downfall of stealing? Or say I stole a twenty-dollar flashlight on a day when a troy ounce of gold had traded three or four percent lower on the New York Stock Exchange?

Another useful piece of information I found in the book was that if a monk stood behind a corner of a building waiting to shoot person A, but instead shot person B, who had somehow managed to turn the corner before person A, the monk wouldn't have committed a downfall because he had failed to properly identify his victim. In a different scenario, if a monk's friend suffered cardiac arrest but the monk decided not to call for an ambulance and let his friend die, he wouldn't incur a downfall because in order to be considered a killer, the monk has to *do* something. Not calling the doctor would constitute inaction, and thus could not serve as grounds for a downfall.

On the day of the second *so jong* in October, I woke up at dawn and grabbed the brick-size monastic manual and my *chogo*, a ragged yellow blanket that all monks attending *so jong* were supposed to wear. I started up the road, the cool morning drizzle licking my face and shaved head. Against my better judgment, I had decided to leave my umbrella at home, so by the time I got to Josh's room, the drizzle had turned into a rainstorm and I was soaked from head to toe. Josh lived in a moss-enveloped monastic compound across from the Main Temple. The door to his room was open, which I interpreted as a sign that he'd been waiting for me for a long time.

"Shall we go?" he asked, getting off his bed. "Did you bring my book?"

I handed him the monastic manual and looked around the room. There were hardly any personal objects, just a bed, a few books, robes, a box of cocoa powder, two cups, and an electric coil for heating water. I couldn't stand electric coils. To me, they symbolized a padded Western experience of India that I absolutely abhorred. To my mind, understanding India began with buying your first kerosene stove and kneading your first ball of dough with tar-stained fingers.

"I made a Xerox copy of the stanzas that you have to recite during the ceremony," Josh said, handing me a few looseleaf Tibetan pages. "It's very easy, you'll see."

"So how does it work?" I asked, glancing at the text. "Is it a confession?"

"Yes, just a general one."

"What if I want to confess specific transgressions, like singing and dancing to a George Michael song while taking a shower? Or tickling another monk?"

Josh stared at me without blinking.

"You don't have to laugh," I told him. "You might break a vow."

"I will certainly not," he said and gestured at the open door.

We walked out and joined a crowd of monks and nuns, all trying to squeeze through the tiny metal gate of the Institute of Buddhist Dialectics at the same time. Standing in line was definitely not part of the Tibetan character. The typical hole-in-the-wall convenience stores in Dharamsala were perpetually besieged by monks, nuns, old people, and kids, pushing one another and shouting their orders at the store vendors. When I first arrived in town, I would stand at the periphery of a shopping crowd and wait patiently for my turn, thinking that eventually everyone would calm down and I would be able to purchase a kilogram of potatoes without having to push frail nuns or elbow the tougher monks in the stomach. It wasn't long before I started taking advantage of my height, my shoulders, and my long hands. Now I was always served immediately. Seeing my unprecedented access, the old Tibetan ladies behind me would often hand me their money and ask me to buy their groceries. "*Kushu-la*," they would call out to me, "*kuchi, kuchi*"—please—"get me two kilos of chapati flour and a can of ghee."

Josh and I forced our way through the metal gate and took the stairs leading to the Main Temple. We passed through the dormitory of the Institute of Buddhist Dialectics, an amorphous, multilevel structure that enclosed a small yard where the monks played table tennis in their free time, and then came onto an intermediate level where a few old Tibetan men scurried between two enormous pots with burning oil to made *tsog*—deep-fried pieces of dough that were consecrated and handed to the people attending the prayers. The Main Temple stood on the very top of all the stacked-up monastery buildings—a spacious, square room rimmed by a balcony on all sides.

"Go with this *gelong*," Josh told me, pointing at a tall monk standing alone by the entrance.

"What do I tell him?" I asked, but Josh ran into the temple and joined a group of monks who seemed to know him quite well.

I approached the tall monk and tapped him on the shoulder. He turned around and I showed him the photocopied Tibetan pages. "Is it all right for us to sit together?"

He nodded and slumped to the floor. I put on my *chogo* and tried to see who was sitting on the throne at the very front. Josh had told me that sometimes *so jong* was led by the Dalai Lama himself. Suddenly the entire gathering started chanting the preliminary prayers and I was overtaken by the self-annihilating and at the same time blissful sensation that one experiences in large crowds where everyone speaks and moves in unison. For the first time I felt that my new identity wasn't just an abstract idea but a reality that had become an inseparable part of me: I was a monk, I had vows, and I belonged to a monastic tradition that spanned over two millennia. I saw myself in the faces of the monks and nuns around me. The smell of old leather sandals and dirty feet, the rustle of a hundred *zens*, the young monks shouting the prayers with sarcastic dramatism, the nuns giggling, the old *gelongs*, hunched up and toothless—this was my world. I had burned all bridges and forgotten my home. I had no other past but this past. There was no future but this future.

I looked again at the front row. The Dalai Lama was nowhere to be seen. The senior monk on the throne concluded the prayer with folded hands as all the monks and nuns turned around to face their confession partners and began reciting what sounded like a well-rehearsed dialogue played on fastforward. I started reading from the pages Josh had given me, but the monk I'd been paired with didn't seem interested in taking part in the ritual: he was staring at the nuns across the hall. Suddenly, the ceremony was over and everyone rushed out, the young *getsuls* clapping their hands in one another's faces, debate-style (the ancient tradition of debate that most Tibetan monks study and practice for hours every day is quite militant, a form of verbal karate), and shouting affirmatives and negatives like "So you can see space directly," and "Then you can't see space directly," and "A human is someone who can talk and understand speech," and "Therefore you're not a human." Shoes and sandals were flying in every direction, old Tibetan ladies were running away with oil-dripping newspapers full of *tsog* offerings, the monastery professors, or *Geshes*, were giving orders, and the nuns were staring stubbornly at their feet, as if fearing that the proximity of so many wild boys could trigger an explosion that would bring down the Himalayas.

"How did it go?" I heard Josh's voice behind me.

"It was pretty manic," I told him. "And the whole time I felt like I was being bitten by a thousand mosquitoes. Now I can't find my left sandal."

"You've got the fleas," Josh informed me, his face beaming. He looked like someone who'd just been released from purgatory.

"So how do you get rid of fleas?" I asked.

"Go home, take your robes off, and spread them on the roof of your house. The sun will chase the fleas away."

"Josh, it's still raining."

"You have to leave your robes out anyway. Otherwise you're going to carry the fleas with you for months."

After I finally found my missing sandal, I went to the monastery restaurant for a glass of chai. I needed to go to the Library of Tibetan Works and Archives to photocopy a text for my first class with Geshe Yama Tseten at the end of the week. The library was a few miles away from the Main Temple, and about halfway between Upper and Lower Dharamsala. I pulled out the note that Geshe Yama Tseten had given to Ani Dawa and tried to decipher it. The only thing I could make out was *lo rig*, an inquiry into the mind's functions, which was one of the main subjects that young monks studied in the first years of their education.

I didn't get out of the library until late in the afternoon. The librarian knew the text that Geshe Yama Tseten had requested, but said that it had been misplaced and I would have a very hard time finding it. He took me to a ceiling-high bookshelf and pointed casually at the dozens of thick binders containing thousands of pages of photocopied material. "See if you can find it," he told me with an apologetic smile. "If you have the time."

I had the time and in fact found the text, though I wasted a good hour or two reading through miscellaneous writings on the "Mind Only" school, Emptiness, and *Mahamudra*. I made it to the Xerox room just as the Tibetan lady working there was getting ready to leave. "It's just ten pages," I told her, opening the heavy binder. She sighed and put her bag down.

"You are lucky," she informed me when she finished photocopying the pages. "I just ran out of paper."

I thanked her and gave her five rupees for the photocopies. She pocketed the money and suddenly jolted forward, as if she'd been pricked with a needle. I pretended that I hadn't noticed and edged out toward the door. The lady jumped again, this time less violently, and her face turned red.

"Did you bring in the fleas?" she asked me angrily.

"No," I lied.

"How am I going to go home now? *Kun chog sum!*"

It was still raining, but I decided to take the long footpath winding through the village because it was less crowded than the main road and I wanted to read the *lo rig* text as I walked along. I recited the first page aloud, and my heart went aflutter. I couldn't believe that I was able to read and understand terms like direct perception, inferential awareness, and prime cognition. There was something incredibly special about gaining access to a body of knowledge available only to a relatively small group of people. Even if I were to die in India, I could at least say that I had tried to look for answers beyond the confines of my Western upbringing. I wished I could explain to my parents—who'd been vehemently opposed to my dropping out of music school and becoming a monk—how important it was for me to have the opportunity to go to someone like Geshe Yama Tseten and discuss, say, the definition of direct perception. Was there a single thing in the world that was more important than understanding one's mind? I didn't think so.

I had come to the point where the village footpath and Jogibara Road converged when I heard loud singing and seconds later saw Tsar emerge at the top of the hill, followed by a woman dressed in baggy pants and a rainbow-dyed T-shirt.

"*Yebem li ti pichku materinu,*" Tsar sang at the top of his lungs, his voice resounding throughout the valley.

I had to stop and laugh. It's not every day that you see a Buddhist monk singing "I'm going to fuck your mother's cunt" in Serbian.

"Nikola!" Tsar called out to me, as he jumped from stone to stone with amazing confidence. He wasn't carrying an umbrella and his robes were completely drenched.

"Your *zen* must weigh about fifty kilograms," I told him when he got closer.

"Oh, fuck the rain," he answered. "I'm not made out of sugar."

The woman, sporting a tiny pink umbrella, smiled at Tsar, and I immediately noticed that there was a weird chemistry going on between the two.

"This is Kaila," Tsar said. "She is from Israel."

"Tsar told me about you," Kaila said, offering her hand. "You and Tsar are the only monks from the Balkans, right?"

"Nikola," Tsar interrupted, "come over to my house, I'll make chai, and then we could cook dinner together."

"I don't know, I am supposed to have a lesson with Ani Dawa at five."

"You could skip one lesson," Tsar said. "Come on, I live in the family compound right over there."

I hesitated for a moment, but Tsar took my arm and pulled me along.

We cut through the waist-long grass and entered a tiled courtyard fenced by a dozen small houses, some coated with slaked lime, some painted cyan, and still others stamped all over with round cow-dung patties. A young Indian woman holding a baby boy and an umbrella greeted Tsar and asked him in Hindi if he needs milk. "*Dood?*" Tsar repeated, puzzled. "Oh, *dood*, yes, *acha*, I need *dood*, *shukria*."

Tsar unbolted the padlock to his room, kicked the door open, and gestured for us to enter.

"Do you know how to work a kerosene stove?" he asked me, hanging his *zen* on a clothesline running across the roofed patio.

"I do."

"Then you put the water to boil and I'll go get the milk."

Tsar's room was dry, immaculately clean, and arranged with great care. A thin mattress, a bookshelf, a low table, and a makeshift easel holding a detailed pencil drawing of Buddha's head marked the living area, which was carpeted. The rest of the floor was covered with linoleum and served as the kitchen and washing area. There were two kerosene stoves set side by side; a large plastic tub with glasses, bowls, dishes, and frying pans; a bucket of water; a wooden chopping board; a metal cup filled with knives and silverware; a banged-up kettle; a jar of oil with a punctured cap, to allow a spoon to fit in; a box of Darjeeling; and an array of spices.

Kaila realized that I was looking for matches and pointed at the pack of India Kings on the floor. I found the matches inside the pack, pushed the stove pump all the way in, and lit the thread of kerosene that shot out of the fuse. Standing up to avoid the subsequent burst of wild flames, I walked to the window and looked out at the jagged Himalayan pinnacles and the valley, a jigsaw puzzle of rice paddies, markets, and tiny villages.

The door opened and in came Tsar, carrying a metal bucket.

"I milked the cow myself," he announced, taking off his monastic vest.

"Are Buddhist monks allowed to milk cows?" Kaila asked.

"Who cares?" Tsar laughed and untied his belt. A second later, his drenched *shanthab* collapsed on the floor and he stepped over it, naked.

"God, it's cold," he shouted and sauntered across the room to get his cigarettes.

I squatted next to the stove, closed the pressure valve, and pumped the piston until I got a steady blue flame. Then I put the kettle on top.

"I haven't smoked all day," Tsar announced, sticking a cigarette in his mouth.

I tossed him the matches and looked at Kaila. It was clear from the way she was trying to avoid staring at his penis that she had never seen him naked before.

"You've got a great view," I noted.

"I love it," Tsar replied, filling his lungs with smoke and rubbing his hairy chest. "On a clear day you could see all the way to Norbulingka. And the window is so low that at night I could lie in bed and watch as people in Lower Dharamsala and Kangra switch their lights on and off."

"So," Kaila said, turning to me, "why did you become a monk?"

Tsar laughed and grabbed a T-shirt and a saffron underskirt from the built-in shelf next to his mattress. "Leave the man alone. He probably gets this question a hundred times a day."

"I think it's a good question," Kaila insisted, putting her wavy hair in a ponytail. She was very pretty, and she knew it, too.

"Well, it's just one of the ways to deal with the fundamental paradox of life," I said. "Everything we do is in inverse proportion to the natural course of things. The longer we live, the more we invest in an identity that is destined to disappear. You could ignore this fact, but if you really think about it for a while, you might start having a hard time getting up in the morning. I was going to a music school in Boston, and one day I came home—after attending a Charles Ives class which gave me a horrendous headache—sat on the dilapidated couch in the living room, and tried to see my life as a whole, not as a succession of events, but as a single event, an act of living. What if I became the greatest composer or jazz pianist of all times? What if I had a family and a house and lots of friends? What if I died young without having a chance to do what I wanted? And did it matter? I had a roommate, Corey, who was unemployed and spent his days hanging out in Harvard Square in Cambridge, bumming joints off the drug dealers. I asked him, 'Corey, what do you think it is that we're running toward?' Of course, Corey was smoking a bong at that moment, so for a while he just nodded energetically, and then said, 'The finish line,' as if this was the easiest question anyone has ever asked him. And that was kind of a turning point for me. I didn't want to run to the finish line, collecting girlfriends, paychecks, apartments, papers, degrees, missed career opportunities, and all sorts of meaningless things on the way. What's the point of that? If we are going to lose everything one day, why not cut through the bullshit and get it over with now rather than later?"

"But what's the point of living as if you're already dead?" Kaila asked.

Tsar crouched between us and poured a glass of milk into the kettle.

"It's about freedom," I replied. "There's a certain pleasure in knowing that you are done with this world, and now you can focus on finding out what you're made of."

"There was this American guy, David, that I got ordained with," Tsar interrupted us, setting three glasses on the floor. "We were part of a group of Westerners that received vows from the Dalai Lama. After the ordination, David and I were walking, and he asked me what I was going to miss the most from my life as a layman. I said, going to the red light district in Amsterdam. I told him about these two Ethiopian girls, Saba and I don't remember what the other was called. I'd take them home once a week and we'd party until the morning. Poor David, he seemed absolutely terrified. I told him that we in the Balkans take sex very seriously and fuck for five or six hours at a time, and he said he's going to pray that I don't end up in hell. I don't know what's wrong with people. Everyone is trying to save me from going to hell, as if it's a bad place."

We heard a man shouting in the courtyard, someone ran past our door, and a powerful explosion shook the compound. Tsar threw himself on the ground, covering his head with his hands, then quickly got up and stormed out of the room.

"Who did this?" he shouted.

"It's Diwali, Guru-ji," a woman answered.

Tsar came back in and removed the kettle from the stove. "I could swear that Diwali was last week. I am surprised that these kids haven't blown a hole in the wall. You should see the size of the firecrackers that they play with."

"Have you ever been in a war zone before?" Kaila asked him, looking suspicious.

"Why?" Tsar asked.

"Because you have the reflexes of a soldier who has seen a lot of fighting. I knew an Israeli guy who used to put his head between his knees every time he heard a loud noise."

"I served in the army," Tsar said, "but I've never been in a war zone. I took the last train out of Sarajevo before the fighting started."

He filled the three cups with chai and leaned against the wall, stretching his feet. Kaila smiled at him and he smiled back, but there was something in his eyes that betrayed his smile, a cold, sinister undertow mixed in with desire and a sense of weariness, the kind that you see in the eyes of people who carry many secrets. I wondered how I'd ended up in the middle of this perverse love game. I sipped my tea and pretended not to notice what was going on.

"So you lived in Amsterdam?" I asked Tsar.

"I did, for a couple of years. It's a nice place—people there grow a lot of tulips."

"Fuck!" Kaila screamed and jumped to her feet. "Something bit me. Do you have bedbugs in your room?"

"Maybe," Tsar said. "But they are not going to kill you, I promise."

"There's something in my pants, I can feel it crawling around," Kaila cried and started jumping and kicking in the air.

"It's fleas," I told her.

"How do you know?" she asked.

"That's what it sounds like."

I grabbed my bag and got up to go. Tsar begged me to stay for dinner, but I told him that I had an appointment with Geshe Yama Tseten on Friday and I had to study the text that he had asked me to bring. "Stop by sometime," he called after me, and I promised that I would.

Ani Dawa's door was locked, which meant that she had gone into town with her mom and wasn't coming home for dinner. I thought about rolling a few chapatis in my room, but then I remembered that I had nothing to spread on them, not even a pack of the everlasting Amul butter, and so I walked upstairs to the chai shop owned by Mr. Singh, my landlord's son, and ordered two parathas. Mr. Singh was playing a tape of traditional Sikh hymns (harmonium, tabla, and a small choir) and I asked him what they were about. He said that they were about Guru Nanak, and that in the Golden Temple in Amritsar there were musicians who played these hymns twenty-four hours a day. I asked him why Sikhs carry a knife and he looked at the silver sheath poking under his shirt, almost surprised to see it there. "It has to do with defending our faith," he explained and then added, jokingly, that if he had to pull the knife one day, the blade would probably break off and he would have to fight with the handle: that's how old and unused his knife was.

I returned to my room, sat up in bed with the massive Tibetan-English dictionary that Lobsang had given me as a gift when we had first met, and went over the *lo rig* text, highlighting the unknown words and writing their definitions in the margins. I read until my eyes began to close involuntarily, but as soon as I turned off the light and assumed a horizontal position, I realized that there was no way in hell I was going to get any sleep that night. My bed was crawling with fleas, the table was inhabited by a mammoth woodworm that made loud, drilling sounds every two seconds, the moon was shining in my window, and Balu, my landlord's giant old dog, had parked himself outside my room and decided to have a barking match with the dogs in the neighboring village. For a good hour or two, I just lay in bed, motionless, giving my body to the fleas and trying to ignore all the noise. Then I went absolutely mad. Why does a woodworm eat only at night? And what the fuck does a woodworm look like? Is it a worm, is it like a beetle, or is it something the size of a flea? I wanted to chop the table to pieces and get to the motherfucker, just to hold him in my fist for a while—I couldn't kill him, of course, because of my monastic vows. *Vrrrr-vrrrr-vrrrr*, went the woodworm. I got up, cleared off the table, grabbed it by its legs, and slammed it on the ground as hard as I could. It was a well-built table, I had to acknowledge that. I opened the door and looked for a stone that I could throw at Balu, preferably something substantial and heavy. Seeing Balu dashing my way in what appeared to be a preemptive strike, I quickly retreated and crawled into bed again. *Vrrrr-vrrrr-vrrrr*, continued the woodworm. As I contemplated setting the table on fire and assassinating Balu in many different ways, the image of Tsar standing naked in the middle of his room popped into my mind. I tried to understand what it was about him that was repulsive and fascinating at the same time. There were the Eastern European traits: the tough stride, the joy of making other people uncomfortable, the bragging about prostitutes, the blatant irreverence—I knew all of them too well. But there was also something else—the fearlessness, the creative energy, and the warmth of a friend who would risk his life for you. The question was, did I want to be associated with someone who was certain to get a bad name in the Tibetan community? Of course not. I had come to India to study the texts of the Indian Buddhist philosophers, and that required winning the trust of the Tibetan teachers. Tsar and I were just treading two very different paths.

Eight

It was Thursday morning, and the Katwali bazaar was swarming with people. Barefoot boys waiting tables in chai shops and restaurants dumped leftover food in the open sewer and rinsed the dirty metal dishes and silverware in buckets of soapy water. On the flat roofs of the village houses, women hung wet laundry and combed their hair. Monkeys stood guard at the entrance of the crumbling Bank of India building, looking everyone up and down as if they had been paid a salary to catch thieves. Taxis, packed with passengers and groceries, roared up the hill and disappeared into the clouds enveloping the higher Himalayan villages.

Ani Dawa walked ahead of me, cutting in front of long lines and arguing with shopkeepers and vegetable vendors about the prices of their merchandise.

"Are you sure you are fine, carrying all the shopping bags?" she asked, handing me a twenty-pound sack of potatoes.

"No problem," I assured her.

"I have to run into the mill to get some gram flour. You should wait for me here."

I put the grocery bags on the ground and sat on the concrete embankment that enclosed the dried-up fountain statue of Hanuman, the Monkey God. There was something about this spot, right at the bottom of the steep Himalayan slopes, that always made me feel intoxicated. I could sit there for hours, just letting the outside world seep into my senses. Fuel exhaust, the roar of buses, a whiff of cumin-spiced potato samosas, yellow-blue-red parrots in the banyan trees, monkeys fighting on the tin roof of a phone booth, stacks of flat one-story houses, hammocks filled with sleeping children, bamboo thickets and squat palm trees, *kulis* carrying cages with chickens, vegetable vendors clinking with their scales—I closed my eyes and suddenly time didn't seem linear anymore; it skipped like a record, repeating itself again and again. A hammer banged in the distance, someone shouted *Panch rupees!*, a bus blew its horn. A hammer banged in the distance. I'd always been here, and the Katwali bazaar had always been the way it was today. Becoming a monk had brought an array of complications, such as maddening erections, adhering to a newly constructed identity, answering to a new name, and having recurrent dreams of playing piano and kissing old girlfriends. It had also brought a surprise treasure—an overriding, blissfully benumbing feeling of resignation to the moment, a resignation that made you feel like throwing your passport and money belt in the sewer and crawling next to a leper, ecstatic with the realization that you had nothing left to do and no place left to go. You were free to sit around and watch the world unwind for the next couple of million years.

When I snapped out of my reverie, I noticed that Geshe Kyerab was standing outside a hardware and repair shop halfway up the street that led to the Tibetan hospital. He waved at me, I waved back, and he turned around to observe as the owner of the repair shop welded a broken kerosene stove back together.

A tall sixty-year-old Tibetan man with intense small eyes, thin lips, and a laid-back stance, Geshe Kyerab looked like a Japanese poet in search of perfect haiku material. He was everywhere. When I went to the post office,

Geshe Kyerab was there watching the old cow with the broken ankle trying to get up. When I went to wash the pots and dishes at the street tap at night, he was there again, studying a lone firefly doing a zigzag dance in the air. He watched construction workers dig holes or weld metal rods; he watched potters spinning clay ovals and cooks tossing chilies in the frying pan; he watched worms split in half, each half going a separate way. He watched mother monkeys drag their stillborn babies everywhere they went. He watched the clouds for hours at a time.

Geshe Kyerab was a teacher at Nechung monastery, but he was not a typical monastery professor—he lacked the stuffiness and the ubiquitous geeky expression of those who replace their own thoughts with the building blocks of a particular dogma.

I first saw him in a chai shop. He was sitting in the back looking at a jar of mango pickles and I was eating parathas. When our eyes met, both of us instantly raised a hand and pointed at each other, as if saying *"Is that you?"* It was a very spontaneous and odd experience.

Geshe Kyerab left the hardware shop and sauntered my way.

"How are you?" I greeted him.

"I'm well," he said, clutching his hands behind his back. "Shopping?"

"Helping Ani Dawa," I explained, pointing in the direction of the mill. "She went to get some flour."

"She told me that you are starting lessons with Geshe Yama Tseten."

"Tomorrow. He asked me to bring a *lo rig* text."

"Good. You're going to get a lot of new ideas."

"Geshe-la, I was wondering if I could stop by your place sometime and ask you a few questions about a text I'm reading."

"What text?" Geshe Kyerab snapped, and his face suddenly darkened.

"Shantideva's *Entry into the Bodhisattva Realm*."

"Oh, I don't know anything about that," he said, shaking his head. "You could stop by, I'd be glad to see you, but you should find someone else to talk to about these things. I don't read better than you do."

Geshe Kyerab held my hand for a few seconds, then took a step backward and hesitated.

"Do you think you can learn to love all beings the way you learn to drive a car?" he asked casually.

"Shantideva says that you can," I answered.

"It doesn't matter what he says," Geshe Kyerab said. "Everyone's free to think whatever they want. Is love something that you can get used to, the way you get used to cold or hot weather?"

"What do *you* think?"

Geshe Kyerab shrugged his shoulders and smiled. "I've been thinking a lot about how we met in the chai shop," he told me. "It was strange, wasn't it? I felt like I'd seen an old friend. We must've known each other from before, from a previous life."

"Who knows?"

"There's no other way," Geshe Kyerab insisted. "People don't just fall from the sky. Look at you: wearing monk robes, speaking like a Tibetan . . . How do you think you ended up here? It's karma."

"Probably," I replied, remembering my first encounter with Buddhism and the excitement I had felt when I had begun reading about emptiness, back in Boston. In bed late at night, in coffee shops, on the T, at work, during classes, and even while walking around Cambridge, I had read every book on emptiness I could find, watching with astonishment as my view of the world had become more fluid, allowing me to examine the very reality of existence. For the first time in my life things had made sense. Reality was a construct; because it was a construct, it never worked the way you expected it to; perpetuating this construct was the same as perpetuating sorrow; dissolving this construct was the end of sorrow.

Emptiness—the core of the Buddhist teaching—is the idea that exteriors don't represent the inner essence of objects. Everything that the mind comes in contact with—colors, shapes, thoughts, feelings—is just a hollow façade, an empty present box, a house without interior walls, a face without an owner, a flower without a purpose. Emptiness is the idea that every experience is superficial, a mere gloss, a concept that cannot be traced, grounded, or defined. Emptiness is returning home and discovering that you've never lived there. It is looking in the mirror and seeing somebody else's face, searching the depths of one's mind and falling through, endlessly, because there's nothing to hold on to. It is getting drunk and observing yourself throwing your hands about, laughing, and speaking in foreign tongues, as if everything that you are, including your sense of time and space, is manipulated by strings, invisible strings controlled by no one and leading nowhere. To someone who is earnestly searching for answers to the fundamental questions about existence—Who am I? What do I see? What is the meaning of all this?—emptiness offers a mind-boggling hypothesis: There has never been an I. There is no subject-object duality. Everything is a play of the mind.

When I was eight, on a quiet winter night, I accompanied my dad to the government-run collection agency to pay the electricity bill. In Sofia, my parents and I lived across from the Russian embassy, an enormous and lavish building complex at the periphery of a state park, a thirteen-foot wall shielding the privileged Russian apparatchiks from the curious eyes of the not-so-privileged Bulgarians. Even on a dark night, with snow falling and none of the streetlights in the neighborhood working, the projectors illuminating the main embassy building—a five-story celebration of Soviet kitsch combining the functionality of a Kremlin ballroom with the feel of a Salvador Dalí ruin, a wide, high, and purely decorative round tower jutting from one side—turned the sky red and made the air seem phosphorescent, almost tangible. Treading silently through the unplowed sidewalk, my torn, oversized shoes filling up with snow, I stared at the hollow open-top tower across the street, waiting for the moment when two of its windows would merge into one frame and offer a glimpse of the red sky. I had been fascinated with the Russian embassy tower for a long time. Whenever I walked past it on the way home from school, or going to the supermarket, I would stop and study its shape and dimensions. I had a very big problem with the tower: I didn't believe it was real. "Dad, how do we know that the tower is round?" I asked timidly, deciding that it was time for me to fill him in on my ideas about the tower. "Are you stupid?" my dad answered briskly, stopping for a second to light a cigarette. My father's no-nonsense approach to parenting never failed to inspire in me a deep sense of suspicion and contempt for the world of grown-ups. "But if you climbed up there," I argued, "and closed your eyes and then touched all the stones, the stones wouldn't feel round because they're flat and rectangular, and if you opened your eyes, you wouldn't see the whole tower, just one side. Why then does the tower look round?" "I don't want to discuss such idiotic bullshit," my dad shouted, speeding up. "What? You can't see that this house is square and the tower is round? These are simple geometric shapes! Why would you bother me with such nonsense?"

Of course, he was right: the house was square, the tower was round. The problem was that I just couldn't understand what made them so. If I looked at the tower for a brief second, I would think, okay, a round tower. But when I spent half an hour staring at it, its roundness disappeared and what emerged in its place was something that had no shape or purpose, a ridiculous something that no one, except me, paid any attention to. The round tower argument I had with my father on that winter night was a momentous event in my life. It was the first time I realized that I saw things differently from other people, that people have different perceptions. What was obvious to me sounded absurd to my dad and vice versa.

Twelve years later, as I lay in bed in my Cambridge apartment reading Aryadeva's *Four Hundred Verses*—a second-century text focusing primarily on the understanding of emptiness—I stumbled upon the following verses: "When someone looks at a vase, he doesn't see it in its entirety. What reasonable person could claim, then, that a vase is objectively perceived?" (13, 1) "One can never see something objectively, i.e., in its entirety, at once. Why is that? Because everything is made of parts: back parts, front parts, and middle." (13, 4)

Suddenly, I remembered the snow and the red sky and the Russian embassy tower, my father smoking and walking ahead of me, the enormous collar of his long, military-style coat concealing his entire head. What did all this mean? There was definitely a link, a narrative between me at eight and me at twenty. Was it karma? Chance? Natural tendencies? Weird brain architecture? Or was it simply that every child was born inquisitive, distrusting their senses, and only later, after a long brain-washing process that included incessant treatment with geometry, math, and empirical materialism, came to accept reality the way it supposedly appeared to most people?

"I have everything now," Ani Dawa said, handing me three enormous bags of flour.

"Why did you buy so much?" I asked her.

"It's cheaper here."

She raised her hand and a taxi minivan pulled over.

"Going up, Ani Dawa?" the driver asked, checking the back of his car to see if there was enough space for us and the groceries. "Get in."

"Five rupees." Ani Dawa set the price and pushed the sliding door open.

The driver wobbled his head adamantly and held out his open palm. "Ten."

"That's not a nice way to talk to old people," she scolded him. "I've known you since you were five and walked around the village with a lollipop stuck to your hair."

The driver, a twenty-year-old Indian man, cursed all Westerners and Tibetans for being the cheapest people on the planet and started off, stamping the clutch and the gas pedal with a vengeance.

The higher we ascended into the mountain, the harder it poured. Soon we were driving through a wall of water. On every turn of the road, the wheels got stuck in the dirt and the engine stalled. The windshield wipers, swishing manically, revealed a world made of quicksilver. A line of taxis behind us honked their horns, urging us to move forward.

Ani Dawa pulled a plastic bag of traditional Tibetan pills out of her vest pocket and dropped a few in her mouth.

"Do you know that some of those pills contain cow dung?" I asked her.

"Cow dung is good for you," Ani Dawa replied.

The driver hit the brakes and the taxi made a hundred-and-eighty-degree spin. An old man kicked the bumper and told the driver to find another profession. "Cows," the driver shouted, backing up to the edge of a precipice. Ani Dawa laughed with a mouthful of chewed-up brown pills.

"Next time I am going to charge you ten rupees for the ride," the driver said as he pulled over. "The rate has changed. No exceptions."

"We will see about that." Ani Dawa giggled and jumped out of the car.

At the door of Ani Dawa's small room, we were greeted by Ama-la.

"What is he doing here?" Ama-la snapped, puckering her lips at me—the Tibetan way of pointing at someone.

"He is going to help me make lunch," Ani Dawa replied, pushing me into the room.

"Help?" Ama-la scoffed and climbed onto her bed, a glass-bead rosary in hand. "I would like to see that!"

The room where Ani Dawa and Ama-la lived was a square, low-roofed cubicle big enough to fit two beds, a portable gas stove, a table, and a chair. There were two miniature windows in the room but their green shutters invariably stayed closed because Ani Dawa used the windowsills to store spices, flour, rice, and big jars of mango pickles. A seven-foot-high butter tea mixer—a heavy wooden cylinder with a giant pestle inside—stood in the corner of the room behind the door, a reminder of Ama-la's heroic flight from Tibet in 1956. Being Tibet's singular technological invention to date, the butter tea mixer had always been an object of fascination to me, not least because it looked like an ancient prototype of a rocket-propelled grenade launcher.

According to Ama-la (Ani Dawa didn't remember a thing and couldn't confirm the story) she had left her home in Tso Ngon (Blue Lake) in the winter of 1956 and had set out on a thousand-mile journey to the Holy Land, India, traversing the most perilous mountain passes on foot, with an infant baby in one hand and a hundred-and-sixty-pound butter tea mixer strapped to her back. Ever since I heard this story I have been unable to separate the image of a butter tea mixer from the image of Ama-la walking in the foothills of Mount Everest, a glass-bead rosary on her neck, her braided hair fluttering in the wind.

"Would you like to eat okra curry for lunch?" Ani Dawa asked, placing a chopping board on the floor next to the gas stove. "I'm also going to make a dozen chapati."

"That's fine with me," I replied, kneeling beside her. "Do you want me to knead the dough?"

"Here," Ani Dawa said, handing me a plastic sieve. "Sift the flour first. Mice always find a way to poop in the flour, even if it's stored in a metal container."

After spending every morning and afternoon of the past seven months cooking, reading, studying, and practicing my Tibetan in Ani Dawa's room, the space, which had once seemed like a tiny prison cell where a mother and daughter lived cramped, shoulder to shoulder, had now become infinitely bigger, as if by growing accustomed to each other, the room and I had modified our sizes—the walls had retreated and my body had become smaller. Rooms are like people—they transform space with their personalities. Some rooms are loud and happy, others are sinister and gloomy. Ani Dawa's room felt quiet and slow, almost suspended in time, yet restless, like the reverberation of an unresolved seventh chord. Everything in Ani Dawa's room was in a state of suspended anticipation. The open door was waiting for a visitor; the door curtain was waiting to be lifted; the two cups of cold milk tea on the table were waiting for the flies to drown; the rats, peeking down from the wooden roof beams, were waiting for an opportunity to ransack the bags of vegetables hung high up on the walls across the room; the moths were waiting for the sun to go down. Ama-la was waiting for her six children who died in Tibet to miraculously appear at her front steps.

"Tell him not to whistle," Ama-la snapped, slipping off her bed.

"Ama-la says you have to stop whistling," Ani Dawa said.

"But I am not whistling!" I protested.

"That's good," Ani Dawa replied, dumping the okra in a bucket of water. "Mother doesn't like when people whistle in the house."

"Last night he whistled, and I had nightmares," Ama-la said, brushing past me. "If he wants to whistle, he should go to his house."

"Why is she getting so upset about this?" I asked.

"She believes that if you whistle in someone's house, you are calling in the ghosts," Ani Dawa explained. "Can you hand me the bag of onions? It's hanging on that nail over there."

"Look at him," Ama-la snickered behind me. "Next life he is going to be reborn as a cow."

"Why is that?" I laughed, returning with the onions.

"If you use your fists to get off the floor, you will be reborn as a cow," Ani Dawa said. "A clenched fist looks just like a hoof."

"Great. I suppose I should quit eating grass and stop mooing at night as well."

"Don't make fun of Mother," Ani Dawa reprimanded me, suppressing a smile. "She knows a lot more about life than you do. Here, take this."

Ani Dawa pulled a pestle and mortar from a niche in the corner and handed it to me, together with five bags of traditional Tibetan medicine. It had been agreed for a while that crushing Ama-la's medicine was solely my responsibility. I knew the prescription by heart: seven of the grain-size balls, two of the big ones, four of the black ones, and three of the gray and the brown ones each. I filled a cup with hot water from the thermos, mixed in the powdered medicine, and offered it to Ama-la with both hands—the proper way—my head bent slightly in respect. Ama-la was clearly pleased. She took a sip, puckered her lips, and shook her head violently, suppressing a powerful urge to vomit. Ani Dawa got off the floor and stared at her mother's face, ready to rush in with an empty bucket.

"It tastes different today," Ama-la complained, giving me a dirty look. "He probably messed up the prescription."

"He didn't, Mother," Ani Dawa said in my defense. "Can you please try to drink the rest of it?"

Heroically, Ama-la downed the remaining medicine, and went to check on the butter tea mixer propped up in the corner.

"Dawa, have you washed this lately?" Ama-la asked, caressing the mixer's dusty surface.

"No," Ani Dawa replied, rolling her eyes. "Why do you need it?"

"Someone will stop by, and we will have no butter tea to offer them."

"Someone who?" Ani Dawa asked, intrigued.

"I don't know," Ama-la mumbled. "People stop by all the time."

As if to confirm this statement, at that moment we heard the roar of a scooter pulling over by the paratha shop up the road, followed by the sound of clapping sandals.

"The egg man," Ani Dawa informed me and unlocked the small cupboard under the main table. Ani Dawa kept her money scattered between the pages of dictionaries and notebooks to give thieves a hard time.

The egg man left a dozen eggs at the doorstep, took the money from Ani Dawa, and ran back to his scooter.

"Crazy *Engies*," Ama-la burst out laughing as she began combing her hair. "If the earth was really spinning, Dalai Lama's palace would be up the hill in the morning and down in the valley in the afternoon."

Ama-la, of course, was referring to our ongoing argument about the nature of the universe and the behavior of the heavenly bodies. She held, among other things, that the sun shut down at night like a candle and that the moon cycle was the result of hungry ghosts nibbling at the moon's body, which was really the size and consistency of a pancake, only a glowing one. Every month the moon was devoured completely and then restored to its original state by a karmic mechanism designed to keep the moon-eating ghosts perpetually hungry. Presented with photographic evidence of the moon's harsh, un-pancake-like surface, Ama-la would look thankfully at the small statue of Manjushri, the Buddhist goddess of wisdom, standing on the altar next to her bed, and cry, "*Engie kugpa!*"

"Where are you going?" Ani Dawa asked Ama-la, who had put on her *chuba* and vest and was pacing nervously around the room. "Are you coming back for lunch?"

Ama-la ignored the question and sat on a chair, taking her shoes in her lap. Closing her eyes, she mumbled a long prayer, something about all living beings going to Tushita heaven, then spat repeatedly on the soles of her shoes and got up to go, wielding her glass rosary like a metaphysical weapon. Ani Dawa explained to me later that the prayer and the spitting were part of a shoe-consecrating ritual that Ama-la performed every day before going out into the world. Once consecrated, Ama-la's shoes acquired the power to send each bug and worm that she inadvertently stepped on directly to Tushita heaven, where they would spend no fewer than seven days in the company of Maitreya, the coming Buddha.

Ama-la walked out without saying good-bye or even looking at us, and I noticed that Ani Dawa grew pensive and distant. I wanted to ask her about her childhood, about the time when she was a girl and not a nun, about her antagonistic relationship with her mother, and about her six brothers and sisters who were killed in Tibet, but instead I just sat beside her and watched as she chopped the onions and the okra and dumped them in the wok, together with a spoon of ghee.

The door curtain, patched up with auspicious blue symbols, moved with the wind, and I caught a glimpse of the slate-tiled courtyard, the old rhododendron tree coated with pale-pink blossoms, the goatherds' shanties on the other side of the river, and the splintered gray Himalayan pinnacles rising above them. The courtyard, enclosed on all sides by shacks and houses, functioned as a sort of hands-off daycare where the neighborhood's two-year-olds, ragged and covered with snot, were left all day to do as they pleased—which mostly consisted of eating ants, throwing stones at one another, and digging out long red worms from under the stones. Since they only had one doll, the kids were forced to share it: one carried a leg, another a head, the third a torso. I had a soft spot for Yanki, a Tibetan girl with pigtails and huge, searching eyes who never smiled. When she came in with the other kids to ask Ani Dawa for candy, she didn't say anything. She just extended her hand and waited for her turn.

"You should buy them all balloons," Ani Dawa said, noticing that I was looking at the kids. "They would be so happy."

"I will. I should've thought of that before."

"If you buy them balloons just once, they will start following you around like ducklings."

Ani Dawa rolled a perfectly round chapati and tossed it on the hot pan.

"I hope I didn't offend your mother by saying something stupid. She looked quite angry when she left."

"It's no problem," Ani Dawa said and walked over to the plastic tub filled with dirty dishes. I grabbed a pitcher and poured water over her hands as she peeled the crust of hardened dough off her skin. "This life, I am just a servant."

"What do you mean?"

Ani Dawa sighed and dried her hands in a towel. "If I didn't have to take care of Mother, I would've left this place a long time ago."

"Where would you go?" I asked her.

"Far away," she said, sitting on her fold-up chair. "But this is my duty: I have to help Mother. I have no other choice."

"What about all the other nuns? They don't live with their parents."

"When Mother contracted tuberculosis ten years ago, all the doctors told her that she wasn't going to live. She was so weak, she couldn't even swallow. I left the nunnery and stayed with her day and night for six months. I had to feed her like a baby. We didn't have any money or a place to live, so I started working in a little shop. You know, nuns are not supposed to work with money, but I did it, and at night I studied English so that I could start giving Tibetan lessons. Now we have a room and a gas stove, we eat three meals a day, but this is not what I want to do."

"And what do you want to do?"

Ani Dawa paged through one of the small notebooks lying on the table and pulled out a photograph of a dark blue lake surrounded by snowy mountains and endless barren fields. "This is Tso Mapam, the highest lake in the world. They say that if you look into its waters you can see the future, or have a vision that answers a question that you've been thinking about for a long time. If Mother dies before me, I will sell everything and go to Tso Mapam. I'll find a cave in the foothills of Mount Kailash, seal its entrance, and spend the rest of my life reading the texts and meditating. What would probably happen, though, is I will die first while Mother will live to be a hundred and ten."

I studied the photograph and tried to imagine what it would feel like to wake up every day in a cave on top of the world, knowing that you might never see or talk to another human being again in your life.

"But Tibet isn't even your country," I said. "You've grown up in India. How do you know you're going to like it there?"

"I know," Ani Dawa replied. "Tibet is very special. If I could just see Tso Mapam with my own eyes, that would be enough."

"And what about all your friends? Do you think you'd be happy living absolutely alone?"

Ani Dawa put the photograph back in the notebook and looked at me with a coldness that I hadn't seen before. "I don't need anyone. I'm tired of people."

Her eyes filled up with tears but I just stared straight ahead, saying nothing. I didn't want to make her feel exposed and vulnerable.

"You don't know what I have to go through every day with Mother," she continued. "From the moment she wakes up, she starts yelling at me. Her *tsampa* isn't prepared right, her chai is too sweet. She hides the money that I make, and when I try to defend myself, she tells me that decent nuns don't invite men to their houses. That's why she left today without eating lunch—because she felt ashamed to see us talking."

"Well, maybe I shouldn't come to your place anymore," I said. "I didn't realize your mother felt that way."

"It's not just you, it's everyone who comes to visit me. She wants me to go back to the nunnery, but if I leave her alone, she is going to die. So what do I do? I am a bad nun if I live like a laywoman, and I'm a bad nun if I let Mother die. I just pray that I'll make it to Tso Mapam one day. Maybe in my next life."

"You don't want to go to Tibet," I told her. "People there share their houses with yaks and wipe their asses with stones."

"They don't do that," Ani Dawa said, shaking her head.

"They sure do. Even the old Tibetan ladies in Dharamsala use stones. I've seen them."

"Well, it's better to use stones than to wipe yourself with your bare hands, the way the Indians do it," Ani Dawa countered. "Then they go and make the dough for the samosas that you love so much."

"I'll remember that next time I walk into a chai shop."

We ate the okra curry cold, and every time Ani Dawa turned to me and smiled, I felt as if I heard Ama-la clicking her tongue and whispering ominous mantras behind me. Who knows—maybe in addition to transporting worms and bugs to Tushita heaven, Ama-la's shoes also had the power to make herself invisible.

Nine

My appointment with Geshe Yama Tseten was at eight o'clock in the morning, which meant that I had to leave my room by seven-thirty to have enough time to buy some fruit at the market. Unsurprisingly, it was raining, so when I went to shave at the street tap, I not only had to hold my rather large mirror, but an umbrella as well. Using the street tap on Jogibara Road was undoubtedly a unique experience. First, there was the fact that seventy percent of the time the faucet spouted only highly pressurized air and drizzle. When the water finally came out, after excruciating hissing, it erupted like a geyser and almost immediately began choking again. This weird behavior of the street tap accounted for a lot of Charlie Chaplin–type scenes: a woman carrying a pot of rice would approach the tap, turn it on, and wait: nothing. She would start to go and the water would explode, spraying all over her sari. She would return, wait twice as long as the first time, but get only drizzle. In the end, she would give up and cross the street, only to see the water flowing freely behind her.

Oftentimes there was a long line of locals waiting to wash their dishes, fill up their empty buckets, brush their teeth, or take a shower. Taking a shower was the most time-consuming activity involving water, to say nothing about the absurdity of soaping yourself without taking your clothes off and flapping under the faucet for minutes on end like a seal.

The third annoying factor was that when it rained hard for more than six hours, the aboveground pipes, channeling water from a spring high in the mountains, became clogged with mud and the street tap on Jogibara Road stopped working completely—which is why I ended up going to my first lesson with Geshe Yama Tseten with a half-shaved face.

Geshe-la's room was located in a rectangular, flat-roofed compound facing the entrance of the Main Temple. There were five rooms on each side of the corridor, and as I walked past the first door, it suddenly occurred to me that I'd forgotten which room Geshe-la was in. It was on the right, that I remembered. And it wasn't the last one, or Ani Dawa would have said so. The first door was bolted, so I knocked on the second one and waited. I heard footsteps and the rustling of papers, then everything went silent. I knocked again; this time, the door opened and out came an old Tibetan monk holding a portable radio. I had seen Geshe Yama Tseten once before, and so I knew I had the wrong room. I apologized and continued down the corridor. I pressed my ear against the third door and knocked: not a single sound from the inside. I began to wonder if there was some sort of description in the annals of Tibetan customs of the proper procedure for entering into people's rooms. Maybe Tibetans just didn't knock on doors. Was I supposed to shout out my name? I pushed the door open and peeked in: it was the right room. Geshe Yama Tseten was sitting on his bed, reading a *pecha*. He was a tall and bulky Khampa in his early fifties (Tibetan men from the Kham region are notoriously tough and combative) with an enormous head, small ears, and a perpetual sneer. Something about him reminded me of Mike Tyson—maybe it was his mouth and his eyes, or the way he held himself.

"What are you doing here?" he asked scornfully, and gestured at me to leave the room. "I'm busy right now."

I nodded and stepped back into the corridor. What did I do wrong? It was five minutes after eight: I wasn't early. Was I supposed to wait outside his door until he called me? And if that was the protocol, how would he know that I was indeed waiting outside? It would be kind of silly if he started yelling "*Lodro Chosang!*" without knowing whether I had come or not. I sat on the ground and listened to the sound of raindrops tapping on the leaves outside. The corridor opened up onto a small balcony overlooking the square in front of the Institute of Buddhist Dialectics. There was a travel agency advertising flights to Katmandu and I thought about distance and how the notion of "arriving" implied that we were confined to a specific location: we could stretch like an elastic band from Boston to Dharamsala, but the essence of who we were remained somewhere else, at an imaginary starting point far behind. It was as if traveling through space made us less real, as if the self that arrived at the end of a journey was a faded copy of the original. *I arrive.* Obviously, if I *am*, I am here now. I couldn't be sometimes here and sometimes there. And if I am always here, there can never be space and distance. To *arrive*, then, meant to be in two different places simultaneously.

The door to room number two opened and the old monk with the radio stepped out into the corridor. Turning the tuning knob, he walked past me and leaned against the balcony railing. A beat-up jeep pulled over at the gate of the institute compound and the sound of soft tabla thrumming echoed across the square. Namgyal Monastery's bull, a beautiful, dark brown animal with fully intact, weapon-grade horns, sauntered to the middle of the road and stopped to sniff the air. Immediately, a pack of dogs charged at him, trying to scare him away.

I came to India—this was certainly the wrong way to go about figuring out what I was doing sitting in a dark corridor at eight o'clock in the morning, a bag of apples in my lap and a photocopied Tibetan text folded in the inside pocket of my *tonka.* Wasn't this enough for me? The barking of the dogs, the soaked granite Himalayan pinnacles in the distance, Jagjit Singh singing a slow *ghazal,* the monk with the radio struggling to pick up a signal in the rain. What was the use of holding on to an imagined trajectory of a self whose coordinates were nothing but a series of flickering memories? There was no invisible string connecting here and there, no glue strong enough to create a concrete person out of fleeting thoughts. Why were memories so painful, then? I could do without them now, and all the past information crammed into my head—the ninety-three exits on I-95 in Connecticut, Chopin's ballad in F major, Coltrane's *Naima*, the inebriated high school days in Sofia drinking eight beers at a local pub before going to classes, the one-night stands in Boston, clove cigarettes and bongs, cruising around the Cape in a pickup truck full of booze, the steamy dishroom of the Berklee cafeteria where I worked every day from four to eight-thirty, including weekends.

The monk with the radio walked back into the corridor, now significantly wet, and returned to his room. "*Sho*," I heard Geshe Yama Tseten say in a barely audible voice. I took my shoes off and opened the door, just a crack. "*Sho!*" Geshe-la repeated, this time forcefully. I walked in, propped up my umbrella on the wall behind the door, and put the bag of apples on the table. Then I sat on the floor and adjusted my *zen*. Geshe-la's room was quite nice by Indian standards—sixteen feet by twenty, carpeted, walls painted dark yellow, a large window looking onto a spacious courtyard where monks from Namgyal and the Institute of Buddhist Dialectics converged twice a day to practice debate. At the end of the courtyard, shielded by a canopy of trees, stood the gates of Dalai Lama's private residence.

Geshe-la wrapped the *pecha* that he'd been reading in a saffron cloth and leaned on a pillow, folding his hands in front of his chest.

"You're a little weird," he said, chuckling. "Why did you come to me looking like that?"

Geshe-la brushed his cheek with one hand to show me what he meant.

"The water stopped," I explained. "I was trying to shave . . ."

"The water stopped!" Geshe-la exploded. "There's water everywhere! It's even coming down from my ceiling."

I looked behind and up, and indeed, there was a wet spot with a few drops bulging at its center.

"Now, if you were doing it the Tibetan way, you'd never end up looking like that. It's all that Western stuff that never works."

Geshe-la stood up on his bed and brought down a wooden box from the top of his bookshelf. Sitting down again, he opened the box and pulled out a pair of traditional Tibetan tweezers, the size of tongs.

"Here," he said, handing me the tweezers. "Try them. You don't need water or soap. Just pluck the hair right out like that."

Geshe-la pretended to yank the hair off his face, closing one eye, and making a sour expression. "The Dalai Lama uses one of those, too. It saves time and money."

"Plucking each hair one by one?" I asked incredulous.

"Just try it," Geshe-la urged me excitedly. "It doesn't hurt."

I looked at the tweezers with great admiration and placed them on the table. "Thank you, Geshe-la, but I'm going to try it some other time."

"What other time?" Geshe-la shouted. "You look like a retard! Here, just see how it works, then you can buy yourself a pair from the market and do the rest at home."

"I'm sorry, Geshe-la, but my facial hair is very thick. If I pull it out, I'm going to bleed."

"Bleed!" Geshe-la jumped. "Are you out of your mind? You think *you* have thick hair? I have thick hair. Have you ever seen a bald Tibetan man?"

I shrugged my shoulders and looked down, determined not to go any further into this subject.

"No, tell me," Geshe-la insisted, all fired up. "Have you ever seen a bald Tibetan man?"

"No," I admitted.

"And what does that say? It says that if I grew my beard, I'd look like a crazy saddhu."

I didn't have to be an anthropological expert to know that this was total nonsense. Geshe-la had exactly three lonely hairs sticking out from the bottom of his chin.

"Fine, I'll try it," I finally conceded and grabbed the tweezers. I clasped a few hairs as hard as I could and pulled: nothing. I tried again and again, but the tweezers just couldn't grip tightly enough to do the job.

"It doesn't work," I announced triumphantly. "My facial hair is too thick."

"It doesn't work! Your fingers are too *weak*, is what it is. Just leave it."

Geshe-la looked out the window and sighed. A small crowd had gathered outside the gates of Dalai Lama's residence and a few Indian policemen were trying to push them back. I took the photocopied *lo rig* text out of my pocket, straightened it out, and glanced through it.

"*Yeah-yeah,*" Geshe-la said absentmindedly, his eyes still fixed at the crowd outside. *Yeah-yeah* is a Tibetan expression that can mean *I see,* or *Let's start,* or even *Good-bye.*

Geshe-la put on his reading glasses and paged through a collection of miscellaneous looseleaf texts laid out on the table.

"Ah!" he shouted suddenly. "*Kun chog sum,* what is that over there?"

I looked back in the direction where he was pointing, but saw nothing that warranted such urgency.

"Why would you bring your umbrella into my room?" Geshe-la asked, transforming into a wrathful deity. "What kind of behavior is that? First you come with a funny face, then you bring your umbrella and ruin my floor. Look at that puddle! Get a towel and soak it up."

I grabbed the towel next to the kerosene stove and pretended to soak up the puddle that Geshe-la was referring to. The floor was absolutely dry, save for a raindrop-size wet mark that had formed under the umbrella's metal tip.

"In the West, do you bring your umbrellas into people's houses?" Geshe-la asked, entering into what I later came to recognize as his debating form.

"Sure," I replied adamantly.

"Do you bring in your horses?" Geshe-la leaned forward and smiled smugly, confident in his imminent victory.

"We don't have horses," I replied.

"Of course you have horses, there are horses everywhere!"

I was starting to get a feeling that ours was going to be a very difficult and thorny relationship.

"Well then, no, we don't go into people's houses with our horses," I conceded. "But umbrellas are not horses."

Geshe-la tilted his head and looked at me as if I were trying to sell him rotten tomatoes for twenty rupees apiece. "An umbrella is something that you use when you travel, right?"

"Right," I agreed.

"Like your shoes and your horse," Geshe-la continued.

"Right, I guess so."

"So why, then, would you bring your umbrella into my room, *kun chog sum!*"

I could have argued more. I could have said that my bag is also something I travel with and that I've never seen Tibetans leaving their bags outside the Main Temple, but I thought better of it.

"I'm sorry, Geshe-la. I'll take it out." I started to get up, but he gestured for me to remain seated. "Leave it," he commanded. "You've already destroyed my floor."

Taking modest pleasure in his unparalleled command of logic, Geshe-la dug out a two-foot-long wooden stick with a rake-like appendage from under his blanket and began to slowly scratch his back with it. I remembered that Terchen Migme Rinpoche, the Mo Lama, had used a similar tool, shaped like a hand and made out of metal and plastic. Reaching out with the rake, Geshe-la detached the metal hooks that held the windows closed, and the smell of wet pine trees and burning incense entered the room. I wondered what it was about Tibetan teachers and their fascination with artificial hands. Were they too lazy to stand up, open their windows, and turn their lights on? Or was the use of the extra hand part of a tradition developed by meditators who wanted to avoid getting up from their cushions by all means?

The crowd outside the gates had dispersed and the courtyard had filled with monks grouped in pairs. One pair sat on the ground defending an arbitrary philosophical position; another stood up and did the strike-a-point dance, a two-part movement that consisted of raising your right hand and left foot and simultaneously bringing your foot down and slapping your hands in your opponent's face—to drive the message more forcefully.

"*Yeah-yeah,*" Geshe-la said, and placed a small *pecha* in his lap. "Go ahead, start from the top."

"A short exposition of *lo rig,*" I began reading the text's title, but Geshe-la slammed his rake on the table, interrupting me.

"Put the pages away," he ordered, pointing at me.

No wonder he was named after Yama, the Buddhist god of death.

"A short exposition of *lo rig,* called wish-fulfilling jewel," I recited the title from memory and then looked at Geshe-la, awaiting further instructions.

"And?" Geshe-la asked.

"Well, that's the title."

"I know that's the title. Go on!"

"I don't have it memorized."

Exasperated, Geshe-la took off his reading glasses and wiped them on a towel. "What are you doing here, then?"

"I'm sorry, Ani Dawa didn't tell me I needed to learn the text by heart. It's quite long—over twenty pages."

"That's long? How am I supposed to teach you anything if you haven't even learned the text?"

"I know a few definitions," I replied humbly.

"Really? Which ones?"

"I know the definition of direct perception: a nonconceptual, unmistaken perception."

Geshe-la seemed very amused by the fact that I had volunteered this information. He chuckled, jerking his shoulders and making high-pitched meowing sounds, then turned serious and began clicking his tongue.

"Do you have a direct perception?"

"I do," I said.

"And what do you see?"

I pointed vaguely at the table. "Apples."

"I don't see apples," Geshe-la announced belligerently.

I looked at the bag of apples and then at Geshe-la, trying to understand what he was getting at. "They look like apples to me."

"If a cloud looks like a rabbit, is it a rabbit?"

"No."

"Then how do you know you're seeing apples?"

"They're not anything else," I said after some thought.

"So before you knew that they were apples, you knew that they weren't anything else? Before I know which way to take, I know that I shouldn't go east, west, or south?"

"I remembered," I corrected myself.

"You knew what you were looking at, and then remembered, or you didn't know what you were looking at, and then remembered?"

"I'm not sure," I admitted in a defeated tone.

"That's enough," Geshe-la said and placed a tattered linen handkerchief on his shaved head.

Was he cold or sweating? I tried to think of a legitimate reason why Geshe-la would cover his head with a cloth that he'd clearly used to wipe his nose, but the longer I looked at him, sitting on his bed with a stern expression, loose threads dangling over his face, the harder it was not to laugh out loud. Granted, I couldn't help grinning, but at least I put a lot of love into it, so as not to look disrespectful.

"Get out of the room!" Geshe-la ordered, giving the handkerchief a shake.

I grinned wider but remained seated.

"What an arrogant *Engie* you are!" he went on. "You ruined my floor, then you argued with me and gave me a terrible headache. Now get out. Go home, and don't come back anymore!"

I didn't move an inch. It felt great just to sit there and defy his orders. My stubbornness, albeit irrational, was the only thing I had left to fight him with.

A minute or two passed, and I rose slowly and reluctantly—to demonstrate that I was leaving because I didn't feel like staying any longer, not because he'd kicked me out. I took my umbrella and shook off whatever raindrops remained on it. Then I opened the door and exited the Western way, showing Geshe-la my ass and back.

Ten

Was this what I had come to India for? Dropping out of school, giving up piano after fifteen years of practice, ending friendships, destroying my parents' hopes, changing my name and identity—to be humiliated by some belligerent old monk who hated Westerners and couldn't talk to people unless he was debating?

I walked out of the monastery compound and started down the road, moving mechanically, without any sense of purpose, holding back tears. I desperately needed to talk to someone but the thought of trying to convey my frustration to Ani Dawa made me cringe. I knew what she would say—that I had to be respectful of older monks and teachers and never argue with them. Of course, there was Lobsang, who was going to take my side no matter what, but the problem with him was that he was a lot more interested in talking about sex and girlfriends than about matters of existential and metaphysical magnitude. Damien was also someone I could go to, assuming that I was willing to subject myself to a one-hour lecture on the importance of trusting your guru and the rest of the crap that's administered to the thoughtless in every ashram across India.

Suddenly, I thought of Tsar, and the image of him going down the path of mossy volcanic rocks, soaking wet, and singing obscenities in Serbian made me smile. If there was one person in the vicinity who was going to make me feel better, it was probably him. There's nothing like a taste of healthy Balkan irreverence after overdosing on emptiness.

I didn't want to run into Ani Dawa or her mother, and so I swerved off Jogibara Road and took a narrow goat trail that made long, unnecessary loops and eventually ended at the river.

Tsar's room was locked, so I sat outside and waited. At the far end of the courtyard, isolated by a foot-high wall made from stacked slate, three bony black cows demolished a heap of hay. A newborn calf, still unsure of what its body could do, galloped back and forth, tripping and slipping, rubbing its forehead against walls and wooden beams and sniffing the wet laundry hanging from the clothesline. I loved the simplicity of village life in the Himalayas: the smell of chapatis, dal, and cumin at noon; the bundles of firewood in the shed and the balls of hay drying in the trees; the dripping aboveground water pipes insulated with rags tied in knots; the houses built of mud, wood, slate, and cow dung, their protruding second floors enclosed on all sides with a balcony.

The young Indian woman that I had seen the first time I had visited Tsar's room came out of the biggest house in the compound and yelled at the calf who was chewing one of the shirts drying on the clothesline. She saw me, hesitated for a moment, and went back into the house. Seconds later she came out again, this time followed by an older woman, presumably her mother-in-law. The two women looked at me, arms akimbo, and I started to get the feeling that something wasn't right. I nodded at them and pointed at Tsar's door. "I am waiting for Guru-ji," I said.

"Guru-ji *kamra no*," the older woman said, doing an affirmative head wobble.

"I know," I replied. "I am waiting for him."

The two women began discussing something, keeping their voices down, and the older stepped forward and said, "Guru-ji is not coming."

"Not coming today?" I asked, puzzled.

"Not coming," the older woman repeated.

I got off the ground and walked over to the patio, where the women were standing. "Does he still live here?" I asked.

The women shook their heads in unison.

"He left?" I offered.

More head wobbles. This was a typical Indian situation. I knew I wasn't going to get anywhere with my questioning, but I pressed on, pretty much out of frustration. "Is he coming back? Yes or no."

"I don't know," the older woman said.

There wasn't much else I could do, so I left Durga Nivas and took the steep path that connected with Jogibara Road. I must have been completely lost in thought because when I heard a distant shout—"Nikola!"—I didn't know whether I was imagining things or someone was really calling my name. The only living soul around me was an old goatherd dressed in an oversize gray *salwar kameez* and smoking a *biddie*. We exchanged *namastes* and I walked on. A second later I heard "Nikola!" again, and this time I saw a man emerge from the cedar grove on the left. Was this Tsar? I stared at the man in disbelief: he was wearing black sweatpants and a black T-shirt; his face was covered with a beard.

"What happened to you?" I asked as I started to recognize Tsar's features—the lips, the eyes, the prominent forehead.

"A lot happened," Tsar replied with a sigh. "Come, let's not stand here. I can't be seen walking near my room."

I followed Tsar back into the cedar grove, trying to think of all the possible scenarios that could explain his new attire and the behavior of the women in Durga Nivas. He refused to pay his rent and was kicked out. Or he looked at his landlord's daughter-in-law in a weird way, and now her husband was out to kill him. Or he was accused of stealing something.

"I was just at your place," I said to him. "The older woman told me you weren't coming back."

"Let's walk down to the Tibetan Library and grab a taxi to McLeod Ganj," Tsar replied, speeding up. "I'll explain everything."

The taxi driver dropped us off in front of a dilapidated shanty that Tsar called the Last Cow Chai Shop because it was located halfway between McLeod Ganj and Shiva Waterfalls, and the wandering cows, who typically gravitated toward the vegetable market and the garbage heaps in the center of town, never ventured beyond that point. Propped by a few frail wooden beams, at an angle that was a generous five to ten degrees off horizontal, the Last Cow Chai Shop looked as if it had just been pushed off the road by a truck or a bus and was about to tumble into the precipitous gorge. Floorboards had been applied sparingly, allowing for shoe-size gaps that provided a breathtaking view of the bleak, rocky scenery three hundred feet below.

We sat by the window overlooking the valley and ordered chai. For a minute or two Tsar didn't say anything, and I didn't push him. When our chai arrived, he pulled a packet of India Kings from the pocket of his sweatpants, slammed it on the table, and got up to borrow matches from the owner.

"I feel bad about taking my robes off," he said, sticking a cigarette in his mouth. He tried to light a match but the phosphorus crumbled. He took out another match, swiped it carefully across the friction surface, and got a small spark but no flame. After a dozen unsuccessful attempts, he gave up and tossed the box at me.

"You try it," he said, infuriated. "You might have better luck."

He was right. My match lit just fine.

"So, do you still have your vows?" I asked him, cupping my hands to shield the flame.

"Everything went to hell," he answered, smiling deviously. "You know, with Kaila."

"You did it with Kaila?" I cried, unable to hide my disappointment. To give in to desire—for me, that was the ultimate admission of weakness. Suddenly I felt very sad and alone. How could I ever respect Tsar after this? How could I complain to him about my disastrous meeting with Geshe Yama Tseten? It was

one thing to be an irreverent monk and another to be weak. Of course, I was in
no way an ideal Buddhist monk—I was always ready to poke fun at those who
took the vows too seriously; I even questioned the very premise of establishing
a monastic tradition of any sort—but despite everything, I respected the act of
renouncing the mundane world and believed that what I was going through
was extremely important for me. It was a challenge and an opportunity to look
at life and myself in a way that I would never have been forced to, had I carried
on practicing piano and working and studying and dating and doing all the
things that people do to get through life, half-consciously.

"Don't give me that judgmental bullshit," Tsar said and snickered. "I had
the fucking Gestapo looking for me. What was I supposed to do, stuck with
Kaila in a hotel room in Norbulingka for three days?"

"The Gestapo?" I asked, incredulous.

"The fucking Indian secret service," Tsar explained. "They and the
Mossad are the best in the world. Every year the Chinese send someone to
assassinate the Dalai Lama, and every year the Indian secret service guys
catch him as soon as he arrives in Dharamsala."

"Okay, but why were they looking for you?"

"I have no idea. I got home four days ago and my landlord took me to his
house and told me that two plainclothes officers had raided my room while I
was gone. He had told them that I don't live there anymore. My landlord is a
really great guy, you should meet him sometime. During the day he makes
omelets in the main square in Dharmkot, a few miles down the road from
here. He has a little stand and a kerosene stove, and constantly drinks. This
man can withstand so much alcohol, it's incredible. When I first arrived in
Dharamsala, I didn't have any money, and he offered to reduce my rent if I
helped him at the omelet stand in the afternoons. I made a million omelets
for him. By three o'clock he'd be so drunk, he'd just sit on the ground and
sing, and he'd sing really well, he'd make you cry. That's how his wife would
know that he was coming home at night—you could hear him from miles
away, his voice echoing across the river."

"Tsar, you're not really telling me what happened."

"Well, I packed my most important stuff and went looking for Kaila. I didn't have a place to stay, or money for a hotel room, and my landlord had advised me to leave town for a few days, until the dust cleared and the police stopped looking for me."

"So you decided to go to Norbulingka?"

"Well, Kaila suggested it, and I thought, why not, it's only a forty-minute bus ride from here. And then everything just happened—I mean, I'm a male, she's a female, what can possibly go wrong? For a while I thought of wearing the robes despite having sex with Kaila, but when I walked out of the guesthouse the next morning, everything felt wrong. I can't cheat, you know, that's not me. I'm going to tell everyone what I did. I don't feel embarrassed at all."

"Did you even have time to renounce your vows? There's a kind of formal ceremony for giving up the monastic life."

Tsar lowered his head and looked at me like I wasn't thinking clearly. "Who has time for ceremonies, man? Where I come from, sex is considered a serious matter. You can't sit around blabbering prayers or eating dinner or watching TV."

I suppressed a smile and took a deep breath. Here was a guy who didn't give a damn about anything, and was proud of it. Absolutely unapologetic. Honest to the point of sounding obscene.

"Why, what's the sentence?" Tsar asked, lighting a second cigarette off the first one. "What does Herr Buddha say about it?"

"Well, Herr Buddha says that you broke your vows and are going straight to hell," I said, laughing.

"Oh, what do you know. Hell's got the best sunsets. And the best Turkish espresso."

"What's with this 'hell's got the best sunsets' stuff," I said. "It's the second time I've heard you say it."

Tsar adjusted himself on the bench and looked smug. "It has to do with the first law of thermodynamics."

"I have absolutely no idea what you're talking about."

"Come on, energy changes its form but it can never be created or destroyed—everybody knows that. The quantity of energy in the universe is a constant."

"So?"

"Think about it," Tsar told me in a conspiratorial tone. "What's energy if not the external manifestation of existence? Existence meaning experience, perception, you know, consciousness. So in reality the one constant is existence—it changes its form, but can never be created or destroyed. And what's more important is that, just like the quantity of energy is a constant, the taste of existence is a constant, too. It can never change. You think it's going to make a difference if you're poor or rich or dying or in hell or in Nirvana, but the fact of the matter is, it never does, the universe is like this metaphysical reactor where opposites cancel each other, pleasure is canceled by pain, highs by lows, reality by emptiness, Enlightenment by inexhaustible boredom, and at the end it all adds up to zero. Heaven isn't going to be too sweet, hell can't be too bad. It's like this: the rich have everything but are desensitized, the lepers have got nothing but are closer to life—they feel every passing moment in their bones. Monks are missing one thing, laypeople are missing another. Ordinary beings are stuck on this shore, the Buddha is stuck on the shore beyond. You could say that everyone is fucked in some way, or you could say that everyone's in a state of equilibrium. It makes no difference, really."

"So why become a Buddha, then, if it's all the same?" I asked.

"What else are you going to do? We've been sitting here for too long. It's time to move on, to stand on the other side of the equation. The equation is going to be the same, of course. You can change the form, you can't change the taste."

"There you are!" someone shouted from the street, and a second later in the chai shop walked Vinnie, Tsar's chess partner. His tattered and heavily stained white shirt was completely wet, as were his baggy striped pants, rainbow-colored rucksack, red mustache, and long, frizzy red hair. I noticed that his sideburns were rather yellow-orange and for the first time it occurred to me that Vinnie might use hair dye.

"What are you two discussing?" Vinnie wheezed, clenching his fists. "Conspiring to overthrow the government?" His voicebox, as I discovered later, had been removed and so he had to squeeze his entire being just to produce a whisper. As a consequence, he always sounded—and even acted—like a turbojet that was about to take off.

"That's definitely an option," Tsar replied.

"We've actually been discussing thermodynamics." I stepped in.

"Thermodynamics!" Vinnie exploded. "That's the spirit! Only in the Himalayas!"

"Do you have the board?" Tsar asked him.

Vinnie sat next to me, pulled a paper chessboard and a box of pieces out of his bag, and began lining up the black pawns.

"I was out of town for three days," Tsar noted, arranging the white pieces with incredible speed and precision.

"I heard," Vinnie said, suddenly looking very concerned. "Two police officers came to your room to arrest you."

"Where did you hear that?" Tsar asked.

"I have my sources," Vinnie replied mysteriously. "I've lived here, on and off, for more than fifteen years."

"I always end up in situations like this," Tsar said, pushing his king's pawn to e4. "Wherever I go, I run into problems with the authorities. Someone told on me, and I think I know who it is. It's this Indian guy that runs an STD phone service next to the travel agency, across from the Institute of Buddhist Dialectics. He's got two golden teeth, a forelock the size of a broom, and does this really slimy handshake—you feel like you're holding a slug. Kaila and I had gone there once to make a phone call, and he must've overheard us talking about my passport situation. It all started with Kaila asking me to go with her to Israel, which was a great proposition, the only problem being that I had thrown my passport out the window of a moving bus."

"You threw your passport away?" I repeated in disbelief.

"What the hell am I going to do with an expired passport from a country that had just been scratched off the map?" Tsar asked, all fired up. "I mean, first they tell you that you're born in Yugoslavia, then they give you a passport that says Yugoslavia on it, and then they bulldoze the whole place and tell you that you haven't really been born anywhere. I personally don't give a crap if I have a nationality or not. Everywhere I've been it's the same: trees are trees, hills are hills, and the people are dumber than rocks. It's just that governments don't like people who don't wear tags. Everyone has to wear a tag. Dogs have it better than humans."

"It's him," Vinnie said after some thinking. "The guy with the golden teeth running the phone booth. He must've filed a report about you in the police station."

Tsar's face lit up. "You think so?"

"I'm positive," Vinnie confirmed, nodding. "When are we going to kill him?"

Without waiting for a response, Vinnie jumped to his feet, fists clenched, and burst into an agonizing, hiccup-like laughter that drained the blood from his face and filled his eyes with tears. Tsar and I both looked at him blankly.

Still giggling, Vinnie returned to the bench and moved his king's pawn two squares. "E takes F," he announced with the intensity of someone who's on the verge of a life-altering revelation. "King's Gambit, accepted."

Vinnie admired the opening position for a minute, and then got up to order chai.

Suddenly the shanty squeaked and shook ominously, and all three of us turned around to look at the owner of the Last Cow Chai Shop, a good-natured, middle-aged man in scraggly pajamas squatting next to a mound of freshly peeled potatoes.

"Baba?" Tsar called out to him. "Are we going down?"

"The wind," the owner replied, making a circular motion with his forefinger.

"There's no wind," Tsar noted.

Holding their heads between the palms of their hands, Vinnie and Tsar leaned over the board and went into battle. If the way people play chess is an indication of how they act in real life, then one could say that Vinnie was timid and passive-aggressive, while Tsar was conceited and belligerent. "You could do that if you want," Tsar would say mockingly each time Vinnie moved. "I'm still going to have my way. Come on, Vinnie, just let it go, man. You're German—German people are supposed to die with dignity." Ten minutes into the game, Tsar was so sure he was going to win, he started singing all the good-bye and break-up songs that came to his mind: "Love will tear us apart, *again*!" and "Every time we say good-bye," and "Don't walk away, *in silence*!" Vinnie, for his part, ground his teeth and said, "I see!" and "Nice!" as if he truly enjoyed what was being done to him by his opponent—a notion that was immediately betrayed when he slammed his pieces down on the board with a trembling hand.

Around the twentieth move, Tsar knocked his king down, resigning, and lit a cigarette.

"On his dying bed," Vinnie began, barely able to contain his excitement, "Hegel turned to his wife and said—"

"We've heard it." Tsar interrupted him.

"He hasn't," Vinnie said, pointing at me. "He turned to his wife and said, 'Only one man ever understood me . . . and he understood me wrong!'"

Vinnie got off the bench to do his epileptic laughter and this time Tsar and I joined him—not because of the absurd desperation in Hegel's last words, but because of Vinnie's astonishing ability to laugh, again and again, at his own jokes.

"He wins once every two weeks, so he has to make a big deal out of it," Tsar explained, smiling compassionately at Vinnie.

"That's not true," Vinnie protested. "I've won the last three games: the one we played in Om Restaurant, the game we played on the bus . . ."

"I've never played on a bus," Tsar snapped.

Vinnie thought about it for a moment, and then nodded gravely. "You are right. It was Rosenkrantz. On the bus. He has a magnetic chess set."

"Who is Rosenkrantz?" I asked.

"It's this fat Dutch former taxi driver who rides homeless cows, smokes hash, and reads Jalal al-Din Rumi," Tsar answered, always happy to summarize someone's entire life in a few words. "And has lice."

"Only in the Himalayas!" Vinnie exclaimed.

"I think I'm going to go pay a visit to my friend with the golden teeth," Tsar confided. "Then I'm going to look for a new room."

"You are a brave man," Vinnie commended him, stuffing the chess pieces and the board back into his rucksack. "One has to face his enemy."

We paid for our chai and walked out to the street, where Vinnie wished us good luck and hurried in the opposite direction.

"Where are you off to so fast?" Tsar called after him.

"The ladies are waiting for me," Vinnie said, smiling like a little kid that's been taken to the merry-go-round.

"In the nursing home?" Tsar suggested.

Vinnie snorted and walked away.

"Nikola," Tsar turned to me, "I need you to come with me when I go in to talk to this guy at the phone booth. It'll make a huge difference if I'm accompanied by someone, especially someone wearing robes."

I agreed instantly, even though it was clear that Tsar was a source of chaos. He was the type of guy who caused trouble wherever he went. There was an internal contradiction that was splitting my personality in half, and I was quickly becoming aware of it. On the one hand, I wanted to think of myself as someone who was very serious about what he was doing. I had come to India to gain knowledge and find the path to salvation. I had become a monk solely for the purpose of getting as close as possible to the people who possessed the knowledge I was seeking. I was really a scientist, though of a different kind. Why was it, then, that I found myself so irresistibly attracted to the world of Tsar—his been-there-done-that weariness of existence, his larger-than-Nirvana attitude, his amendment to the first law of thermodynamics, his irreverence, his free and uncompromising spirit? Was it that I was ultimately more interested in the story of the underdog and the sinner who, if for a very brief moment, succeeded in defying all gravity (the gravity of good and evil, of sorrow and peace, of purpose and nihilism), than in the fable of the Buddha, who followed the path of the noble ones and achieved a state of perfection? Or did I just crave a genuine adventure?

IT HAD BEEN A LONG DAY—first meeting with Geshe Yama Tseten, then hanging out with Tsar and Vinnie—and I still hadn't eaten anything. We returned to McLeod Ganj and ordered parathas at a dim Punjabi joint right across from the spot where all the lepers gathered to beg and share their proceeds in the afternoon.

I told Tsar about my fight with Geshe Yama Tseten, and he said that I was taking people too seriously. "Fuck him," he concluded, dumping an entire jar of pickled mangoes on his plate. "What's so special about him, anyway? He still has an ego, right? Everyone's got an ego. You could think about the ego as just another form of gravity—it's a pull. The greater the sphere of influence, the greater the ego. The Buddha has an ego, a giant one, too. By the way, he might not be able to tell the difference between his ass and a tree or between a subject and an object, but he still has an ego. Just like the sun—it doesn't intend to, but it holds all the planets together. So, what I'm saying to you is, you can't let this Geshe's ego crush you. Even Buddha's ego can kill you if you don't keep at a safe distance. Get too close and he'll suck the life force out of you. The first day I arrived in India and looked around, I felt like everyone was on drugs. What the fuck was wrong with all these Westerners walking around like a bunch of brain-dead fairies? Then it hit me—they had given in. They hadn't survived the pull."

We finished our parathas and got up to go, when the owner of the joint, a heavily built Punjabi man with a porcupine mustache, droopy chicken pox–jagged cheeks, and betel-reddened teeth, blocked our way and demanded that Tsar pay for the jar of mango pickles that he had eaten. "It cost me twenty-five rupees when I bought it," the owner said tersely. "There is no way I'm going to pay for that," Tsar replied and went on to explain that, as far as he was concerned, a jar of mango pickles was no different from the salt, the chili paste, and the ketchup that were offered free of charge in every restaurant in town. The owner agreed with him, but pointed out that the jar had been absolutely full prior to our arrival. "One paratha—one hundred grams," he reasoned, holding Tsar's empty plate. "You ate two parathas— that's two hundred grams. Now look at the jar—it says two hundred and fifty grams. That's a quarter kilo of *ajar*."

I opened my money belt to pay for the *ajar* but Tsar wrapped his arm around my shoulder and ushered me out of the restaurant. Exasperated, the owner tossed his hands in the air and picked up our mess.

"You can't give them money for mango pickles," Tsar told me as we started to stroll toward the Main Temple. "If they start charging us for stuff like that, soon we'll have to carry our own jars of mangoes every time we go to a chai shop."

Perhaps to illustrate that he'd much rather give his money to a stranger than to someone who didn't respect his right to eat as many mango pickles as he wanted, Tsar stopped in front of a beggar woman with sunken eyes, a dreamy smile, and iodine-soaked bandages wrapped around her finger- less hands, and dropped all of his change—about ten rupees—into her tin can. The woman pressed her forehead to the ground and whispered a thank-you.

"I understand the untouchables," Tsar said. "They're just like me—no tags, no passports, no country."

When we approached the STD run by the alleged government informer, Tsar paused to give me instructions.

"It's very important for me that this goes well," Tsar began, tossing away his cigarette. "All I need from you is to agree with me. When I say, 'Right, Nikola?' you answer, 'That's absolutely right, Tsar, I remember.' And try to look mean and angry. Can you do that?"

"Sure," I replied, thinking nothing of it.

"All right, then," Tsar concluded, taking a deep breath. "Let's do it."

The STD was about six feet wide and ten feet long and consisted of a bench, a counter, and a cardboard cabin with a phone in it. The owner of the STD sat dwarfed behind the counter, staring at three identical white clocks mounted on the wall opposite him. The handwritten labels under the clocks read *Dharamsala, New York, Sydney*. The Dharamsala and Sydney clocks had stopped, and the third one, apparently still in working condition, showed four o'clock, which was perhaps the correct time in Papua New Guinea. Next to the clocks hung a high-tech representation of Hanuman made of yellow plastic and surrounded by blue and red lights, which blinked from left to right, then from right to left, and then simultaneously to the accompaniment of deafening car-alarm sirens that went off every ten seconds and made the STD owner swell with pride and flash his golden teeth. The bench was occupied by a young Scandinavian couple and an American woman in her forties whom I had seen once at Ani Dawa's house. I nodded at her, and she nodded back, but I didn't get the feeling that she had recognized me. Was she doing her Ph.D.? Or teaching at Columbia? I couldn't remember. I had met her before I became a monk.

A Tibetan lady in the cardboard cabin was speaking in a mixture of English and Tibetan: "School *kan dre dug? Re pe?* All right, then, *ma shag gi yin ta.*"

It was clear that the STD owner wasn't very happy to see us. For a good minute or two he busied himself with the scraps of paper scattered across his counter and pointedly avoided making eye contact with us. Finally, Tsar leaned forward, elbows on the counter, and put his face two inches away from the owner's.

"Do you remember me?" Tsar said quietly and with a wicked smile.

The owner jumped to his feet, said, "Yes, yes!" rushed out the door, and yelled at a boy across the street to bring three glasses of chai.

"Take a seat," the owner said, pointing at the bench.

"There's no place to sit," Tsar observed. "You should really buy a longer bench."

"I'll get a chair," the owner suggested and started toward the door.

"Come back here," Tsar said. "I just want to ask you a few questions."

The owner returned behind the counter and scooped all the scraps and bits of paper into one big pile. The Tibetan lady in the booth was having a hard time hearing. "*Ka re sa?* Say it again!"

"So what's my name?" Tsar asked casually.

The owner looked up, did a conciliatory head wobble, and said, "*Acha.*"

"Did you hear that?" Tsar turned to me. "What was this called? I say, what's my name, and you answer *acha*? Does anyone know?"

The Scandinavian couple shrugged their shoulders; the American woman looked away.

"A non sequitur," I offered.

"Right," Tsar said dreamily. "A non sequitur. Say, Nikola, do you remember when we were on a train to Amsterdam and there was this guy who just couldn't remember my name? He thought and thought, and finally got so frustrated, he jumped off the train. And we were going about ninety kilometers an hour."

Everyone looked at me, awaiting my response. I scratched my head, adjusted my *zen*, and said, "Yeah."

"I don't know what's wrong with people," Tsar went on, getting excited. "Jumping off trains like that. And then there was this immigration officer in Amsterdam who got so concerned with my visa situation that he fell into an open sewer and broke both of his legs—in broad daylight! Nikola, remember that guy?"

"I do," I said, blushing.

"Everywhere I go, people want to help me!" Tsar exclaimed and pulled out his pack of India Kings. "Like the other day, two police officers came to my room to help me find my passport and spent three whole hours going through all my stuff. I don't know who told them that I had lost my passport—Nikola, do you have any idea?"

"None," I confirmed.

The door opened and in rushed the boy with the chai. The owner of the STD gave him three rupees and yelled at him to get out.

"I mean, it's really too bad that these police officers didn't get a chance to meet me in person," Tsar said, sipping his chai. "I really don't want anything bad to happen to them. You see, I bring bad luck to people—they try to help me, and suddenly the most horrible things happen to them. That's why I came to you—I just had this feeling that you want to help me, and I got very worried."

"No, no, no," the owner said, waving his hand.

"You don't want to help me, then?"

"No, no. Not me."

Tsar lit a cigarette and looked triumphantly at the American woman and the Scandinavian couple. "You hear that? The man doesn't want to help me. Good! I don't want you to get on your scooter one night after work and fly off a cliff because for some strange reason your brakes had malfunctioned."

With the cigarette clasped between his fingers, Tsar demonstrated with his hand what happens to someone who goes straight at a road turn and plummets to the bottom of a yawning precipice. "Like the coyote in *Road Runner*," he noted. "Have you seen *Road Runner*? I love that cartoon."

The owner hadn't seen *Road Runner*.

"Oh, and by the way, I like your golden teeth," Tsar complimented him, as he pushed me toward the door.

"*Acha*," the owner replied, smiling.

Outside, Tsar pointed at himself, and smirking as if to say, *Who is the king now?* he ran his thumb and middle finger down his chin, stroking an imaginary goatee. This was, I later realized, Tsar's signature gesture, a little theatrical touch that he used to announce that he had or he was going to come out on top again. And that was a fundamental part of Tsar's character, this sense that he was always getting away with something or getting even. He didn't win battles: he dodged bullets. He was the underdog, the outlaw on the fringes of society, the refugee who wasn't welcome in any country on the planet.

"Fucking pussy," Tsar said. "There's definitely something wrong with people."

"What if this guy had nothing to do with the police officers that raided your room?"

"Come on, Nikola, he was shitting his pants!"

Tsar took a few steps, then stopped, and waved at me to follow him.

"He probably didn't even understand English," I said, trying not to sound furious. "We basically went in and acted like total buffoons, talking about people jumping off trains and breaking their legs. And the only thing the owner said was *Acha*."

"Nikola, you're going to have a heart attack if you continue like this." Tsar laughed. "Relax! Come, let's go see a movie."

"I don't want to see a movie," I protested. "The woman that was sitting next to the door—she knows Ani Dawa. Do you understand what that means? Tomorrow everyone in town will look at me like some runaway criminal."

"And what's wrong with that?" Tsar asked innocently.

"What's wrong with it is that I'm trying to be a monk."

"'Trying' is the right word. You can't get anywhere by trying."

"Well, it took supposedly three million years for the Buddha to reach Enlightenment."

"Exactly," Tsar cried out. "It took him that long because he was trying."

"Right, and you're probably going to get there tomorrow."

"I'm not in a hurry. I'll get there when I get there."

Quarreling, we entered McLeod Ganj, walked past the vegetable market, and stopped in front of one of the local movie theaters, a dilapidated shanty covered with a thick blue plastic sheet.

"I'm not going in," I told Tsar as he pulled out a ten-rupee bill to pay for two tickets.

"Of course you're going—what else are you going to do?"

Tsar lifted the door curtain and gestured for me to get in. "Come on, we're going to miss the beginning."

"I'm going home," I said stubbornly.

WE WATCHED AN UNMEMORABLE Hong Kong kung fu movie on an old TV, model indeterminable, which behaved as if it had been placed on top of a powerful magnet: a vibrating rainbow rendered one-third of the screen completely useless, while a constant snowflake effect created the impression of watching a live broadcast from Mars. The video player didn't exactly run smoothly, either—it jammed every fifteen minutes, and the Video Supervisor, a generously mustached Kashmiri entrepreneur, had to turn on the lights, extract the cassette tape using a combination of knives, screwdrivers, and parts of umbrellas, and then try to revive the chewed-up mechanism by banging the tape against his knee, pulling the magnetic ribbon, and rotating the cogwheels with his fingers. Halfway through the movie, Tsar stepped out and returned with a small bottle of Indian brandy, which he promptly consumed before the final tape jam, when the Kashmiri entrepreneur ushered everyone out onto the street.

Drinking a half-liter of hard liquor didn't seem to have much effect on Tsar. He walked in a straight line, greeting restaurant owners, shopkeepers, and barbers, who all knew him and seemed surprised to see him dressed in lay clothes once again. I asked him if he was going to miss Kaila, who had left early that morning for Israel, and he said that letting go of someone was the best feeling in the world. Then he went on to explain, in graphic detail, the different techniques that he had employed to bring Kaila to climax. These included, but were not limited to, scratching her back, pulling her ears, massaging her temples, stimulating the pressure points on the crown of her head, squeezing the back of her neck, pulling her hair, and pinching her ass. Tsar said that he was very happy about the way things had turned out, because, if it hadn't been for him, Kaila might never have experienced real sex in her life. Kaila, apparently, had suffered from an orgasm block, acquired from dating sloppy boyfriends, and Tsar had helped her to break free from it.

It was getting dark, and the setting sun had colored the mountains bright orange. The nunnery's gong was calling for dinner; from the temple on top of the hill, Om Giridi was blasting his evening tape of Shiva hymns through a loudspeaker. And underneath all the village noises—the distant honking, the kids shouting and laughing, the clinking of metal dishes and silverware, the clapping sound of horseshoes—there was the ever-present roar of the river, a pedal point that sustained the pulse of the Himalayas.

Approaching Jogibara laundry, I asked Tsar what his plans were for the future, now that staying at a monastery was out of the question for him. He said that his first priority was to find a new room and buy some normal clothes—he had thrown out all of his old clothes on the day he was ordained. Without thinking twice, I took him to my room, pulled the army sack from under my bed, and handed him the clothes that I had brought with me to India. Tsar immediately took off his black sweatpants and T-shirt and put on what used to be my favorite beige corduroy pants and a cream-colored sweater.

"I owe you a big one," he said as we parted on the street.

I could see in his eyes that he really meant that. Under all the posturing and the Balkan bravado, there was a sincerity and openness that's nearly impossible to find even in one's closest friends. I felt bad that I had been so apprehensive and judgmental from the moment I had met him. Whether self-inflicted or imposed by outside circumstances, Tsar's problems were real. He had run away from a war that had destroyed his country, then had been tossed around from one immigration camp to another, across Western Europe, and finally he had ended up in India, without a passport and a future, at the age of thirty-seven—only to find himself on the run again. It was quite apparent that he was having a hard time living in the world.

Watching Tsar recede into the distance, dressed in my pants and my sweater, was truly a weird sight. On the one hand, it was like watching my alter ego slip back into its old clothes and walk away from the life that I had chosen. On the other, it felt deeply symbolic, as if by putting on the clothes that I had renounced, Tsar had tied a karmic knot, the kind that fastens two people's paths together, for better or for worse.

Eleven

Following a day of deliberation, prompted by fears of a new police raid on his room, Tsar packed his belongings and moved fifty feet up the road to a spacious room on the second floor of a mud-plastered house, which was also part of the Durga Nivas family compound and belonged to Tsar's perpetually inebriated landlord. The rent was five hundred rupees a month (about twelve dollars), which by most village standards was considered expensive. In comparison, my room on Jogibara Road cost four hundred rupees a month, and Tsar's old room cost two hundred and fifty. A six-dollar difference might not seem like a lot, but for me and Tsar it equaled two weeks' worth of basic life-sustaining groceries. Tsar and I weren't tourists. We had no credit cards, bank accounts, stash of traveler's checks, or parents who were eager to send more money as soon as we went broke. We had come to India to stay, and each of us lived on a budget of about thirty-five dollars a month, or fourteen hundred rupees, which bought us the following amenities: room (four hundred rupees), ten kilos of chapati flour and a packet of baking soda (forty rupees), five kilos of fast-cooking orange dal—the yellow and green kind took about four hours to cook—(eighty rupees), ten kilos of rice, two grades below basmati (fifty rupees), five kilos of red beans (eighty rupees), ten kilos of potatoes (fifty rupees), five kilos of tomatoes (seventy rupees), ten kilos of onions (forty rupees), four kilos of the strongest, weapon-grade chilies (fifteen rupees), a carton of sunflower oil (twenty-five rupees), Amul butter, which had the fantastic shelf life of one year, at temperatures over 100°F. (thirty-five rupees), masala and spices (twenty-five rupees), five kilos of bananas (twenty-five rupees), one kilo of apples (twenty rupees), a branch of lychees (fifteen rupees), a box of long-leaf Darjeeling tea (seventy rupees), six kilos of sugar (thirty rupees), five liters of contraband kerosene (sixty rupees), two taxi rides (twenty rupees), ten local bus rides (twenty rupees), four show-ers at the Green Hotel (forty rupees), a haircut (ten rupees), twenty parathas and ten glasses of chai at a third-class chai shop, or ten rice-and-dal meals at Smiley's hole-in-the-wall restaurant behind the bus stop (one hundred rupees), toothpaste (twenty rupees), hair and body soap (seven rupees), dish soap (three rupees), salt, matches, flashlight batteries, a movie ticket, incense, and miscellaneous other items (fifty rupees).

What thirty-five dollars a month didn't buy was: a room not populated by lizards, scorpions, crabs, snakes, rats, mice, bedbugs, birds, and praying mantises; access to a bathroom within two miles; a private sink with running water; a chocolate cake from the German bakery at least once a week; a plate of potato *momos* for lunch; a daily dose of mango *lassi*; basmati rice; vitamins; bottled water; the option of taking a taxi when it was raining; the freedom to drop off your dirty clothes at the Jogibara laundry and pick them up clean and folded the next day; a shiny and quiet gas stove in place of a kerosene one that spouted soot and tar and scorched your eyelashes; a pillow in place of a heap of clothes; a comforter in place of nylon blankets buzzing with static electricity; handmade leather sandals; books from the English-language bookstore; high-quality Tibetan incense; a working flashlight that wasn't made in China.

Once Tsar and I sat down and calculated how much each of us was spending a month, it became obvious that it would make a lot more sense if we moved in together and split the rent. I knew that Tsar had only a hundred dollars left (Kaila's farewell gift) but I wasn't worried about it. Even if Tsar were to go completely broke—something he stubbornly dismissed as impossible—I would've still been able to pay for food and shelter for both of us without going dangerously over budget.

Ani Dawa's face darkened when I broke the news to her. "With Tsar? You know, it's bad karma to live with a fallen monk."

We were sitting in Ani Dawa's room, eating tofu chow mein and sipping salty butter tea.

"What did I tell you, Dawa," Ama-la shouted excitedly. "Next thing you know, he's going to find some American girl, throw away the robes, and bring shame on all of us. All *Engies* are like that—they come here, pose as monks for a while, and then they run off and get married."

"You're acting as if Tsar has killed someone," I said, trying hard not to explode. "Just because he broke his vow of celibacy doesn't mean that he is a bad person. It's not like he has rabies and he's going to start biting people left and right."

"You're going to get a lot of bad karma," Ani Dawa repeated ominously.

"I don't care about bad karma." I laughed belligerently. "And I'd like to see one text where it says that it's a crime to live with a monk who has broken his vows."

Ani Dawa put her plate on the table and leaned back in her chair. "It doesn't have to be written anywhere. I'm just trying to help you. I've seen many Westerners come and go, without learning absolutely anything. When we first met, you said that you wanted to study all the texts, from beginning to end, and I believed you. If you want to live with Tsar, that's your choice. But you should think about what you're doing with your life."

It was strange that I felt obliged to ask Ani Dawa for permission to move into a different room. On the one hand, I was happy that there was someone who was truly concerned about my future, but on the other, I was worried that Ani Dawa had begun to project onto me the qualities and responsibilities of a male figure that was simultaneously her son, her husband, her father, and her brother. And as much as I cared for her, I realized that I couldn't possibly be all the people who had always been absent from her life, and still manage to not disappoint her. So, in a sense, leaving Jogibara Road was good for both of us. We had gotten too close, and that wasn't healthy.

Tsar and I spent about a week making our new room in Durga Nivas livable. The biggest problem with the room, we quickly realized, was the dust. When we woke up the first morning, there was so much dust everywhere, we felt like we had survived a massive earthquake. There was dust in our mouths, in our eyes, in our blankets, in all the cups, plates, and pots, and even, unbelievably, in our box of expensive, long-leaf Darjeeling. And this wasn't the kind of fine dust that was largely made up of dead human skin. This stuff was grainy, red-brown in color, and mixed in with rat poop, dried leaves, dead spiders, moths, flies, wooden splinters, and an occasional piece of what appeared to be patterned snakeskin. There was only one place where all this junk could be coming from: the roof. In addition to the cracked, disjointed, or missing slate tiles, there were fist-size holes between the roof beams and the mud-plastered walls, which allowed small birds to enter the room, make a few circles, steal some crumbs, and exit through another hole. "There must've been a pretty powerful storm last night," Tsar commented after we spent our first morning in the new room sweeping the floor, dusting all the surfaces, shaking our clothes and blankets, and rewashing the cups, plates, and silverware. The same thing happened the next morning, and then on the morning after that. On the fourth day, Tsar woke up spitting angrily on the floor and told me to get ready, because we were going shopping in Lower Dharamsala. Halfway down the road, we stopped at a chai shop and Tsar told me his plan: we were going to buy a plastic sheet big enough to cover the roof, and then buy two real beds (we had been sleeping on the floor) and some rope and hooks so that we could hang everything that we owned in the air, away from the rats. I instantly had a vision of living in a postmodern installation, with pots, pans, monk's robes, books, kerosene stoves, and bags of rice floating in space, suspended on barely visible strings. We succeeded in finding a thick blue plastic sheet bigger than our room, but when it came to buying bed frames, we realized that we would need to hire an army of *kulis* to carry them back to Durga Nivas. Lacking the money to do that, we settled on a pair of plywood sheets that we could place on mud bricks and stones, and at least get our blankets off the ground. One thing we couldn't find anywhere was hooks, and so the whole plan of suspending our belongings on strings went to hell, or, as Tsar phrased it, to Pichku Materinu. Pichku Materinu (literally "mother's cunt") was the place where, according to popular Serbian folklore, everything went, ultimately.

When we returned home, we tried to spread the plastic sheet across the roof, but quickly decided instead to insulate the room from the inside. Tsar had a very strong sense of symmetry and managed to nail the sheet to the roof beams and the upper part of the walls so tightly and perfectly that there wasn't a single place where the plastic flopped or ventured below the designated line. After we set up our plywood beds and hung Tsar's old monastic robes as curtains, the room began to feel quite decent. In fact, it looked pretty impressive, considering that, in reality, we had rented a hollow mud cake. As soon as we sat down to admire our achievement, a delegation of village elders, headed by our landlord, ascended the external staircase and entered the room, silent, hands clasped behind their backs. Our landlord inspected the novel roof insulation, studied the plywood sheets propped up on mud bricks, tapped on the low tea table that Tsar had crafted the previous day, and performed an approving head wobble. Each of the remaining members of the delegation repeated this sequence of movements, as if they were practicing a pantomime: they looked up at the roof, kneeled down to look at the beds, tapped on the table, and then shook their heads sideways. After the village elders came the women: our landlord's wife, her daughter, and her daughter-in-law. They were followed by Purba, the twenty-seven-year-old ex-monk from Tibet's Amdo region. Acknowledging our presence with a nod, he went straight for the pressure cooker, and without waiting for an invitation, poured himself a bowl of the spicy dal that Tsar and I had cooked for dinner. Opening the lid of the pot next to the pressure cooker, Purba found the rice. As he ate, sweating excessively from the pound of chilies that Tsar had dropped into the dal, he informed us that Tibetans refer to Westerners as *na ring*, or "long-nosed," and then went on to tell us about his uncle from Amdo who would catch dragons with a lasso, right in the middle of a raging storm, lock them up in a barn like chickens, and then starve them until they became compliant and agreed to do favors for him.

"You're making this up," I concluded matter-of-factly. "You also told me that your grandfather would go into a secret cellar and teleport himself to Mount Kailash."

"And what do you know about the world?" Purba asked with a smug smile. "Tibet is a different planet: people there talk to dragons all the time."

"Right," Tsar jumped in. "And my grandmother in Sarajevo is ninety-four and drives an F-16."

After Purba left, we were visited by Lobsang, who ate the rest of the dal and rice and asked us if we knew of something that one could do in order to have sex for a long time. He said that he was seeing a half-Swiss, half-Tibetan girl who was so pretty that he would always get too excited too quickly and ruin the whole thing. Naturally, Tsar had a lot to say on this subject. Recalling the days when he used to visit Amsterdam's red light district four times a week, he advised Lobsang to drink seven beers, or half a bottle of brandy, depending on his mood, then memorize ten sentences from some utterly boring and worthless book, preferably a religious text or the universal declaration of human rights, then put on two condoms, one on top of the other—for double protection, and as a kind of local anesthetic—and proceed with the fun part, all the while thinking about the fact that we, as unenlightened humans, almost never do what we want, meaning, that all of our actions, including sex, are actually forced upon us by a combination of peripheral factors, such as delusion, genetics, and quantum mechanics, and the whole business of dancing around and wiggling like monkeys, with half of our brains gone numb, is nothing but a samsaric drag, one that we have to put up with, but with great displeasure. Tsar stressed this last point, saying that in order for his method to work, it is imperative that you feel like you're doing the whole thing against your will.

Lobsang was absolutely blown away by this presentation, and said that he was going to try everything Tsar had suggested as soon as possible.

"I hope you realize what you've done," I told Tsar after Lobsang had left. "Now he is going to get wasted, go to see his Swiss girlfriend who has just graduated from high school and has come here for the summer to visit her Tibetan relatives, and act like he's about to have an epileptic seizure. I mean, how much fun are they going to have?"

"You're a monk," Tsar reminded me smugly. "You shouldn't worry about people's sex lives."

Some weeks passed and Tsar and I established a routine. We'd set the alarm clock for seven-thirty, intending to get an early start and arrive at the Library of Tibetan Works and Archives in time for the eight o'clock Introduction to Buddhist Hells class, which we were both mildly curious about, and every morning we'd wake up at half-past nine, with neither of us having any recollection of an alarm going off at any point. This phenomenon prompted Tsar to conduct a series of experiments with the alarm clock (an Indian make, with a winding mechanism) where he'd observe the alarm going off from different corners of the room, and even from behind the house, to monitor the area for mysterious interferences. After repeatedly taking the clock apart and putting it back together, Tsar reached the following, apparently inevitable conclusions: 1. The clock wasn't equipped with a mechanism that could make the alarm go off at seven-thirty at night and not go off at seven-thirty in the morning. 2. There were no perceivable outside forces that could prevent the alarm from going off at seven-thirty in the morning. 3. The alarm was not audible from the outside, hence no independent observers, such as neighbors, could affirm or deny whether the alarm actually went off or not. 4. At seven o'clock in the morning our door was locked and the likelihood of someone, say our landlord's wife, climbing on a ladder, pushing our window open, crawling on the floor, and turning the alarm off was quite slim.

Taking into account all available evidence and the conclusions derived from it, Tsar announced that there were only three possible answers to the alarm mystery: 1. One of us got up every morning, sleepwalked across the room, and shut the alarm off as it was about to go off. 2. At seven-thirty in the morning the Himalayas underwent an electromagnetic shift that rendered all mechanical alarm clocks useless. Hence, all the dirt and debris that we found on the floor. 3. The alarm clock was affected by the Indian law of probabilities, which states that some things happen or don't happen, again and again, for absolutely no reason.

So we'd wake up at nine-thirty, make some really strong black tea, and try to guess what the teacher at the Tibetan Library had talked about in his Intro to Buddhist Hells class. "They probably discussed the sixth hot hell," Tsar would say dreamily. "The one where you disintegrate into trillions of quarks, and each quark becomes an additional hurting body which is pulverized by radiation and then brought back to its original state. I love that hell. You get the feeling that one of those Indian guys who first wrote about it, back in the days, was reading a textbook on quantum physics."

"I personally don't care so much about the hot hells," I'd interrupt. "The eight cold hells are a lot more appealing to me, from an aesthetic point of view."

"You're right," Tsar would agree. "We have to get a new alarm clock before they start talking about the cold hells. God knows what will happen to us if we keep on living such ignorant lives."

At around ten-thirty we'd walk out of the house and split at the fork in the road: Tsar would go to play chess with Vinnie at a chai shop in Lower Dharamsala, and I'd go to see Gedun, a thirty-year-old Tibetan monk living nearby who had agreed to teach me Tibetan grammar and poetry writing. Gedun, who was undoubtedly very smart and extremely well-read, thought of himself as a scholar on a mission to write a treatise that would change the world. Every day he managed to read a five- or six-hundred-page Tibetan book, take twenty pages of notes, and still find the time to give me writing exercises and to inscribe in my notebook the etymology of the more obscure and complex words in the Tibetan dictionary. His ambition was to publish the first secular Tibetan history, a virtually impossible task since all of his reference material consisted of biographies and autobiographies of famous Tibetan teachers and dignitaries who claimed to have conversed with dead or invisible beings, remembered their past lives, or recounted the past lives of others, and who treated all historical events as miracles brought about by supernatural forces. Gedun openly despised Tsar, referring to him as "lazy" and "a hippie"—arguably the most offensive words in his vocabulary.

I spent long hours in Gedun's room doing exercises and memorizing the definitions of words. Gedun lived alone in an Indian family compound, away from the clatter and bustle of communal monastery life, which he believed was designed to make people stupid. He was handsome, self-confident, and very polite to strangers, but he was also extremely introverted and short-tempered. Oftentimes, when I had trouble following him or couldn't memorize something quickly enough, he would make me repeat everything that he'd said to me in the past hour, and then he'd throw my notebook on the floor and walk out of the room, slamming the door behind him. His fits didn't last more than five minutes, but were powerful enough to set the dynamic of our relationship forever. Another thing about Gedun was that he had no sense of humor. He always looked very concerned and preoccupied, staring into space with knitted eyebrows, conceiving plans of running off with the entire collection of books in the Tibetan Library of Works and Archives (to preserve them), or exposing the hypocrisy of Tibetan lamas, or initiating a guerrilla campaign against the Chinese forces in Tibet. I asked him once if he could tell me the single most important thing that he'd learned after reading hundreds and hundreds of documents, memoirs, and biographies going as far back as 800 A.D. He said that all of his research pointed to one conclusion, which was that all the wars, atrocities, and suffering experienced by the Tibetan people until the middle of the twentieth century had been perpetrated by Tibetan lamas and *Geshes*. This was, needless to say, an extremely radical view for a monk educated in the Tibetan monastic system, and it wasn't at all surprising that Gedun was secretive and paranoid about his work, often lying to others about the nature of his project. He confided in me that he feared for his life and that if word about what he was writing got out, he'd be killed by a Chinese spy or a Tibetan monk.

Despite his army style of teaching, or perhaps because of it, I learned more from Gedun in one month than I had learned the entire time I had studied with Ani Dawa. Interacting with Gedun also taught me a great deal about what happens to people who have been socially, sexually, and ideologically isolated for a long time. Gedun exhibited a set of idiosyncrasies that I later observed in almost all my monk friends in the Institute of Buddhist Dialectics, and some years after that, in Drepung Monastery in South India. First, there was the obsession with doing things the *right* way. "Lodro," Gedun would say to me, shaking his head, "this is *not* the way to boil water. You have to wipe the bottom of the pot," Gedun would explain in all seriousness, "then you have to lower the flame, and place the pot in the very center of the stove, with the handle pointing at the window. If the handle is pointing at the wall, it'll get very hot and ruin the pot." Or: "Lodro, give me the knife. You don't know how to cut onions. You're making rings." "I'm going to chop it very fine and you won't see the rings, I promise." "It doesn't matter," Gedun would say, exasperated. "You can't cut an onion in rings."

Then there was the obsession with putting things in the *right* place. "Put the dictionary under Gyaltsab Je's commentary of Abhisamaya Alankara." "Why? It's just a stack of books." "That's where it belongs."

Gedun was also very particular about the things that he could buy. "These potatoes have spots; we'll look somewhere else." "All potatoes have spots," I'd observe. "Yes, but *these* spots are different."

There was really no end to the rules that stipulated what was permissible and what wasn't. Taking a walk before lunch was verboten. Doing homework on the roof of the house was permissible. Eating at cheap Indian joints was verboten. Eating at cheap Tibetan joints was permissible.

Finally, there was the irrational deference to authority. I told Gedun once about a Swiss guy I'd met in McLeod Ganj who had left Switzerland as a teenager in order to avoid the mandatory military service.

"Switzerland doesn't have an army," Gedun snapped, looking at me the way a high school teacher looks at a student who's telling stories.

"Why do you think that?"

"I've heard the Dalai Lama speak on this subject," Gedun replied.

"He probably meant that Switzerland is a neutral country," I suggested.

"No," Gedun insisted. "He said they don't have an army."

"Well, they do. I could introduce you to three Swiss people tomorrow, and you could ask them about that."

"I don't need to ask anybody. Why would the Dalai Lama lie?"

There were tears in Gedun's eyes, tears of compassion, frustration, and total astonishment. I had assumed the unthinkable: that the Dalai Lama would mishandle the truth.

"Gedun, I really don't care what the Dalai Lama has said and what you've heard. There are newspapers, libraries—you should find out who's right and wrong on your own."

I reminded Gedun that in Tibetan one of the expressions for "universe," *si pa*, also means "a possibility." Things are possible. It's possible that someone is wrong. It's possible that someone heard wrong. It's *possible* that Switzerland has an army.

"But why would the Dalai Lama lie?" Gedun repeated stubbornly.

That logic really killed me.

IT WAS THE END OF DECEMBER and the Himalayan ridges were covered with a thick cap of snow. The weather was still pretty warm, about sixty-five, seventy in the sun, but most of the people in Lower Dharamsala were already

dressed in their winter attire: the *kulis* wore woolen vests; the street juicemak-
ers wore hats and scarves; the vegetable vendors wore sweaters on top of their
pajama *kurtas;* the saddhus were wrapped up in heavy blankets. Tsar, for his
part, wore light gray linen pants, a cream-colored striped dress shirt, and sev-
enties sunglasses. Leaning back in a chair outside a chai shop above the main
bazaar, one leg over the other, a lit cigarette in his hand, his head tilted back
for maximum sun exposure, he looked like a croupier from the French
Riviera.

"What took you so long?" he asked as I walked into the chai shop to get
an extra chair. "It's almost four-thirty. I have a game with Erick in ten minutes, and the bus to McLeod Ganj just left about a minute ago. We'll have to
get a taxi."

Erick was a Dutch guy in his mid-forties who was regarded by everyone as
the local chess wizard. Playing against him was considered an honor, and
those who managed to beat him, or even force him into a draw, instantly
acquired the patina of champions.

"I didn't know Erick was going to play tonight," I said, by way of apology.

"That's what Vinnie told me. We'll see who shows up."

"Is everyone meeting in Om Restaurant?"

"Either Om, or at the Green Hotel terrace."

I turned my chair around to face Tsar directly and stared at him, inviting
him to spill the beans. It was obvious that there was something going on, not
least because he was wearing clothes that I've never seen him wear before.

"What?" Tsar said, adjusting his sunglasses, also a brand-new acquisition.

"Did you rob a bank?" I suggested, pointing at his pants and shirt.

"Well . . ." Tsar began, stroking his chin and smiling smugly. "This morning I went to the mailbox in the Tibetan Library and found this letter,
addressed to Tsar Tenzin Dorje. You know, Tenzin Dorje was my monastic
name."

Tsar handed me an envelope bearing Israeli stamps and a return address
written in Hebrew.

"It was already opened when I got to it," he explained. "The postmen always open the letters to look for money."

In the envelope was a folded card depicting a sunset over Jerusalem. A message in English read: "Here is something for you. Look for it. Miss you, K."

"So Kaila sent you money?"

"Of course," Tsar said, reaching for the card. "It took me half an hour to figure out where she'd hid it, though. Look at this!"

He opened the card and pointed at a nearly invisible incision running parallel to the groove in the center. Tsar stuck his finger inside and pulled out a piece of tinfoil.

"Genius work, isn't it?" he exclaimed, putting the card back into the envelope. "Who would've thought that I'd end up in India, without a passport, and I'd have an Israeli girlfriend sending me money in the mail?"

"Nobody," I agreed.

Suddenly Tsar jumped to his feet, with a cigarette in one hand and a glass of chai in the other, and ran across the street to intercept the McLeod Ganj bus that had just appeared at the bottom of the hill. I left three rupees on the table and dashed after him, my zen flapping behind like a pair of wings.

"Quick!" Tsar shouted as he blocked the door with his back. I wrestled with the crowd of Indian and Tibetan men who were screaming at Tsar to let them through, and stumbled into the bus, just in time to secure the last two empty seats.

"I don't remember ever getting a seat on the McLeod Ganj bus," I admitted as the driver rammed into first gear.

"That's because you don't know how to do it," Tsar replied. He was still holding his glass of chai and his fuming cigarette, but not even the ticket collector dared to reprimand him about it. Tsar had entered combat mode and all he wanted to talk about was chess openings and mid-game strategies.

"Erick prefers the bishop opening," he informed me, the wind ruffling his hair. "Getting your king's bishop out early on can do a lot of damage. I, on the other hand, like to work with rooks. I'd sacrifice the f-pawn any time: once I get an open rook line, you're in trouble, my friend. One wrong move and everything goes to Pichku Materinu. Erick knows that very well. That's why he never takes my f-pawn. When I play the King's Gambit, he just looks the other way, like he doesn't see the free pawn. He knows it's poisoned."

I wasn't a good chess player and half the time I had no idea what Tsar was talking about. Still, I nodded and pretended to care. What was interesting to me was how chess had become the most important thing in the lives of people like Vinnie and Tsar. Was chess a form of communication? Or was it that in the absence of everything else—a family, a home, a career, a purpose, a cause to fight for, an identity—the chessboard and the laws that governed the movement of the pieces became a reality, an archetypal narrative where kings really died, where ordinary pawns actually reincarnated as queens, where bishops sacrificed themselves for something bigger, where control of the vital squares brought victory? I asked Tsar why he was so obsessed with chess, thinking that he'd say something along the lines of "Chess brings people closer," but instead he got offended and announced that chess teaches survival techniques and instincts that can't be learned anywhere else. When I asked him if he was saying that a good chess player was better prepared to face challenges in the real world than someone who had no chess knowledge, Tsar said absolutely.

"*Dobro,*" Tsar began, dumping his chai out the window and lighting a new cigarette. "Here's a scenario for you. Say you want to take the five o'clock bus to New Delhi because, I don't know, you have to go there. By the way, you step out of your house and *boom!* a donkey."

"What do you mean, a donkey?" I asked.

"You hit a donkey, what do you think? A donkey is galloping, you get in the way, and there you have it. By the way, your ankle is broken in half and now you have to make an important decision. You can go to the hospital and miss your bus, you can wait for a taxi to take you to the bus station, or you can just go back home. Watch out here: a good chess player would see *all* the options, not just the obvious ones. How many people do you think would decide to jump on the back of the donkey and gallop to the bus station?"

"Not many," I agreed.

"That's right. When a good chess player calculates his moves, he doesn't think, 'Oh, I can't do this, it's too weird.' The best move is the one that takes you somewhere in the shortest time. By the way, you get to the bus station but the five o'clock bus to New Delhi has been canceled, and the next bus doesn't leave until the following morning. The other option is to get a taxi to Pathankot and jump on a train, but the last taxi on the plaza is already full and is just about to leave. Say you were in this situation. Would you ever consider throwing yourself in front of the taxi?"

"No," I replied.

"A pretty surprising move, right? I tell you what: Indian taxis are very light and can't do much damage to you, plus you already have a broken ankle, so what do you care? It's called making small sacrifices in return for gaining a tactical advantage. *Dobro*, the driver agrees to take you to the hospital on the grounds of having run you over, but you tell him, listen, better take me to Pathankot, I have a train to catch. So far, so good. By the way, you're in the taxi going ninety miles per hour when suddenly you see your opponent's next move and realize that you need to do something about it. It's called preventive action."

"Wait a second," I interrupted. "Who is my *opponent* in this case?"

"There's always an opponent," Tsar explained, adjusting his new Boss sunglasses. "If you haven't figured this out so far . . . you're what, nineteen?"

"Twenty-two."

Tsar shook his head in disbelief and flicked his cigarette out the window, whereby all the ashes flew back in and dispersed evenly across the bus. "Watch your step here: one wrong move and your entire strategy goes to Pichku Materinu. First of all, you have to consider the facts. Pathankot is a city that has a train station: that's a fact. Dharamsala doesn't have a train station: that's also a fact. Trains aren't easy to catch: that again is a fact. You put two and two together and what do you get? Don't say four. The answer is, you need to go to the next big town south of Pathankot. That way, you'd double your chances of catching the train, and what's more important, you'd move closer to New Delhi. *Dobro*, you get to the next big town and everything is the way you've calculated it: the trains are running and there are omelet vendors on every corner. By the way, you are standing on the platform and, indeed, the train from Pathankot to New Delhi is in sight, the only problem being that it's an express and doesn't stop in every town."

"So you miss the train?"

"Naturally. But that's part of the game. Most people would say, 'What the fuck am I doing here? There's no way I'm ever going to get to New Delhi.' And they'd go home."

"And what would you do?" I asked.

"I'd jump on a train going in the opposite direction," Tsar said, smiling deviously. "By the way, it's a train that's heading to Bangladesh, but that's all right. It's like a flank pawn that no one notices until it's too late. You're losing the game, your opponent has pushed you in a corner, and what do you do? You move your only pawn. At first your opponent doesn't pay any attention. He thinks you're doing it out of desperation. Suddenly, the pawn is unstoppable and you get a queen: the game's yours."

Our bus entered McLeod Ganj, circled the main square, and pulled over next to a cigarette stall. Tsar and I remained in our seats, deciding to wait until all the passengers got off.

"I don't really see your point," I confessed. "First you break your ankle, then you ride on the back of a donkey, then you throw yourself in front of a speeding taxi, miss the Pathankot–New Delhi express, and finally end up on a train going to Bangladesh."

"So?"

"Well," I hesitated. "What is this example supposed to demonstrate?"

"It demonstrates that a good chess player always has a move," Tsar explained. "Look around you—most people act without any imagination. They plan to do something, and if it doesn't work out, they get stuck. Not a grandmaster. You take a guy with real understanding of chess, he can never be surprised. He's always twenty moves ahead."

Steering clear of mud puddles and mounds of cow dung, Tsar walked over to the cigarette stall to buy a new pack of India Kings and then sauntered across the street, staring brazenly into people's faces. We were a strange couple: me wrapped up in my maroon monastic garments and Tsar wearing a dress shirt and hip sunglasses. It occurred to me that India had given me everything that I had asked for, and more. I was studying metaphysical ideas that I'd always longed to know, and I had found friends who understood both the implications of a reality disentangled by emptiness and the notion that doing nothing was the highest act of being. There was something final, transcendental about sitting in the shadow of Enlightenment and passing time, idly, with degenerate mystics like Tsar and Vinnie. It was a perfect balance. I had arrived at a mountaintop from where my past, my piano career, and my birthplace seemed tiny, insignificant. Where was Nikolai the pianist now? Where was Boston? Where was Sofia and the Iron Curtain and the red fascists who marched the streets holding portraits of Lenin and Marx? They were just a collection of old names.

"Here they come!" Vinnie announced as Tsar and I entered Om Hotel and Restaurant, a three-story accretion of amorphous pieces built in the hanging-onto-a-precipice style of architecture typical of Himalayan hill towns. Vinnie was sitting with Erick and Rosenkrantz, the Dutch taxi driver and chess aficionado. Since there was only one chess set, it was agreed that Tsar would play Rosenkrantz, the winner would play Vinnie, and the winner of that game would play Erick. Rolling up his sleeves, Tsar ordered hot lemon water with ginger and honey—one of Om Restaurant's signature drinks—and began the game with Rosenkrantz, playing fast and with great determination. In less than ten moves Rosenkrantz had lost a knight and a rook and was running with his king all over the board. Facing forced mate, Rosenkrantz resigned and went outside to smoke a joint, "To clear the clouds," as he phrased it, pointing at his head.

Vinnie took Rosenkrantz's chair and spent nearly five minutes contemplating his answer to Tsar's e4—a psychological tactic intended to stall Tsar's desire for a quick victory and set a pace that was comfortable for Vinnie.

"We're not going to be here all day," Tsar said, blowing smoke in Vinnie's face.

Vinnie played c5 and announced the name of the opening somberly: "Sicilian." Then he got up and walked over to the counter to ask the Tibetan waitress, Chungda (Little Moon), to turn the music down. This was another tactic that Vinnie used against Tsar: frequent interruptions of the game made Tsar less focused and damaged his ability to devise long-term strategies. By the time Vinnie returned to his chair, Tsar had lost interest in the game and was checking out the women sitting in the restaurant. Vinnie immediately took advantage of Tsar's lax attitude and won two pawns.

"Tell them I said something!" Tsar shouted, realizing that he was in trouble.

Vinnie exploded with laughter and shook Erick's arm. "He learned that from me."

"What is it?" Erick asked.

"It's Pancho Villa, the Mexican general," Vinnie explained. "He was dying and he couldn't think of anything important to say to the crowd of people that had gathered outside his house. So he turned to his attendant and said, 'Tell them I said something!' And these were his last words."

"Well, I'm sure the guy was very sick by that point," Erick observed, smiling politely.

"You can't understand the joke," Vinnie said, winking at me. "Laughing isn't part of the Dutch character."

Vinnie switched to German and Erick countered, also in German. Tsar, for his part, sacrificed his bishop and took Vinnie's queen with his knight.

"*Scheisse!*" Vinnie roared, grinding his teeth.

I had ordered muesli with homemade yogurt and honey (Tsar was treating) and was having a great time eating and listening to the conversation.

Suddenly, something cracked inside my head and a paralyzing burst of pain shot through my body.

"What the fuck was that?" Tsar asked with a concerned look.

I pulled a dime-size pebble out of my mouth and dropped it on the table, to demonstrate how heavy it was.

"Christ," Vinnie exclaimed. "Good luck finding a dentist around here."

I groped around my mouth with my tongue, and sure enough, I found a large chunk of tooth. The weird thing was, I didn't seem to be missing any of my teeth.

"I know it sounds crazy," I said, "but I don't think this tooth is mine."

I opened my mouth and Tsar agreed: "Yeah. You've got all your teeth."

"Which can only mean one thing," Vinnie observed, nodding slowly.

Tsar rolled his sleeves, took the stone that I had found in the muesli, and headed for the kitchen, jerking his shoulders as if he were warming up for a boxing match.

"Call the owner," he shouted at Chungda, who had just come out of the kitchen carrying a plate of steamed momos and a bowl of tugpa, a traditional Tibetan soup.

"What's the matter?" Chungda asked, leaving the plates on the counter.

"What's the matter?" Tsar repeated, raising his voice. "First of all, I want to know how long your cooks have been spitting in people's food!"

The chatter in the restaurant ceased and everyone looked at us.

"They would never!" Chungda answered, trembling.

"Tell them to come out," Tsar said, pointing at the two Indian boys— both under fifteen years old—who were making momos in the kitchen.

Chungda shouted something in Hindi and the young cooks appeared in front of us, looking scared.

"Have you seen this?" Tsar asked them, dropping the stone from the muesli on the counter. The stone bounced twice and fell on the ground. Chungda picked it up and returned it to Tsar.

"I'm really sorry," she said. "A lot of things come with stones. There are stones in the rice, in the flour . . . We try to get them out but sometimes it's very difficult."

"There's more," Tsar announced. "Nikola, show her."

I placed the broken tooth on the counter and stepped back. Chungda let out a cry and covered her face with her hands.

"I'm sorry, Kushu-la," she whispered, lowering her head in deference. "*Kon dag.*"

"It's not his tooth!" Tsar interrupted her.

"Which can only mean one thing," Vinnie added from the back.

Chungda ran out into the hallway and disappeared into the room where the restaurant owner lived with his wife, son, grandson, and daughter-in-law. After a short while Chungda returned, followed by the owner, a slightly overweight middle-aged Tibetan man wearing sweatpants, sneakers, and a T-shirt. He must have just woken up from a siesta because he couldn't stop yawning. He looked at Tsar and the broken tooth, rubbed his eyes, and looked at the tooth again.

"Let me tell you what happened," Tsar volunteered. "My friend Lodro— you know, he quit the best music school in the world, in Boston, to come here to study Tibetan language and philosophy. Look at him, he's a good monk, he deserves to be treated better—he ordered muesli with yogurt and honey and bit on a stone. By the way, he pulled the stone out but he also pulled this tooth, and it's not his tooth. Anyone with half a brain can add two and two together. The obvious conclusion is that one of the cooks took a bite from Lodro's muesli, cracked his tooth on a stone, and spit everything back into the bowl. Then they brought the bowl to our table."

While Chungda translated for the owner everything that Tsar had said, I pulled Tsar aside and asked him to end his investigation. There was nothing we could do, and I didn't want Chungda or the cooks to get fired because of me.

"I'm not going anywhere," Tsar responded, loud enough so that everyone could hear. "Once they start dropping their teeth in our meals, what's next?"

I turned around and glanced at the panic-stricken faces of the guests. No one was eating. Perplexed and still yawning, the restaurant owner told the two cooks to open their mouths and say *a-a-ah*. "A-a-a-ah!" the cooks bleated in unison. The owner inspected their teeth, turned to Tsar, and shrugged his shoulders. Tsar folded his arms and shook his head: he wasn't satisfied. The owner checked Chungda's teeth and shrugged his shoulders again. "No problem," he said, managing a smile.

"Yes, problem," Tsar exploded. "I'm not leaving until I find out who dropped his tooth in my friend's muesli."

The owner walked to the mirror hanging on the wall by the entrance, looked into it, and opened his mouth: "A-a-a-ah!"

Tsar was furious. "Nikola, do I look like an idiot? I must look like an idiot. We come here to study their culture and language, and how do they treat us? We find a human tooth in our food, and they can't even say sorry."

"Sorry," Chungda offered.

"Well, that's not enough," Tsar went on. "It's about respect. Tibetans are so good at playing victims, but they don't give a shit about other people who are also suffering." He went on, speaking like a baby: "'The Chinese stole our country! The Chinese are destroying our culture!' By the way, I don't have a country, either. Millions of people lose their countries every year. And, by the way, countries are just names. A bunch of made-up names and cheesy national anthems, and you should know this better than anyone else if you're really Buddhists. So give it up."

At that precise moment, my tongue snagged on something sharp and I discovered that one of my molars was practically missing. The only part still standing was the inside wall, and I realized that after the initial shock of biting on the stone, I must've mistaken the wall for a whole tooth. Bursting into sweat, I took Tsar by the arm and pushed him toward the door.

"What is up with you, Nikola?" Tsar protested. "Don't you see how they're treating us? If you're not offended, man, I am, and I'm not moving one millimeter until they deliver the person who dropped his tooth in your bowl."

"Tsar!" I shouted, opening my eyes as wide as I could, to give him a hint that there was something I needed to tell him in private.

"What?" Tsar snapped. "If you have something to say to me, say it here. I'm going to find the person responsible for this and make him swallow his broken tooth, and a few extra ones, to give him a sense of what it feels like to mess with other people's food."

"I'm going to wait for you outside," I said and left the restaurant.

A minute later Tsar came out, still in fighting mode, and walked over to me. "Why the fuck did you leave me there like that? They were about to give up."

"The broken tooth is mine," I said apologetically. " I didn't realize it until the very end."

Tsar lit a cigarette and stared angrily at the big metal sign that read "Om Hotel and Restaurant, McLeod Ganj, Himachal Pradesh."

"Still," he said, shaking his head. "Still."

Twelve

By the end of December, Dharamsala looked almost deserted. Most of the tourists had gone home; others had moved south to Varanasi or Goa. The Tibetans, especially the *Geshes* and the monks and nuns who could afford to buy train tickets, had left for Bodhgaya to take part in the Monlam Chenmo, the annual teachings and celebrations commemorating Buddha's Enlightenment. One person who was still around was Geshe Yama Tseten. It was hard to miss him, walking slowly through the empty streets, a six-foot-four heavyweight champion of Buddhist metaphysics, his chin tipped slightly upward, indicating his contempt for the myopic world of ordinary beings where every object was removed from its natural state of duality, of being and nonbeing; where the gray winter sky was just that, where people had things to do, where a kilo of apples was equivalent to twenty rupees, where the crystalline eyes of the dead fish piled on the fisherman's pushcart were windows into the future, the quiet stillness of the afterworld awaiting us.

Geshe Yama Tseten never showed any sign that he recognized me, so I was quite surprised when one afternoon I turned a corner and saw him standing in the middle of the street, arms akimbo, looking at me as if he'd been anticipating my arrival.

"What are you doing walking around?" he asked, with a heavily exaggerated Tibetan intonation—covering two octaves in just one sentence.

"Uh, no special reason," I said, taken aback. I was with Tsar, who was smoking. Vinnie was trailing behind with the chessboard. Geshe Yama Tseten chuckled in a rather mean way and pointed at Tsar with his lips.

"Who's this?"

"He is from Bosnia," I explained.

"Every day I see you walking around like a headless chicken," Geshe Yama Tseten said with disgust. "Up, down, up, down. Lead a meaningless life and die a fool."

"I study every day," I replied in defense.

"Study! What, the alphabet? It's all very good. Very good! Incredibly good!"

Now Geshe Yama Tseten was shouting and Tsar looked at me, trying to figure out what was going on.

"What's the difference between someone who has seen emptiness and someone who hasn't?" Geshe Yama Tseten pressed on.

I was so confused about the situation I had found myself in that I didn't even pay attention to the question. Was Ani Dawa behind this? It was very possible. I could see her going to Geshe Yama Tseten's room and asking him to save me from ruin. I knew that she resented Tsar and was convinced that he was going to lead me astray.

Geshe Yama Tseten looked at me intently, waiting for an answer. I had spoken to him only once before, when he'd kicked me out of his room for alleged disrespectful behavior, but I knew that all of his questions were traps. He was prepared to destroy me no matter how I answered.

"Even a little kid knows this," Geshe Yama Tseten snickered.

"What's the difference between a person who has seen emptiness and one who hasn't?" I repeated, buying myself time.

Aside from the obvious answer—one understands reality, the other doesn't—I had no idea. Difference. In what sense? Unable to calculate what

Geshe Yama Tseten was getting at, I focused my attention instead on the two dogs behind him who were dealing with the humiliation of postcoital entanglement.

"There is no difference, is there?" Geshe Yama Tseten laughed. "You have someone who walks up and down, up and down, busy-busy, very busy"—Geshe-la closed his eyes and contemplated the meaning of "busy" with a sour face—"and you have someone who thinks about the way things are and the way they appear"—here, he put on a blissful expression to demonstrate what that felt like—"and in the end, no difference. Very good. You could waste your life and die a complete idiot, and you wouldn't have to worry about it. Don't worry, you understand? Dying empty-handed is a good idea. Very good."

Geshe Yama Tseten turned around, laughed at the adjoined dogs with disdain—"Huh! Huh hu-u-uh!"—and walked away slowly, with the grace of a three-ton hippopotamus.

"This guy has great acting skills," Vinnie commented. "Laughing, shouting, pausing to contemplate, his intonation as well . . . I didn't understand anything he said, but he looked great."

"Vinnie used to stage plays in nursing homes across Germany," Tsar said, winking at me.

"Not true," Vinnie protested. "Not across Germany, and not always in nursing homes."

I THOUGHT HARD about my exchange with Geshe Yama Tseten, and in the end decided to do something rather irrational—to show up for class as if nothing had ever happened.

Two days later, at exactly eight o'clock in the morning, I entered the monastery compound and pressed my ear against Geshe-la's door. I hadn't brought fruit or even a *katak*, but I didn't care about rules and customs anymore. I heard the clink of a porcelain cup and knocked three times. "*Sho,*"

Geshe Yama Tseten answered. I opened the door wide and walked straight in—no hello, no how-are-you. Geshe-la gestured at me to sit down without lifting his eyes from the text that he was reading. Suddenly I froze. I had committed the number-one offense again: I had brought my umbrella into the room. I stepped out into the corridor and propped my umbrella against the wall.

The first thing that I noticed when I sat down on the floor was that Geshe-la had an umbrella exactly the same make as mine, only a different color. What was more intriguing was that his umbrella was wet and hung on a nail behind the door. I took a deep breath: did he kick me out just to give me a hard time?

Geshe Yama Tseten continued reading for another fifteen minutes and then asked me to bring him the thermos.

"Yeah-yeah," he said, sipping butter tea. "Where were we?"

I pulled the photocopied *lo rig* text out of my bag and flipped through the pages.

"Start!" Geshe-la ordered and looked out the window, arms akimbo. I began reciting the text from memory but just when I was thinking that I had finally done something right, Geshe Yama Tseten interrupted me and pointed at the door.

"Did you leave your umbrella outside?" he asked, disgruntled. "Are you stupid? Someone's probably stolen it by now."

I raised my hands in a what-can-you-do gesture, but that only made Geshe-la angrier. "Go and get it. *Kun chog sum*, what kind of person are you?"

I rescued the umbrella and propped it pointedly behind the door, next to his.

"You are lucky," Geshe-la noted with a hint of disappointment. "You can't leave anything out there. Even if you drop a cookie, it would instantly disappear."

With this serving as a preface, Geshe Yama Tseten ventured into what I later learned was one of his two favorite subjects of discussion: thieves. The other subject was large marine animals. When he talked about thieves he made the ugliest, most sour faces possible. In contrast, when he broached the subject of deep-water mammals, his face would light up and he would start moving around like a giant whale.

"Everywhere you go—up, down, east, north, what else was there—you see them lurking, with their big, *big* noses, and these, these—what do you call them . . ."

"Ears?" I offered.

"No, these . . . give me the dictionary."

I got up and pulled the Tibetan thesaurus from the top shelf. Geshe-la opened it in the middle and stared at the words, scrunching up his nose. "These disgusting, ugly-colored, hooklike, oily . . . fingers."

Geshe-la tossed the thesaurus aside and took a sip from his cup with such revulsion, I could've sworn he was drinking boiling shit.

"Some of them have two thumbs on their right hands," he went on, joining his thumbs together to show me what that would look like. "With one thumb they search your front pocket, with the other one they dig in the back. You'd know them by their eyes. Their eyes are like this"—Geshe-la focused his eyes on the tip of his nose and shook his head—"I can't do it, their eyes go in opposite directions, one to the left, one to the right, and when they get on the bus, they can watch the driver and the ticket collector at the same time. And their nails. *Ama!*"—Mother!—"their nails are black and twisted, and on their pinkie they grow a nail that's as long as a knife. You're on the bus thinking about something, the sun is shining, mountains, and the thief cuts through your pants with his nail—*khr-r-r-r*—and gets all your money. Gone! Or you're carrying a suitcase with a lock—no problem, he can open any lock with his nail. It's like a key." Geshe-la waved his pinkie and poked excitedly at his desk and then at his pillow. "They can open my door anytime they want. And they have special dust, like flour—you go to a hotel, you're tired, lie down on the bed, and they knock on the door. Who is it? It's me. The door opens, it's the hotel boy, bringing chai. Hello? Hello. How are you? How are you. Then the boy dumps a bag of dust on top of your head, and you can't move anymore. You can see everything, you can hear, but you can't talk, and you can't even move your hand. Then you look at the boy and you count: one, two, three . . . eleven fingers! Three thumbs! Big nose. A long nail on his pinkie: it's a thief."

"Have you ever been robbed this way?" I asked.

Geshe Yama Tseten looked offended. "Many, many, many times," he replied, closing his eyes. "Once, in South India, they stopped our bus . . ." He stopped talking and continued in pantomime. Lips pressed together in anger, he lurked behind trees, holding a rifle and giving orders to other outlaws. Then he was a bus driver, happily spinning a steering wheel the size of a tractor tire. Drowsy and oblivious passengers jiggled and wobbled in their seats, occasionally scanning the unimpressive scenery. The desperado with the pressed lips appeared again, this time holding the reins of a large, domesticated animal, most likely a camel if Geshe-la's wild swinging was any indication. Avoiding a near collision, the bus driver threw himself backwards and fell on the ground, together with the steering wheel, which must have snapped out of the dashboard. Holding his rifle with one hand, the desperado searched the pockets of all the passengers and stuffed bundles of cash under his shirt. An exceptionally crafty passenger who was lugging two suitcases zigzagged between a series of large objects and arrived at a place infested with bird-size mosquitoes.

"The jungle," Geshe Yama Tseten explained. "I ran through the jungle— very dangerous. Tigers, elephants, snakes, what do you call it . . ."—Geshe-la looked around the room, searching for clues—"Peacocks. Finally I got to a hotel and they poured dust over my head. I thought, that's it, I must be dead. Couldn't even move my eyelids. And they took everything."

"What did you have in the suitcases?" I asked.

"Clothes, what do you think? Two sets of robes, sandals, books . . ."

"I see," I said, trying to imagine what a thief could do with a pair of Buddhist monastic robes.

"What is that?" Geshe-la exploded. "*I see*. You don't know anything. *I go, I stay*—you don't even exist."

"Who are you talking to, then?" I countered.

"I'm not talking! You started talking!"

"You said *you*," I observed.

A dark shadow fell over Geshe-la's face and I sensed that I was going to be kicked out soon. "Do you know what *ribon ra* means?"

I nodded. *Ribon ra*, or the horns of a rabbit, was a Buddhist philosophical term used to describe a nonexisting entity. Other such terms were *mo sham bu*, the son of an infertile woman, and *namkhai metog*, a sky flower.

"When you see a rabbit from far away, it looks like it has horns. When you get closer, you realize that what you thought was horns is the color pattern of his ears. In the same way, I say *you* and *Lodro* because you look like a real person. But in reality you are not there at all. There's no Lodro anywhere in the room."

"There must be something, though," I noted.

"Something!" Geshe Yama Tseten giggled. "What arrogance! A person who has experienced emptiness might see *something*. What *you* see doesn't have any substance. Lodro has never existed. *Kun chog sum*, how arrogant you are! Now get out, I have more important things to do."

"I just think it's strange that you won't even allow me to exist on a conventional level," I said, laughing belligerently.

"Your intelligence is very poor," Geshe Yama Tseten concluded with a tragic expression. "I wasn't convinced at first, but now it's quite obvious. *Engies* are stupid in general, but at least some of them are monkey-smart—they can steal a lot of money and make toys like radios and telephones. But you're not even monkey-smart! *Kun chog sum*, what a sad situation!"

I felt completely crushed inside, but I wasn't ready to concede defeat.

"Lodro exists as a mere thought label," I pressed on, quoting the definition that, according to the Prasangika Madhyamika philosophical school, outlined the extent to which things exist.

Geshe Yama Tseten was unimpressed. "These are just words to you. To understand what that means, first you have to experience emptiness, and to do that, you have to go beyond the third level on the Path of Preparation—and you're probably never going to get there. A mere thought label! You don't see labeled things, you see *ribon ra,* things that have never existed. *You* have never existed! And you should be ashamed of your arrogant behavior. I'm not some friend of yours that you could play with. Go back to America and pray to *Yeshu*"—Jesus. "Buddhism is not for you."

My throat was clogged, my jaw was trembling, and I knew that if I tried to make a sound, it would have definitely come out as a helpless howl. I listened to the wild pounding of my heart, to the blood throbbing in my veins. A nonexistent heart in a nonexistent body. Nonexistent flickers of thought searching for a safe ground. Nonexistent memories connecting the present to a nonexistent past. Names of things, names of emotions. Doubt, and the aftertaste of doubt; fear, and the aftertaste of fear. I must go, but who is it that wants to go? I am a musician, I play piano—or was I a monk? Flashbacks, and the aftertaste of flashbacks. I must do something: the present moves into the past, the past is the future. My tongue—a foreign tongue, my mouth—somebody else's mouth, a nonexistent heart pounding in a hollow body. Anger, and the aftertaste of anger. Trembling hands—not my hands. Trying to remember the organizing principle. I must move toward the center; there used to be a center. I'll remember in the future. It'll all come to me, the organizing principle. These are not my eyes, this is not my skin. Things flow in one direction—there is no direction—I'll remember in the future, I must exist in the future. My eyes sting from the tears, there must be some reason—somebody's tears, not mine. I can't look up. I must do something, I was supposed to do something—I'll remember. It all must be a huge theater, it was meant as a theater—this is what I came for, to find the root of the subject-object duality, to see the ego kicking. Somebody's kicking. There was an organizing principle. I'll remember, it's coming, I must hold on. It was meant to be that way, just a theater; I have to go somewhere. Sounds, and aftertaste of sounds. I have to find the center, there was a center. I remember now—this is what I came here for.

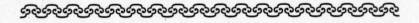

Thirteen

I woke up to the sound of my landlord's daughter-in-law shouting, "*Namaste*, Guru-ji!" right underneath my window. I looked at the clock—it was six a.m., a truly inhumane hour for a jazz musician, albeit a former one—but as soon as I got tangled up again into the net of my interrupted dream, I heard Tsar's smooth baritone, "*Namaste, ab ke se he?*" and my drowsiness evaporated at once. Two things puzzled me: why did my landlord's daughter-in-law refer to Tsar as *guru-ji*, a title reserved only for monks and priests, and, second, what was Tsar doing back in Dharamsala so early in the morning? I got up, unbolted the door, and looked out. Tsar was holding our landlord's one-year-old grandson and making funny faces at him. I tried to remember whether I had ever seen Tsar playing with babies before. Was that a sign that his trip to New Delhi was successful? Was he now officially a Bosnian refugee? I stepped back and started the kerosene stove to make chai.

Stomping heavily, Tsar ascended the stairs and entered the room, ducking to avoid smashing his head.

"*Choveche!*" he sighed, tossing his leather rucksack on his bed. *Choveche* is Serbian for "man" or "dude." "I don't know how people sleep on the bus.

There was this guy, he kept dozing off and smashing his head against the front seat's railing. I'm not kidding—his eyebrows were swollen like he'd fought in a twelve-round boxing match, and he didn't care, I'm telling you. Bang, bang, for twelve hours straight. I tried waking him up—forget it—and he drooled a lot, too, my whole sleeve was wet. By the way, we stopped at some dingy little roadside *dhaba*, and the ticket collector announced a fifteen-minute chai break. I thought, *dobro*, I'll go and get a plate of *aloo gobi* and mango pickles. It smelled good—you know how these places are. So I'm sitting down, eating, and I hear the bus transmission coughing in the distance. I look around, no bus driver, no ticket collector, and I know the rules, too, you can't lose sight of the driver. *Choveche*, I barely made it back on the bus, it was just like in the movies, swinging on the door as the bus driver shifts into fourth and hits sixty. I was swinging so hard, I almost hit an electric pole—*dobro*, I've worked on trains, I know how it is. By the way, there's an Australian girl who's screaming and crying because the driver had left without her boyfriend, so I said to the ticket collector, I said, 'Tell your friend to turn the bus around, and do it now'—I was really polite like that, the girl screaming and everything— and the ticket collector, he just smiled at me. '*Yebem li ti pichku materinu*,' I said, 'Turn the fucking bus around or I'm going to break your neck,' and when the guy tried to get up—he was sitting in the seat next to the driver—I put my hand on his head and pushed him down. I was still acting friendly. 'I'm going to count to three and I'm going to throw you out the window,' I told the driver, but I don't think he understood because he started yelling at me to take my hand off the steering wheel. *Choveche*, you should've seen how upset he got. '*Mister, let go! Accident! Mister!*' screaming like he was in the movies. 'Of course we're going to crash, you stupid motherfucker,' I said. 'How do you think you can drive when I'm holding the steering wheel!' He had to pull over, he didn't have any other choice. Then we went back to look for the Australian girl's boyfriend, and I tell you, it was so romantic, I almost threw up, the way she jumped from the bus and ran to greet him, *choveche*, half of

the passengers on the bus started crying. Unbelievable. I said to the Australian girl, 'You guys are acting like you'd survived World War II. This is
India, things happen again and again for absolutely no reason. Take it easy.'
Then we stopped at a chai shop, right after we reached the first Himalayan
slopes. I got out to walk around and smoke a cigarette; my neck was so stiff
from the cold air gushing through the windows, I couldn't even turn my head.
By the way, I'm drinking my chai, and I look over and see the Australian guy
holding on to the bus door with both hands, like a drunk holding on to a
street sign. He just wasn't going to let that bus take off without him this time.
Learn and live. Or was it live and learn, I don't remember anymore."

Tsar took the small mirror from the wall, grabbed a towel, soap, and a
razor, and headed out the door.

"So what happened in New Delhi?" I yelled after him.

"Nothing," Tsar answered from the bottom of the staircase. "No asylum,
no money. The whole trip was a waste of time and money."

This was bad news. When Tsar, following Vinnie's advice, had left for
New Delhi a week ago to apply for a refugee status with the UNHCR (United
Nations High Commissioner for Refugees) he'd really hoped that he would
finally solve his legal problems. In addition to guaranteeing Tsar certain
rights, a refugee status would have included financial assistance, which Tsar
desperately needed. Ever since Tsar had spent the hundred dollars Kaila had
sent in her December postcard, he and I had lived almost exclusively on the
money that I had originally saved for myself, and were starting to look
anorexic. There were health issues, too. For one, Tsar had to switch from
Western cigarettes, which went for about ten rupees a pack, to *biddies*—
cigarettes made from single rolled-up tobacco leaves, costing one rupee a
bundle. He viewed the repercussions as the difference between dying from a
heart failure at sixty and dying from lung cancer at fifty, *biddies* being consid-
erably more lethal than cigarettes due to the fact that they were filterless and
included stems, sticks, and some unidentified substances. As for me, my lax
attitude toward eating at cheap Indian joints, where water was drawn from a

bucket green with bacteria and plates were rinsed just once, without soap, had finally taken its toll. By the end of April I was diagnosed with severe amoebic dysentery and was forced to check into Delek Hospital. What ensued was ten days of nonstop shitting, high fever, excruciating stomach pain, and a bitter taste in my mouth from the antibiotics. At the beginning, my primary goal was making it to the hole-in-the-floor toilet across the hospital ward in time, and so for the first few days I could be seen storming out of my room, dashing down the hallway and across the open yard, and hurling myself at the toilet door, the way runners throw themselves across the finish line. Gradually, as I got more and more dehydrated and the last grams of muscle on my body melted, I lost my motivation to fight and reverted to walking—slowly, and with the air of a martyr. When I succumbed to the amoeba attack halfway between my room and the toilet (which happened almost every time), I did so with fortitude and dignity, and not even for a second did I feel embarrassed or self-conscious. There was only one other Westerner staying at the hospital, a Canadian girl, whose friend, a Canadian guy in his forties, became very concerned about my condition and started bringing me fruit and cookies. He was curious to find out why I had moved to India and why I'd chosen the life of a Buddhist monk. I answered his questions with little wisdoms such as *Life is short*, and *There is a lot we don't know*, and *If the world doesn't exist as we see it, how can anyone voluntarily take part in it?* One day, I was walking up the stairs, having just purchased a second packet of antibiotics from the pharmacy on the ground floor, when I felt as if my intestines had been shoved into a slow-spinning blender, and fell on my knees, seeing red. The toilet was far away, so there was no point in running, even if I had been able to. The best solution, of course, was to go in my pants, and I was, in fact, wearing pants, just for the occasion. (A Buddhist monastic skirt—being completely open—is not exactly appropriate attire for a patient tormented by amoebic dysentery.) Bent in half and clutching the metal railing with both hands, I resisted a second contraction. Just when I was about to give up, I saw the Canadian guy coming down the stairs with a worried look on his face. This really complicated things because, on the one hand, I couldn't just explode in my pants while having a tête-à-tête on Buddhist metaphysics with someone acting as my patron, and on the other hand, I couldn't survive another amoebic attack without bursting into pieces. I had reached a point where the slightest movement, even opening my mouth, was enough to tip the balance and knock my defenses down. I prayed that the Canadian guy would somehow figure out my situation and just keep going down the stairs without saying a word. Naturally, he did the exact opposite. Shouting, "Are you okay?" he grabbed my hand and pulled me to my feet.

That did it. I don't know if he was missing some of his senses, but what sounded to me like a special-effects blast from *Star Wars* made absolutely no impression on him. He continued to demonstrate his friendliness by patting me on the shoulder and shaking my hand. "You look much better today," he observed with a broad smile. "How are you feeling?"

"To tell you the truth," I said matter-of-factly, "I'm shitting my pants."

The Canadian guy squeezed my hand even harder. "You know what they say about Samsara," he said compassionately. "Everything is impermanent. Even Samsara is impermanent."

"Right," I agreed, fighting off a new spasm. "The thing is, I'm shitting my pants right now, as we speak."

Finally, he got it. His first impulse was to step back, but then he realized that he might offend me, and so he continued shaking my hand, only now he did it mechanically, and with a frozen smile.

I LOOKED OUT THE WINDOW and saw Tsar standing by the communal spigot in his underwear, soaping his head and body. Cursing in Serbian, he squatted under the icy cold water spouting from the faucet, washed off the soap, and started running around the yard, throwing air punches and jumping on one foot to get the water out of his ears. I took the kettle off the kerosene stove and strained the tea leaves. Life was simple: drinking black Darjeeling tea, meditating on the earthen floor, washing clothes in the river, waiting for the first monsoon clouds to arrive. Despite the financial constraints and the diseases, I was happy to be where I was. The only thing that worried me was that one day I might grow stupid and decide to do something else with my life. I had everything that I needed: Geshe Yama Tseten taught me humility six days a week, except Sundays; Ani Dawa believed in me like a mother; Tsar was a friend I could count on for everything; the soaring Himalayan ridges talked to me day and night about the mystery present in all things; the white-throated vultures reminded me of the inevitable end; the lepers showed me how to let go; the wandering cows taught me about detachment and permutation; the monkeys clued me in on the roots of consumerist society; and my parents called twice a month to assure me that I had a past.

"I don't know what's wrong with people," Tsar shouted, storming into the room with a wet towel hung on his neck. "The Romans had running hot water as early as 500 B.C., first in Pompeii, and then in Florence, for saunas and hot baths, and look at us now, at the end of the twentieth century, still freezing our asses off, *choveche*, the water down in the courtyard is so cold, they must be drawing it from under the Siberian fucking tundra. My balls have shrunk to the size of raisins, I'm not kidding. The same thing in New Delhi—when did I get there, was it Saturday? I walk into the first decent-looking hotel in Paharganj and tell the guy at the reception desk exactly what I want: a bed and a shower. The guy says, 'I have the perfect room for you, but I need to see your passport.' I had to give him fifty rupees extra to get him to shut up about my passport, which I threw away a year ago. *Dobro*, I go to my room, turn on the shower, and wait. Nothing. The water is icy cold and forms giant rainbow-colored bubbles, the kind that you see floating on top of the Yamuna River when you enter New Delhi. I wait half an hour and go downstairs. 'Where the fuck is the hot water?' I ask the receptionist. 'Hot voter comingh, sir,' the guy says to me. 'Don't vorry!' Fine, I know this is India—trains are three days behind schedule and letters travel for six months, presumably strapped to the back of a blind donkey in the final stage of Alzheimer's—so I go back to my room, turn on the water, and wait: nothing. Half an hour later I'm still standing in my underwear, and the whole bathroom is covered with pink bubbles, like I'm running a chemical laboratory. I go downstairs and the receptionist again says, 'Don't vorry, hot voter comingh!' Unbelievable. I wait another half an hour, and this time the receptionist starts wobbling his head as soon as he sees me on the top of the stairs. 'Hot voter on second vloor!' he says to me, like that solves everything. 'After van minute, dirt vloor!' At this point I'm pretty angry, but I return to my room on the third floor and turn on the water one more time. Five minutes later I hear a knock on the door. I open it and see an old Indian man carrying a bucket of steaming water: 'Hot voter, sir!' and he's got a big grin on his face, too. 'Yebem li ti pichku materinu,' I said. 'What am I supposed to do with this, make chai?' Unbelievable."

Tsar continued with his monologue, chain-smoking and jumping from one anecdote to the next. He told me about the UNHCR office in New Delhi and how the Western guy working there had refused to review his case after he'd found out that Tsar had already applied for a refugee status twice before: the first time in Germany, right after the Bosnian war had broken out, and the second time in the Netherlands. Apparently, the Indian government had adopted a "safe first country" policy, according to which people running away from war or persecution were expected to seek asylum in the first safe country that they arrived in. When Tsar had showed the UNHCR employee his asylum papers from Germany and pointed out the fact that he'd never been actually granted refugee status, the guy had shrugged his shoulders and suggested that Tsar go to the Indian Ministry of Home Affairs and try to win someone's benevolence. Hungry and without any extra money for rickshaws, Tsar had walked across town to the Ministry of Home Affairs, and joined a line of about two hundred people, all of them waiting to speak with a high-ranking officer. Thinking that he'd finally found someone who would try to understand his predicament, Tsar had walked confidently into the officer's room and immediately begun narrating his story—from the time he'd fled the fighting in Bosnia, to the time he'd arrived in India with the intention to spend his life as a Buddhist monk, sparing no details. At first the officer had appeared friendly, going as far as opening a box of *barfi* (milk-based sweets coated with edible silver foil), but when he'd heard that Tsar had been living in India without a passport for a year, he'd telephoned the guards downstairs and ordered them to come up and arrest him. Tsar had fled immediately and plunged into the crowd outside, sending dozens of people on the ground and tripping a number of civil servants carrying large trays of chai and sweets. Jumping whole flights of stairs at a time, Tsar had landed on the first floor on all fours, crawled between the guards, and bang! popped out on the street, where he'd swiftly thrown himself into a passing rickshaw, then gotten out again around the corner, no baksheesh, no thank-you. Then Tsar's story took an even more bizarre turn.

"By the way, I'm walking down Paharganj—my elbow is bleeding, and my mouth is so dry, I can't even swallow—and I see this guy with long hair and a beard, tattered clothes, about the same age as me, and really dirty. He's playing a bamboo flute—I say 'playing,' but it really sounds like horse farting—and he's got a sign that reads *Help a poor refugee!* written with a pencil. When he hits a really high note, he closes his eyes and starts shaking like an epileptic. *Dobro*, there are plenty of crazy Westerners out there, so I keep on walking, when suddenly the guy grabs my elbow, the one that's bleeding, and pulls me back, unbelievable. '*Yebem li ti pichku materinu*,' I tell him, and before I could react, he takes this fifty-kilogram edition of the Bhagavad Gita and slams it on my head, nearly knocking me unconscious. I was that close to achieving Enlightenment, *choveche*, the madness of Paharganj all around me, and this Western guy is knocking me on the head and then kissing my hands and saying that I've been sent by Krishna to rescue him. Turned out, he was Bosnian—what is the statistical chance of someone like me running into another Bosnian, a refugee at that, in the middle of New Delhi? Zero—and the guy was completely mental, everything he said was Krishna this, Bhagavad Gita that, God is Love—all the signs of a successful spiritual lobotomy, although, to be fair, if I had lost my family during the Bosnian war and then had spent five years as a homeless beggar in India, I would've probably started to speak with Krishna as well. Maybe he was lying about his family, what do I know. He offered to buy me lunch and I thought, *dobro*, I don't have any money, why not. By the way, we walk into this restaurant and the Krishna guy immediately starts talking to some British woman about the way his parents and sister were slaughtered during the Bosnian war. I mean, I've read a few of the works by the Karamazov brothers and so I have a pretty good sense of tragedy, but, *choveche*, this guy was something else. By the time he had finished, everyone in the restaurant was crying and the British woman had counted a thousand rupees to give to him: unbelievable."

I was running late for my morning class with Geshe Yama Tseten, and so I put on my robes and told Tsar that I would meet him later in McLeod Ganj. As I started up the hill, I thought about Tsar's predicament and tried to understand how someone could get into so much trouble. Was Tsar's bad decision-making—like throwing away his passport, or refusing to fight for asylum in Germany and the Netherlands—a form of renunciation, an outright and conscious rejection of the ways of the world? On one level, I understood the impulse to do away with all the names and tags necessary for survival in a world broken up by hatred and violence. I could see how someone like Tsar, who'd witnessed firsthand the stupidity that overcomes those eager to fight over invented geographical notions, could decide to throw away his old identity and become a nobody, a Buddhist monk. Before the bullets start flying, there are other forms of violence: adhering to a nationality, a desire for justice, and a sense of independent existence. The first creates *us* and *them*, the second ensures that everyone suffers equally, and the third provides the philosophical basis for the act of separation. Perhaps it was thinking along these lines that had brought Tsar to India in the first place. Yet Tsar wasn't the kind of person who could renounce everything and spend his life in a cave, subsisting on pine needles. He loved life and people, sex and cigarettes, and he didn't believe in absolutes like pain and happiness, Samsara and Nirvana. For him everything was a fabulous mess, without a middle, beginning, and end.

I WALKED INTO GESHE YAMA TSETEN'S ROOM quietly, without knocking, and sat on the floor. As usual, Geshe-la was sitting cross-legged in bed, only this time his eyes were closed and his breathing was very slow, almost imperceptible. It had started raining and I watched through the window as the heavy raindrops chased away debating monks and old Tibetan ladies circumambulating the Main Temple, coloring the gray asphalt black. I was in no hurry. If Geshe-la decided to teach me something profound, I would listen. If he decided to talk about rabbits with horns or mythical thieves with sawed-off rifles for hours on end, I would listen as well. If he lost his temper and kicked me out, I would simply go home. After months of classes, I had learned to accept his actions as given. He was certainly eccentric, and while some of his views were offensive and flat-out wrong (he claimed that there were four planets in the solar system and that the Buddha had left manuals for constructing airplanes), I had learned a great deal from him about the theory of emptiness according to the different Buddhist schools of thought, and I felt lucky to be part of his life.

Ten minutes went past and Geshe Yama Tseten opened his eyes and looked around the room, disoriented, as if he were surprised to find himself back in the monastery compound. "Yeah, yeah," he mumbled and examined his empty teacup. I contemplated whether this was a sign for me to get up and make a fresh pot of butter tea, but chose to remain seated and not say anything.

"It's so pleasant," Geshe-la exclaimed, closing his eyes again. "Just take a deep breath and watch the mind, from a corner."

When he said "corner," Geshe-la made the kind of face that he'd usually make to impersonate a lurking thief: lips pressed tight, scrunched-up eyebrows, a crooked, self-congratulatory smile.

"Whatever arises goes away on its own," he continued, now groping in the air like a blind man. "And everything is pure, final, there's nothing to be done anymore."

Having spoken thus, Geshe-la drifted away again; if it weren't for his snoring, I would certainly have mistaken him for a great meditator. I sat around for ten more minutes, just to make sure that he wasn't taking a short nap, then edged toward the door on tiptoe. I was already in the hallway when I heard Geshe-la clearing his throat. "Since you're going downstairs, get me a bowl of cold rice noodles," he yelled after me. "And tell the lady to put in a lot of vinegar and chili paste—these street vendors can be very stingy."

I SPENT THE REST OF THE MORNING and the afternoon reading on a beautiful slate-tiled terrace beneath Shiva Waterfalls, an isolated mountain spot in the foothills of the towering granite ridges, about half an hour walking distance from Dharamsala. A year as a Buddhist monk in India—without newspapers, radio, TV, jazz, non-Tibetan books, social obligations, a girlfriend, and a nine-to-five job to go to—is an awfully long time for thinking, and if one concedes that thoughts are the stuff that fill the gap between two moments and, in turn, two points in space, it could be said that a year of thinking is equivalent to zooming through space at the speed of light. By the time the new monsoons descended upon Dharamsala, saturating everything tangible with the taste and smell of pulverized charcoal, I felt so completely removed from my past and so comfortable with the things that defined who I'd become—putting robes on in the morning, shaving my head once a month, accepting silent bows from respectful Tibetans everywhere I went, sitting in large crowds of monks—that when my ex-girlfriend called me one Sunday from New York (my parents had given her the phone number of the STD where I'd hang out for an hour, twice a month, waiting for their call), I felt like telling her that she'd gotten the wrong person, and hanging up. "Sweetheart? You miss me? What are you talking about—the noise? There are monkeys banging on the roof of the phone booth, yes, life is nice, except for the amoebas . . . I said amoebas, yes, I have a nice place, it's a mud house plastered with cow-dung patties. No, it's very clean, well, I'm not in a monastery, maybe next year, I'm sharing a room with a Bosnian refugee—from Bosnia—it's the monkeys again . . . exciting? I don't know. I like riding on the roof of beat-up government buses, bathing in the river is nice, and the sunsets are pretty cool, too—it's not cheesy. When have you taken three hours just to watch the sun drop behind the horizon? Who said that? And why does he think that I've gone crazy? From smoking too much pot? You've got to be kidding me—everyone smokes pot in Berklee, including the teachers, it's a jazz school for crissakes. Right, well, next time you see him, tell him to fuck himself—at least I'm not waiting tables or hauling refrigerators in Roxbury, whatever it is that you guys do to pay the rent. Well, working to pay your rent while your time on earth is ticking—that sounds crazy to me."

After I hung up, I remained in the soundproof phone booth, trying to imagine my ex-girlfriend's life in New York—her new apartment, her friends, her job. Did I care that she was supposedly dating two guys at the same time—one handsome but dumb, the other smart but kind of nerdy? Did I care that she still called me sweetheart and wanted to know if I was thinking about her? I really didn't. Even my memory of her seemed displaced, as if acquired from somebody else. What I did care about, however, was that she had in her possession a long wisp of my hair that she playfully threatened to send to a gypsy seer in Bulgaria for enchantment—that is, if she ever wanted to make me come to her. How on earth had she obtained a long wisp of my hair? Had she cut it when I was sleeping? I found that very disconcerting.

I STARTED GOING TO Shiva Waterfalls because I needed to be completely alone for a few hours every day. It took me a while to realize how lucky I was to live in a place where I could just walk up the mountain and watch the world from afar, with the sound turned off. I enjoyed being alone and, in a sense, it was the natural thing to do, since I was wearing robes originally intended for those who'd vowed to leave their homes and hit the road in search of the Absolute. Leaning against a small shrine—where the local Shiva priests would leave glasses of milk to please the god of snakes, who was presumed responsible for the monsoons—I would analyze the brutal debates that I'd had with Geshe Yama Tseten and memorize a few pages of text, to prepare for my next class with him. Occasionally, a hunter with an old rifle strapped to his back would walk by, and we'd exchange friendly head wobbles. I had often heard people talking about the caves and natural crevices that had been converted into meditation huts higher up the mountain, and sometimes I'd set out to look for them, hoping to catch a glimpse of the meditators living inside. For me this was the ultimate adventure: not taking a train or a bus and traveling thousands of miles through jungles, deserts, and dangerous lands, but sealing yourself off from the world and going inward. As far as I could remember, I've always believed in reincarnation, and ever since I was ten or eleven, I've had this vision of taking thousands of books and secluding myself somewhere—in a cave or a space capsule—with the intention of staying there until I'd figured everything out. More than anything else, it was this vision that brought me to India, and not some sort of pot-induced existential crisis or a mental breakdown, as the people who knew me liked to believe. Once I was in college, away from my parents and free to do as I chose, it was just a matter of time before my metaphysical proclivities came out and reorganized my reality. There were many turning points, but I remember one particularly well, perhaps because it was the first time I sensed that there were processes in my mind that I wasn't quite aware of. I was sitting in Trident Bookstore on Newbury Street, right around the corner from Berklee College of Music, sipping tea and paging through a pocket edition of the Dhammapada. It was spring, the trees were blooming, and I was thinking about a pair of Dr. Martens that I'd seen in the window of the shoestore next door. *Lotus flowers, lions, horses, subdue the mind, don't do this, do that:* all in all, the book was pretty boring and I often caught myself lifting my eyes to check out the girls from the New England

Conservatory strutting by in a ballerina bounce, all of them dressed in tights, and with their hair up in a bun. Then I came across the line *Little spider, why are you afraid to leave your web?* and suddenly it occurred to me how incredible it was that, despite having free will, people were often incapable of altering the course of their lives or even straying from a purely circumstantial narrative. Who said I had to be a musician? Who said I had to go to class? What invisible force made people perform the exact same routine every day? What made people go back to their beds every night? In a world where some people didn't live past thirty, and the entire human population was recycled every hundred years, there had to be *something* that could account for the widespread clinging to prefabricated narratives, or the universal penchant for repetition. I didn't have to be the person everyone expected me to be. I didn't have to work in the dishroom of the Berklee cafeteria four days a week. I didn't have to go on a date with someone just because college students weren't supposed to spend Friday night alone.

Two years later, I was still contemplating the question of free will and identity, but on a different level. Looking at the meditation huts, I often wondered what it would take for me to burn through the fragile seams of my identity and disappear into the world like a Paul Bowles character, resigned to accept every kind of fate, including death, with absolute indifference.

ON MY WAY BACK FROM SHIVA WATERFALLS, I stopped at a barbershop to get my monthly haircut. The barber knew me well and so he gave me the special treatment—a fifteen-minute head massage that involved rubbing, tapping, slapping, and even punching. The idea, I guess, was to soften my head before the actual haircut began, and, looking at the barber's blissful face in the mirror, I felt bad telling him to skip the drum solo and return to the main theme. I walked out of the barbershop dizzy and disoriented, but with a new understanding of things. The old Tibetan shopkeeper with the missing front teeth was smiling because he'd just won a game of *sho*. The one-legged postman, propped up like a broom against the counter of Samosa Shop No. 13, was drinking chai and dreaming of making out with the beautiful forty-year-old postwoman, who was married with four children and spent her days sitting motionless behind the post office counter, her lips coated with a thick layer of bright red lipstick, her neck wrapped in a scented purple silk scarf. The large prayer wheel in the middle of McLeod Ganj was spinning on its own; the sexiest prostitute in town was trying on a new pair of shoes and thinking about her day off, when she would sweep the room where she lived with her mother, scrub the walls and the windows, and then make tea and sit around, waiting for someone to stop by, perhaps a friend. The sun was where it's always been, and everything that was going to take place in the future had already happened.

I entered Om Restaurant and walked over to the corner table by the window where Tsar and Vinnie were sitting with two blond girls in their twenties (later I found out that they were twins, from Switzerland). Tsar looked disheveled, with a loosely buttoned shirt, glossy eyes, and hair sticking out in every direction. No one acknowledged my arrival because Tsar was in the middle of telling the girls about his trip to New Delhi, and when Tsar told stories, he didn't like to be interrupted.

"I waited for two days in front of the Ministry of Home Affairs," Tsar was saying as I pulled up a chair and joined the group. "I slept in a garbage can, just to keep my place in the line. Finally, one of the senior officials in the building agreed to hear my case and I thought, *dobro*, my troubles are almost over. By the way, I went to meet with the guy, and he turned out to be a complete retard. I explained the whole situation, how I've fled the fighting in Bosnia and everything, and he said, give me your documents, I'll review your case next month. Now, I didn't have a passport, so I gave him my asylum papers from Germany. 'Sorry, mister, ve don't luke at applications by people who have claimed asylum prior to their arrival in India.' I couldn't believe it. So I asked him, 'Are you saying that I have a right to seek asylum only in the first country that I reach after escaping a war zone?' 'First country of disembarkment, that's right.' 'Say I left Sarajevo in a hot air balloon. How far do you think I can travel?' 'Vive hundred kilometers, depending on the vether.' I said, 'Let's assume the wind is very strong and I float all the way down to the Mediterranean Sea, drift down the Suez Canal, past Yemen, cross the equator, fly all the way down to Madagascar, and get caught in a storm that drops me on the shore of Antarctica. Is it possible or not?' 'It's possible, but it's very unlikely.' 'By the way, I land in Antarctica, catch a few seals, drink some snow, wrap a piece of blubber around my balls to keep them from freezing, and suddenly I see an icebreaker with the Japanese flag on top. "Do you want to come onboard," the Japanese captain asks me. "We'll take you to Tokyo." Oh, no, I tell him, I can't go anywhere, I'm filing for an asylum here, this is my first country of disembarkment.'"

"And what did the official say to that?" one of the girls asked.

Tsar lit a cigarette and shook his head—slowly, as if he was trying to chase away a painful memory. "He said, 'If you vont to seek asylum in Antarctica, be my guest.' And the way he smiled, I knew he was setting me up. Suddenly the door opened and a dozen guards rushed in, with handcuffs and bamboo sticks, fucking bastards. I was completely surrounded but I still managed to wriggle out and get to the window—in Germany I used to work for a construction company that built high-rises, so, for me, balancing on a windowsill that's three floors aboveground was nothing. I jumped, grabbed on to the drainpipe, and started climbing down, the only problem being that the drainpipe wasn't attached correctly and so I flew across the street, fell through a tree, and landed right next to a bicycle rickshaw—only scratched my elbow."

The twins took note of Tsar's bruised elbow and turned to Vinnie, who was grunting and looked like he was about to punch someone. "*Scheisse!*" he exploded, and stomped his feet on the floor with such force that the two cooks stopped rolling *momos*, and came out of the kitchen to see what was happening. Chungda, the waitress, approached our table and asked me in Tibetan if everything was fine. "There's nothing wrong with the food," I told her. "The old man is having some problems."

"Fucking Indian Secret Service!" Vinnie went on, now banging on the table with clenched fists. "They are much worse than Mossad. Much worse!"

"Vinnie," I said. "You can't act like this—they're going to kick us out. Last time we were here, we accused the cooks of dropping their broken teeth in our food."

"By the way," Tsar interrupted me, "I'm walking down Paharganj, and I see this Indian guy running toward me with a piece of paper in his hand. 'Sir, fax for you, sir, you give me five rupees.' Fine, I give him five rupees, look at the fax: it's from the Red Cross."

"Which can only mean one thing," Vinnie observed gloomily.

"So I'm reading the fax," Tsar continued, "and it says something about an agency responsible for locating missing persons and identifying the remains of victims killed during the Bosnia war."

Tsar paused to allow us to grasp all the implications arising from this information.

"After four years of investigation," he said, blowing smoke through his nostrils, "they finally identified the remains of my grandmother."

"Tell them about the library," Vinnie urged him.

"They found her in the library," Tsar explained. "In what used to be the main Sarajevo library."

"What a pity!" Vinnie exclaimed. "The poor woman had gone in to check out the classics. In a time of bombing and shooting, she turned to literature."

"They only recovered a pair of legs," Tsar observed, burying his face in his hands.

At this point the girls started crying, Vinnie took to grunting again, and Tsar got up and started pacing up and down between the tables—to take some of the heaviness off his chest. I would've been crying, too, if I didn't happen to know that Tsar's grandmother had died of natural causes ten years before the start of the Yugoslav war.

Fourteen

Life in Durga Nivas continued this way until one day in September, when Tsar woke up at around noon and announced that he was thinking about moving out on his own. To see Tsar suddenly cold and resentful really felt like a slap in the face. After all, I had initially decided to rent a room with Tsar because he was broke and illegal, and I didn't want him to end up on the street. Month after month, I had paid the rent and bought groceries, thinking that I was helping him.

I asked Tsar what the problem was. Was I an irritating roommate? He said no. Was there something that I had done that had offended him? He said he wasn't offended. What, then?

It took him a while before he could formulate a coherent complaint. "Every morning when I wake up," he said, "you're up, memorizing Tibetan texts and paging frantically through the dictionary. At lunch, you're reading, meditating, or whatever, and digging in the dictionary. At night when I come home, you're still doing the same thing. When I get up at night to go pee, you're still up, reciting, blah-blah, slamming the dictionary, scribbling things down."

"And how is that irritating?" I asked him. "Considering, of course, that I am really that obsessed with my studies."

"I feel suffocated," Tsar replied. "I also want to meditate and read and think about life."

This was all really strange. Tsar wanted to meditate? I had never thought he was interested. But maybe it was I who had been killing his desire for dharma practice all along. I could see how living with a monk who did nothing else but read Tibetan texts could make you resent everything that was connected with the idea of inner growth. There could be nothing worse than feeling like the dharma was just another area where people compete and try to outdo each other. That said, there was a very big possibility that Tsar's real problem was not having a place of his own where he could bring his girl-friends. Which was also understandable. If you were no longer a monk, you might as well get laid as often as you could.

"What about money?" I asked Tsar. "How are you going to pay for rent and food?"

"I'll be fine," Tsar replied, indignant. "I'm thinking of starting a business, selling things. I've got some ideas."

His business ideas became apparent the next day, when he woke up at sunrise and started sketching the outlines of what looked like a *tankha*-style composition—a traditional Tibetan Buddhist painting in which everything from the length of Buddha's shoulders to the background themes and the colors had to be drawn according to strict rules.

"What do you think?" Tsar asked me when he'd finished filling in the background.

"It's nice," I said, "but if you're planning to sell this as a *tankha* painting, you're going to make a lot of Tibetans very angry."

Tsar was offended. "I've followed all the rules. See: this is the diagram that shows the correct proportions."

"I understand that," I told him, "but aside from the fact that there's never been a mention of the Buddha riding on an elephant, I would say that you've really pushed the sideburns a bit too far. The guy looks like a Chechen terrorist."

"Oh, Nikola," Tsar sighed, "I really don't know what they teach you in the monastery. There are millions of paintings where the Buddha is shown riding an elephant. Millions."

"Where?" I demanded. "Name one shop or restaurant in Dharamsala where you've seen a *tankha* depicting the Buddha riding an animal of any sort."

"But this is so basic, Nikola, I can't believe you learned Tibetan to study the scriptures and you still act like you've never heard of it. Everyone knows this: Jesus rides a donkey, the Buddha rides an elephant. It's basic stuff."

LATER THAT DAY Purba stopped by to see me, and when I told him that Tsar was moving out, he suggested that he and I take a trip to Manali, a Himalayan hill station about eight hours away from Dharamsala, and stay at the monastery of a renowned Tibetan teacher and meditator by the name of Khenpo Rinpoche. Purba said that he had been born in the same village in Tibet as Khenpo Rinpoche and he was certain that Rinpoche would give us a room for free. I told him that it was a great idea. Tsar needed some time alone, and I needed a break from my daily lessons with Geshe Yama Tseten. Besides, the monsoons had really begun to wear me down and I thought that leaving town for a while would help me clear my head.

Purba and I left early the next morning in a lopsided government bus packed with schoolkids, goats, hens, stone-faced soldiers, elderly villagers, and a few saddhus. Two hours into the journey we blew one of the back tires, which were doubled on each side, so driving with three back tires was certainly possible, even though the bus felt as if it was going to fall apart. Instead of pulling over, the driver decided to speed up, kicking the brakes, rotating the steering wheel like he was pulling a rope, and all the while telling the ticket collector a story that spurred furious head wobbles and angry shouting all the way to the back of the bus. The story, according to Purba, who knew Hindi, was about a failed marriage and was told in the form of rhetorical questions for dramatic effect: "If you said to your daughter-in-law that she had to move to a smaller room, would she stop milking the cows? And if your son took your side, would she go back to her parents and tell her brother to come and poison your donkey? And if you caught her brother on your property doing bad things, would you invite him over for chai or would you break his head with a stick?" And so on.

When we entered the precipitous canyons of the Kulu Valley and began driving on a narrow ledge carved into the cliff, in some places chipped by fallen rock and eaten away by rain, in others turning at an angle requiring three or four maneuvers (backing up to the edge of the ravine, then going forward again at a curve, with one of the doubled back tires sticking off the road), most of the passengers grew noticeably religious, mumbling with their eyes closed or clutching pendants and rosaries. Purba, for his part, managed his anxiety by throwing up every five minutes. He threw up so many times that in the end there was nothing for him to spit, and so he would stick his head out the window and just bark like a sick dog. At one point, feeling too exhausted to keep up with the barking, Purba wriggled out the window and climbed onto the roof (while we were going fifty miles an hour on a dirt road) to get some fresh air, as he phrased it. The ticket collector noticed that Purba was missing and immediately opened an inquiry into the matter. "Your friend, where?" he asked me. "Up," I replied, pointing at the ceiling. "Tell him to come down," he ordered. "I can't," I said. "You go upstairs and fetch your friend," the ticket collector demanded. "I'm not going upstairs," I told him and then suggested that he try knocking on the ceiling. The ticket collector knocked three times and waited. A moment later Purba knocked three times back. The passengers were ecstatic: we had just broken new ground in the field of bus communications. Looking fierce, the ticket collector knocked four times, a lot louder than before, and stared at the ceiling, arms akimbo, as if he expected Purba's head to somehow pop through the metal. The answer came promptly: four knocks at even intervals. The ticket collector performed an approving head wobble and smiled at the passengers. He considered the matter settled. We waited for Purba to come down but he didn't. The ticket collector knocked again, and Purba knocked back. This went on for a while, and, finally, the ticket collector gave up and returned to his seat next to the driver, where he fell instantly asleep, with an angry face.

The monastery was located on a steep hill above the main road, about half an hour outside Manali. The climb was really hard because we were carrying two kerosene stoves, pots and pans, a thirty-liter kerosene barrel, bags of flour and dal, cooking oil, and clothes—all packed in three oversized army sacks with broken zippers. Sitting down to get some rest, Purba told me that when Khenpo Rinpoche had begun his retreat in one of the caves on top of the hill many years ago, the area had been completely uninhabited and virginal. As the years passed, word about Rinpoche's commitment to auster-ity spread and people started coming to him for teaching and advice. His fol-lowers grew, the laity built a temple, the monks and nuns built their own meditation shacks, and Rinpoche eventually left his cave and moved—reluctantly—into a newly constructed residence.

Khenpo Rinpoche received us immediately and, as Purba had predicted, offered to put us up in one of the rooms that wasn't occupied at the moment. Rinpoche was a really gentle old Tibetan man, though I got the feeling that he didn't like chatting very much. An elderly nun came and escorted us to our room, which was quite far from the main compound—literally, in the middle of a forest—and looked more like a shed for storing bags of soil and gardening tools. Purba and I unpacked and set out to explore the surrounding area. We discovered that we had settled right at the edge of a vast apple orchard, with trees weighed down by enormous pink and red apples, the famous Manali apples. We approached a villager perched on top of a tree and asked him to sell us some apples. He came down, studied my face for a moment, and said that he couldn't sell us apples because I was a monk. "I'll make you a gift," he announced and promised to stop by our room before nightfall.

Purba and I didn't really expect the villager to keep his word and so we were rather surprised when, later that night, we heard a knock on the door and the villager entered the room, pulling a donkey by a rope. He unloaded the apples right on the floor, sack after sack, until half of the room was filled with apples—about seventy pounds total. We told him that there was no way we could ever eat so many apples, and he replied that we should eat as many as we could and give the rest away.

When we woke up the next morning the smell of apples had seeped into absolutely everything, from our blankets to our clothes. Even the earthen floor and the wooden boards smelled of apples. Purba and I went to see Khenpo Rinpoche and requested that he teach a short text on *Dzogchen* that Purba had brought with him. Rinpoche agreed and told us to come back early the next morning. Everything was working out: we had a dry place to stay, an apple reserve that we could subsist on for a whole month, Khenpo Rinpoche was willing to fit us into his schedule, and the view of the valley was so breathtaking that sitting for just a few minutes on the terrace above the temple pacified all internal chatter.

I went to shave at the spout behind our shack and, as I was admiring a magnificent ganja thicket towering over the surrounding apple trees (Jesus Christ, I thought, who gets to smoke these beautiful things—the Hindu sad-dhus, of course, lucky bastards; if Buddhist monks were allowed to get stoned, at least once in a while, they would have a much better time resisting the world of the senses) I noticed a beautiful young Tibetan nun standing ten feet away and looking at me in a manner that was, well, very un-nunly. She was tall and skinny, with full lips, elegant cheekbones, cute dimples, and rather small eyes that hinted at a strong and daring personality. Although the dress code and strict rules of behavior governing the life of Tibetan nuns were meant to make them look uniform and indistinguishable, I had discovered— after a great deal of observation—that nuns often used subtle and not-so-subtle signs to tell strangers, and monks in particular, about their personality and the things that they were interested in. Right away, just from looking at the nun, I could tell that she was neither the strict and rigorous kind of nun, nor the warm, motherly type, like Ani Dawa. Her pierced ears told me that she must have gotten ordained sometime after she'd hit puberty (a large number of nuns are sent by their parents to a nunnery at a very early age, thus no ear-piercing marks). Her pendant (nuns are not allowed to wear jewelry or makeup, but they can get away with a pendant bearing an image of the Buddha) meant that she didn't mind if boys looked at her. The saffron-colored sleeveless button-up shirt, tailored in a way to suggest the shape of her breasts, told me that she wasn't ashamed of her body. The discreet, transparent coat of nail polish, the curled eyelashes, and the manner in which she wore her *zen*—carelessly, like a rag that she'd picked up somewhere—were all signs that she was bored with her nun life.

"Have you come to see Khenpo Rinpoche?" she asked and, without waiting for an answer, stepped forward and extended her hand. "What is your name?"

"Lodro," I replied.

"I am Sangye. Are you going to attend the evening prayers?"

"I really don't like prayers," I admitted, deciding to be honest. "What's the point?"

Sangye giggled and started playing with her pendant. "It's nice to see someone who is not so serious. There was an *Engie* monk who lived here for a while but he was very intense. You never saw him laugh."

We talked for some time—about Khenpo Rinpoche and the river that had flooded at the beginning of the monsoons and washed away all the bridges and nearby houses—and then, all of a sudden, Sangye got nervous and said that she had promised to be at the monastery kitchen, to help with the dinner preparations, almost an hour ago. "Come," she said with a smile that held many secrets. "You should see our kitchen."

Was I supposed to say no? Even if I was, I had lost all of my willpower to do anything about it. Sangye was very attractive and I couldn't even remember the last time I had talked to a woman other than my mother and Ani Dawa, who was really my second mother. A year and a half ago? Two years?

I sat on a long wooden bench and watched Sangye and five other nuns roll *momos* and cut vegetables to make *tugpa*. The master chef, a monk with the arms of a bodybuilder, stirred a giant ball of dough with a spoon that was bigger than he was. In the brief moments when I regained a degree of self-awareness and managed not to stare at Sangye's ass, I tried to figure out what was happening to me. Just a few days before, I had been going to classes, studying, and talking to Ani Dawa about my plans to earn a *Geshe* degree. Then Tsar had moved out and, after a dizzying bus ride through the Kulu Valley, I had found myself yearning to change my life and start over again. The mind is a strange thing: it works in secret. Oftentimes the most important decisions in life are made while you're not paying attention.

Purba found me right before dinner. As a former monk, he possessed the unique ability to detect sexual thoughts as easily as most people can detect overt hostility.

"This is not going to end well," he commented, sitting beside me. "You guys are really in trouble."

"I know," I agreed. "The only thing that can kill my sex drive at this point is smoking the entire ganja bush behind our shack."

"If something happened between the two of you," Purba noted, "we'd all be kicked out of the monastery and we'd never be able to come back again."

I promised him that I would keep things under control. For about a week and a half, Purba and I went to Khenpo Rinpoche in the morning and then hiked up and down the hills on both sides of the river, discussing what we'd learned. Then one afternoon I came home and saw Sangye sitting cross-legged on what I considered my bed (two blankets spread over the earthen floor), holding a glass of milk. Purba was sitting across from her, smoking a *biddie* and smiling cynically.

"I was in my room," Sangye said innocently, "and I thought, Kushu-la probably hasn't had milk in a long time. I added a spoon of honey, but maybe you don't like it sweet, I don't know."

Oh, I liked it, all right. I sat next to her and began sipping the milk, grinning at Purba like a little boy. Beautiful eighteen-year-old virgins bringing milk and honey to my bedside—how could I complain?

"My roommate and I are making dinner tonight," Sangye announced. "Would you like to come over and help us cook? We could play cards, maybe. I've invited other monks and nuns as well."

Purba and I were very excited—we were invited to a real party. I hand-washed my robes in the communal spout and then dried them on the tin roof of our shack. Purba, for his part, put on his best pair of pants and bought a comb to untangle his long hair.

"We are all going to hell afterwards," he commented on the way to Sangye's house. "And you'll be the first one to go."

"Who knows," I replied. "Maybe I'm about to attain Enlightenment. Just before Buddha found the Middle Way, a woman offered him a cup of milk."

Laughing, we entered Sangye's room and found ourselves surrounded by young nuns, some only sixteen.

"If there is a good time to run, this is it," Purba said to me in English, so that the nuns wouldn't understand.

We stayed until after midnight and when we returned to our room, I saw that Purba was carrying one of the nun's rosaries wrapped around his wrist.

"She is certainly very pretty," I teased him.

"She is," Purba agreed, dreamily. "But at least I'm not a monk anymore. And I saw what Sangye gave you."

"What?" I asked, feigning innocence.

"It's in the inside pocket of your *tonka*," Purba hinted, extending his hand.

I pulled out an envelope and handed it to him. In the envelope was a photograph of Sangye from when she was sixteen and was still in high school.

She was dressed in jeans and a T-shirt, and her long hair, tucked behind one ear, added something to her smile that was no longer there.

Purba clicked his tongue and shook his head. "What happened to her?"

"She contracted tuberculosis and her parents thought she was going to die," I explained. It was common for Tibetans to send their sick kids to a monastery or a nunnery. Taking vows was considered a kind of therapy, a last-ditch cure for those who had run out of all other options.

We spent the next two weeks studying with Khenpo Rinpoche and play-ing games with the nuns. We played badminton and frisbee in the afternoon and cards at night. It was intoxicating to hear the girls laugh, to watch them tiptoe across the floor and breathe the air stirred up by their skirts. Sitting in Sangye's room felt like being in a forbidden world, a secret mandala where bliss was illusory and everything illusory was bliss. I couldn't stop marveling at the dry air and the sweet scent coming from the bedsheets. There were clean shirts mounted on coat hangers, robes folded and put away in the closet. A glass bowl with floating white rhododendron petals sat on top of a bookshelf, postcards hung from the wall by the door, and a pink alarm clock stood on the night table, next to a portable tape player and a stack of tapes. After living for a year and a half like a beggar—sleeping in my clothes and going to the bathroom in the forest—I just wanted to crawl under Sangye's bed and not come out for a very long time.

As the days went by, Sangye and I grew closer, and one morning I woke up and realized that I couldn't wait until the afternoon to see her. Khenpo Rinpoche wasn't teaching that day, and Purba had gone to Manali with the main cook and two other monks responsible for doing the grocery shopping.

I went to Sangye's room and knocked. Sangye opened the door and smiled without saying a word. *Weird*, I thought. It seemed as if I had been transported back in time and I was going over to my girlfriend's house to watch a movie.

"I'm going to make tea," Sangye announced and locked the door from the inside.

Now a warning light went off in the center of my brain and I became paranoid. Why was she locking the door? Somehow everything felt predetermined, as if Sangye and I had been given a script and we were just enacting our roles.

"I don't want any tea," I said. "Thank you."

"Are you sure?" Sangye asked, her voice shaking. She was scared, too.

"I'm sure."

She made tea anyway.

We sat on the edge of her bed, our eyes fixed on our glasses. There was nothing to say. We both knew what was going on. The door of the neighboring house opened and we heard monks talking loudly and laughing. The monastery gong sounded: it was ten o'clock, time for reciting scriptures at the temple. I looked at Sangye, expecting her to stand up and get ready to go. She didn't move.

A group of nuns walked past the door and one of them glued her face to the window, trying to see through the curtain. "Sangye?" she called out.

Sangye looked at me and giggled.

"I know you're inside!" the nun said.

A minute passed and everything became quiet. Sangye set her glass on the floor and fell back on the bed. She was wearing a sleeveless golden silk button-down shirt, and I noticed that one of the buttons had come undone, exposing her breast.

"What?" she asked.

"Nothing," I said. "I'm just looking at you."

"I can't hear you."

I lay down beside her and stared at the white ceiling, hoping that the image of Sangye's nipple would somehow fade or become distorted. It didn't.

"You're not drinking your tea," Sangye teased me.

I turned over on my hip and looked in her eyes. She did the same, resting her head on her outstretched arm. The bottom end of her shirt had pulled over her stomach and I could see her belly button and part of her pubic hair.

She didn't have any underwear on, which meant that we could do it without even taking our robes off. How could I stop this? I wanted to tear the strings that moved my body, to shake off the urge to taste the final moment, when all conceptual entities collapsed, above became below, one became many, in became out, I became none. I wanted to stop thinking; I *had* to stop thinking.

"You are beautiful," I said.

Sangye moved her hand closer to me, and a little closer still, pressing the bedsheet under my thigh. I knew what she was looking at, and I also knew that if she touched me there it'd be all over—I'd reach under her skirt and press my chest against her breasts . . . Why couldn't I put my hand on her belly? It was right there, I could do it so easily in my mind. Just to feel her pulse and touch the hairline.

I moved my head closer to hers, and she moved her hand a bit higher until it brushed against my robe. I could feel her fingers on the outside of the material, as if my tactile sense now extended beyond my skin and into the clothes I was wearing and the bedsheets. Sangye glanced at me and then lifted her head a bit, to see what she was touching with her hand. I was so close to her that I could smell the skin on her neck. Suddenly it occurred to me that I knew how her skin smelled everywhere, on her breasts, on her belly, between her legs. I knew what it would feel like to untie the saffron-colored string, pull down her skirt and kiss her right below the hairline. I knew how she would resist—instinctively, and only for a moment—when I tried to push her legs apart. I knew how she was going to look at me when I was on top of her. I was experiencing a massive, overpowering déjà vu. Everything that was going to happen had already happened, the future was in the past, and then I saw beyond the present moment: Sangye and I were living across the river, in a tiny shanty with a traditional Tibetan door curtain depicting the eight Buddhist auspicious symbols. She had long hair, and held a baby in her arms; the windows were fogged up, and I was kneeling by the gas stove, stirring a pot of *tugpa*. A black-and-white TV in the corner delivered the eight o'clock news from New Delhi in English; on the table was a stack of notebooks that I was planning to grade after dinner. The fifteen dollars a month that I earned teaching English at a high school outside Manali didn't buy much, but we were lucky because Sangye's parents lived next door and were always eager to help with our groceries.

Was this what I wanted? Ours would certainly be a great love story: a Western monk and a Tibetan nun throw away the shackles of celibacy and follow their hearts, outraging an entire Himalayan community. Maybe I would be happy living a small life filled with small wonders: a warm bed, a kid's smile, the whisper of the Himalayas at night.

I jumped to my feet and walked to the door. I paused for a moment, expecting that Sangye would ask me where I was going, but she didn't. Was there anything that I could say to her? I couldn't look back because my eyes were full of tears. I imagined her staring blankly at the wall, resigned to accept every disappointment and heartache as the natural outcome of a life that she had never wanted, a life that stood in opposition to the rise of the oceans, the moon cycle, the blossoming trees in the springtime, electricity, gravity, and the oscillation pattern of every particle in the universe.

I found Purba sitting on the doorstep of our shack, eating an apple and smoking a *biddie*. He wasn't wearing a shirt and his chest was red from the sun.

"How quick can you pack?" I asked him.

Purba pushed back his glasses and chuckled.

"God, you're slower than a turtle," I said and walked inside. I threw all my clothes and blankets in the army sack and started picking up the stuff lying on the floor: a notebook, pens and pencils, an old Walkman, boxes of incense, matches. I tossed Mark Twain's *Letters from the Earth* into the sack and Sangye's photograph dropped on the floor. I kneeled over it and studied Sangye's face as if I were seeing it for the very last time. *When did I become such an inert dork?* I thought to myself. I had done so many crazy things before. Given the option to follow the rules or do my own thing, I had always chosen the second. I had run away from home at fifteen; I had smoked cigarettes and drunk homemade brandy in class when I was in ninth grade. I had stolen and burned my high school's records, leaving all students with blank grades. I had written "Death to the Communists" on the wall of my high school three years before the fall of the Berlin Wall, when all dissenting voices in Bulgaria were sent to camps, correction centers, or simply disappeared. Why this sudden deference to rules and institutions, then? The right thing to do was to run away with Sangye and send everything else to hell. There was nothing more powerful, nothing sweeter than the act of asserting one's free will.

I put Sangye's photograph back between the pages of Mark Twain and looked up: Purba was standing in the doorway, smiling affectionately. This was the special thing about Purba—in difficult situations he didn't ask questions; he understood.

We went to thank Khenpo Rinpoche for reading with us through the text that we'd requested and headed down the hill, followed by the monastery dog, which was in the habit of intercepting and escorting every visitor.

We hopped on the first bus that came by. It made no difference where it was going, Kulu or Manali. Once we got to a city, we were going to figure out the best route to get back to Dharamsala.

The bus was almost empty and Purba and I sat in the middle, each taking two seats. Purba stuffed his lower lip with tobacco and started spitting out the window. I contemplated jumping off the bus and running in the opposite direction, just like in the movies. I'd go back and Sangye would know that I had come to take her with me, and we'd have this big reunion, with a lot of kissing and everything, and even though the rest of the monks and nuns would be outraged, in their hearts they'd rejoice because, at the end of the day, everyone likes love stories.

I counted the roadside chai shops, I counted the buggies overfilled with apples, I counted the goats and the trees, I counted the miles. The bus didn't move forward. It made space disappear. The villages, together with the houses and the cows, rolled up like rice paper; the road folded into itself and went up in smoke, incinerated in the great dichotomy of here and there. The driver just chose the direction, like an archer pointing one of Zeno's motionless arrows, while the internal combustion engine did the hard work, breaking space down and then reconstructing everything backwards, so that whatever used to be near became far and whatever used to be far became near. I could hear the transmission struggling to cut through the strings that bound Sangye and me, and I felt the pull in my bones and in my stomach, but it really didn't hurt much, it was a lot like getting a root canal with a ton of anesthetic, and soon the sun was setting and the bus was still completely empty and smelled of apples because the ticket collector had a huge bag and would eat an apple every five minutes; and I still wiped my eyes but I wasn't in pain, not really, the internal combustion engine had pulled almost everything out and I felt relieved. The sweet, stinging sensation in my navel had disappeared, opening my senses to the world around me, the bitter smell of the dusty windows, the hint of burning wood in the wind, the dizzying gorges and the eagles flying overhead.

We arrived in Mandi after dark and switched to a bus headed for Dharamsala. As we waited for the driver to get in, Purba sat beside me and asked me to give him Sangye's photograph, which I did, mechanically.

"You have no idea how many Tibetan boys would've died for this girl," he said, pulling out a lighter. He lit a *biddie* and then lit the photograph. I didn't stop him. I knew that he was doing the right thing.

When the flames reached his thumb, he tossed the burning photograph out the window.

"Now I'll never know what she looked like," I observed.

"It's better that way," Purba said.

AFTER SPENDING THE NIGHT at a guesthouse in McLeod Ganj, I got into a taxi and went to the Tibetan Library, hoping to find someone who knew of Tsar's whereabouts. I didn't have to look far. Tsar was sitting on the patio of Nechung Café reading a newspaper, his feet resting on a chair opposite him.

He was wearing a plaited button-down shirt, cream-colored cotton pants, sandals, and sunglasses, despite the fact that the magnificent branches of the old oak tree formed a canopy that blocked almost all direct sunlight. It struck me again how different he was from other people. No matter what was happening to him, he always looked like he was on vacation. Even if he ended up in a concentration camp or in hell, he'd still sit around, imperturbable, one leg over the other, smiling a dirty, Mickey Rourke smile and giving the impression that he was just waiting for a gin and tonic. If it's true that ordinary souls are those who feel sad when they are sad and happy when they are happy, then Tsar was certainly a metaphysical character. His mood always transcended what was happening to him.

"Tsar!" I shouted from the bottom of the stairs.

Tsar put the newspaper down and lowered his sunglasses. "*Choveche!* Stay there!"

He descended the stairs and grabbed one side of the army sack that contained all my belongings. When we reached the top we dropped the sack on the ground and hugged. It occurred to me that home was simply a place where your friends waited for you to come back.

"You want chai?" he asked and without waiting for an answer walked to the entrance of the café and shouted an order for two chais.

"Why didn't you call me?" he reprimanded me when he returned. "I got worried."

"They didn't have a phone," I replied in defense.

"You should've written a letter, then. Just a few lines to tell me how things are going."

"They didn't have a post office."

"What the fuck did they have there?" Tsar exclaimed, pulling out a pack of India Kings.

"Pretty nuns," I answered. "Lots of them."

Tsar let out a string of smoke and studied my face for a clue that would give away my secret. "*Choveche*," he said at last, "don't make me sit here and pull the words out of your mouth. Did you score or not?"

"Dirty old man," I said, very much enjoying Tsar's cynical perspective on the events of the past month. "Of course I didn't score. Other things happened, though. There was a nun who invited me to her room all the time and there were a few occasions when we almost crossed the boundaries."

"Oh, don't give me that platonic shit," Tsar replied, disappointed. "You either fucked or you didn't; that's all there is to it. For a moment I really thought you'd done something exciting."

I told Tsar that I was looking for a new room and he suggested that I sleep over at his place for a few nights. He warned me that his room was too small even for one person and we'd practically have to share a bed.

"Come and see my palace," he said and tossed the army sack over his shoulder.

We walked downhill for about fifteen minutes until we reached a deserted area off the main road marked by nothing but a few large volcanic rocks and some leafless bushes. Tsar's house stood alone on a hill overlooking the river, away from the mooing and the ceaseless clamor surrounding every family compound in the village. It was constructed entirely of mud, with an economically tiled roof and a rusty metal door.

"Are you comfortable in here?" I asked him, stunned by the size of his bedroom and the austere look of the cracked cow-dung-plastered walls. "There's barely enough space for one person to lie down."

"I love it," Tsar said. "I've got everything I want. I bathe in the river, and at night I make a fire outside to keep the leopards away."

"What leopards?"

"The Himalayan leopards, of course! This is where they come first when they cross the river at night. You can hear when they catch a dog, there's a lot of howling and crying going on. One night they surrounded my house, five of them, they could smell that I was inside and I could hear their breathing. I stayed up all night holding the cleaver in my hand, ready to chop their heads off if they found a way to get in through the roof."

"How would they get on the roof?" I wondered.

"But they *were* on the roof!" Tsar said. "They were shaking the whole house."

This was a role that Tsar hadn't played before: Tsar the hermit, Tsar the leopard fighter. What had happened to him? Was this his way of getting used to the fact that he was stranded in a foreign country, without any prospect of ever getting out?

"Do you still have the sheet of pressed wood that I used for my bed?" I asked him. "I'll need it when I get a room."

"I hope you're not going to be mad at me," Tsar said, giggling. "I know that you spent a lot of money on it, but I wasn't sure if you were coming back or not, and so I used it to make some improvements—for my new business that I'm starting tomorrow."

Tsar lifted a blanket serving as a curtain and invited me into the kitchen, which was as tiny as his bedroom but had a window so that smoke could escape freely. In one corner of the room lay half of the sheet that I considered my bed; next to it stood a three-foot-high folding ladder bearing a sign that read:

BOSNIAN BREAD!
TRY IT! ONLY 5 RUPEES!
Real bread tastes different

The sign was written in black marker and framed with green tape. As much as I was mad at Tsar for chopping my bed to pieces, I couldn't help but burst out laughing.

"What do you think?" Tsar inquired, eyeing his creation with pride.

"Are you really going to sell bread?" I asked him, laughing harder and harder.

"Why the fuck do you have to be so negative!" Tsar exploded. "You've got a passport and money for a return ticket, and your parents will always bail you out if it came to it! I don't have anything! This is my only shot at getting some independence."

"I just wonder if bread's the best thing to sell here," I explained. "They have chapati masters sitting on every corner. And the price, too. Five rupees sounds like a lot, considering that you could get a paratha for three or four."

"Give me a break," Tsar said exasperated. "Chapati isn't bread—it's like eating shoes. There isn't a single person who knows how to make bread here. You know this very well. Tell me one place in Dharamsala that sells bread—not hammered rubber pancakes, I'm talking about real bread."

"I guess you're right," I agreed. "But how are you going to cook it? You need a big oven."

"You are standing on it," Tsar informed me, pointing at the mud floor and looking smug, as if he were about to give me a ride in his new Porsche.

"I really don't get it," I said, looking around. "It's just a mud floor. Unless you're planning to set your house on fire."

Tsar walked back into the bedroom and picked up a cable sticking out of the floor. "All I need to do is plug this end into the lightbulb outlet. In five minutes, the kitchen floor is going to reach two hundred degrees Celsius."

I looked at the floor again and this time I noticed that it wasn't made of ordinary dried mud but of something more resilient, perhaps clay.

"I've buried a hundred electric coils like this one," Tsar said, showing me a hollow metal pipe wrapped up with thin wires. "It took me a whole month to do this. Then I found some fresh clay to put on top. All I have to do now is knead the dough, break it into pieces, and spread the pieces across the floor."

Tsar rubbed the palms of his hands together and ran his fingers down his chin, as if to say *Who's the king now?*

"Have you tested it?" I asked him.

"Not yet. I've been waiting for the clay to dry. By the way, I'm going to test it tonight. We'll do it together, since you're sleeping over. I've made enough dough to bake about forty small loaves."

"It's a genius idea," I admitted. "To turn the floor of your house into an oven! That's pretty out-there. I've never heard of anything like that. How did you integrate all the coils into one electric circuit? It must've been very hard."

"Oh, it was a nightmare, and mostly because I couldn't get the things I needed from the hardware store. *Choveche*, they didn't even have a screwdriver that can measure the polarization of a circuit. If I have the right materials I could make anything. My brother was a licensed electrician and I used to work for him, back in Sarajevo. I've been shocked hundreds of times. Look at all these toys: I bought them just to get their transformers."

We admired Tsar's buried invention for another hour and then started up the hill to meet Vinnie, who was waiting for us at Om Restaurant.

"NIKOLA, GIVE ME THE SCREWDRIVER!"

I handed Tsar the screwdriver and stepped back, afraid that some of the live, exposed wires hanging from the ceiling could brush against my face and shock me.

"Yebem li ti pichku materinu!" Tsar yelled as he fell off the chair and landed on the floor.

"Are you all right?" I asked him, rushing to help him get up.

"Dumb motherfuckers!" he shrieked, showing me the wire that he had ripped from the cable leading to the lightbulb. "How can they put such a thin wire! You can't even run a hundred-watt lightbulb. And Nikola, please, you have to point the flashlight at my hands, I almost got killed up there. You're constantly moving around."

Five minutes later, Tsar came down and grabbed the flashlight from my hands. "Ready?"

"Just a second, I'm going to wait outside," I told him, putting my shoes on.

The air was cold and carried traces of pine trees and night-blooming flowers. Do rhododendrons blossom in September? I filled my lungs and listened to the distant sound of dogs barking. I could feel the pulse of the river in my feet. The jagged pinnacles above were enveloped in a corona of white light; the ascending moon was about to peek in.

"Three, two, one," Tsar counted inside.

I expected a loud explosion and perhaps a dramatic conclusion to Tsar's life, but everything remained quiet. Then the lights started going off all around me, neighborhood by neighborhood, house cluster after house cluster, like lined up domino pieces, until all of Lower and Upper Dharamsala turned completely black.

Tsar came out of the house and looked around. "What the fuck happened?"

"You just left the Dalai Lama in the dark," I replied.

"Fucking India," Tsar shouted, kicking a stone. "Nothing ever works here. Nothing."

Fifteen

After his unsuccessful attempt to convert his room into an oven, Tsar bought three new kerosene stoves and started baking his bread three loaves at a time, using a combination of frying pans, paint brushes (for the oil), forks, wires (to prevent sticking), and cracked Bakelite plates serving as lids. With the flame turned down to low, it took about twenty minutes to cook a bun-size loaf, and so in order to cook thirty loaves, Tsar had to get up at four o'clock in the morning and work until eight, flipping bread, pumping the stoves with air, adding kerosene, unclogging the valves, and slipping the baked bread into a special, thermo-insulated sack that he had stitched up just for the occasion. I had rented a room halfway between the Tibetan Library and Tsar's house, and I was at the communal spout brushing my teeth when I saw Tsar coming up the steep, stone-tiled path on the morning of his first day as a bread salesman. He was wearing his fake Boss sunglasses and used the folding "Bosnian Bread" sign as a walking cane; the thermo-insulated sack with bread was strapped to his back. I couldn't believe that he was really going to do it, that he was going to join the throng of lepers, *paan wallahs*, and chickpea masala vendors camping out in front of the Tibetan library and stand there all day, trying to sell his bread to the foreigners

attending the classes at the library. Not many Westerners would do it. I would
say almost none. On the one hand, I admired Tsar for having the humility to
admit to the world that he was broke, stranded, and illegal, and that he was
willing to do anything to get by. On the other hand, I was worried that if his
new venture failed miserably—which to my mind was the most likely scenario—he would sink into a hole that he wouldn't be able to get out of. After
all, he hadn't chosen his nickname *Tsar* for no reason. His bravado, metaphysical stubbornness, and cynically exaggerated self-importance was his act
in life. It was what he did best. Whether he was a good or bad person was
beside the point; he was Tsar, and I liked him that way. What would happen if
the reality of his predicament—the war in his home country, his shady life in
Amsterdam, the lack of legal documents and steady income—became too
overpowering and crushed him? Would he be able to spring back and rein-
vent himself? I decided that it was very important for me, as his best friend, to
buy some of his bread and spend an hour or so with him every day, as a show
of support. Walking back to the library after my class with Geshe Yama
Tseten on the day Tsar went to work for the first time, I thought hard about
what I should say to Tsar to give him confidence and show that I didn't look
down on him because he had been forced to sell buns on the street. I imagined myself in his place and realized how humiliating it would be for me if my
friends came by to see me and started making fun of what I was doing.

Turning the corner of the Tibetan Government in Exile building, I was
stunned to see how gravely I had underestimated Tsar's resilience. It's true:
Tsar was sitting in a crowd of toothless lepers, *paan wallahs*, and masala snack
vendors, just as I had imagined, but whereas the *paan wallahs* shouted their
paan mantra, waving betel leaves, and the lepers pressed their palms together
and whimpered to capture the attention of the passersby—in this instance, a
robotic Swiss lady—Tsar was sitting leisurely in a fold-up chair, sunglasses on,
cigarette in hand, and ordering a teenage beggar boy to bring him a bottle of
Indian Coke.

"I'm going to give you extra ten rupees if you run to Lower Dharamsala

and buy me a kilo of paneer and a pack of foreign cigarettes," Tsar was saying
to the kid as I approached him.

"Fifteen," the kid argued.

"No way," Tsar told the boy and nodded at me. "Have you come for my
bread?"

"Of course," I said, handing him ten rupees. "May I have two, please?"

"It's all gone," Tsar announced proudly. "Actually, I have one left, but
I'm saving it for Geshe-la from the library. He already paid for it."

"Geshe Sonam Rinchen?" I asked in disbelief.

"Same one. *Choveche*, you should've seen the crowd: they were fighting
to get in line. The bread was gone in five minutes. I made a hundred and fifty
rupees just sitting around. I could easily sell sixty pieces a day—by the way, a
guy came and said to me, you should really make sandwiches as well. So
tomorrow I'm going to bring ten pieces with paneer and tomato slices in the
middle, to see if people like it."

FOR THE NEXT FIVE MONTHS I saw Tsar only briefly, when he stopped by at
my place at eight o'clock each morning to give me two warm pieces of bread,
and then later in the afternoon for an hour in front of the Tibetan Library. He
woke up at four o'clock in the morning and went to sleep at eight. He didn't
play chess anymore, and in his free time he bought groceries and kerosene
and made yogurt, which he added to his dough to improve the taste of his
bread.

Then spring arrived and I was given permission to join the new class at
the Institute of Buddhist Dialectics (I was fluent in Tibetan and there were
spots available). It was a great opportunity, considering that a new class
started only once every four years. The Institute of Buddhist Dialectics—
originally established by the fourteenth Dalai Lama with the intention of
offering an unbiased approach to the study of Buddhism—was a small monastic school that more or less followed the curriculum of the three big Tibetan

monasteries, Sera, Drepung, and Ganden. For a period of seven years, the students enrolled in the school covered subjects such as logic, mind science, Indian schools of thought, Maitreya's *Ornament of Metaphysics*, and Chandrakirti's *Entry into the Middle Way*. At the end of the program there was a final exam in the form of a public debate overseen by the entire theological community.

In addition to the daily ten to twelve o'clock morning lecture, my classmates and I were required to take part in the afternoon and evening debate sessions held in the courtyard in front of the Main Temple, which lasted two hours each. Buddhist debate, or what had survived of it in the Tibetan Buddhist tradition, appeared to me to be a cross between ballet and chess. The debaters never entered an argument from an equal position: one always stood on his feet and attacked, dancing around, while the other sat on the ground and defended himself. Each one had a predetermined set of possible and *allowed* questions and answers, and so a good debater calculating his opponent's answers was no different from a chess player calculating, say, fifteen or twenty moves ahead. Not surprisingly, Buddhist debate was the one area where young monks channeled all their masculinity and sexual frustrations. Hovering over their opponents like giant maroon crows, they finally got to kick someone's ass and triumph over other people's intellect. Here, they enjoyed all the forbidden sweets, from rapidly pumped adrenaline to revenge, pride, and victory. There was also something explicitly erotic in the way the monks enacted the master-slave archetype, their peacock-like moves, the passionate head and ear grabbing, the slow-motion foot stomping, the clapping of hands, the sound of flesh against flesh, the cute little pirouettes that the master performed after driving a point home.

For me, debating was just a way to improve my knowledge of Tibetan. I liked the game side of it, and I was fascinated to see the analysis and line of reasoning that empowered the fundamental Buddhist concepts concerning the nature of the mind and emptiness, but when it came to spouting out memorized definitions or defending categories that I didn't believe existed, there wasn't a more jaded debater in the courtyard. (Time, for instance, was placed in a category that was neither matter, mind, or space. I claimed that it was a property of the mind, and no one succeeded in proving me wrong.) I was so uninterested, in fact, that once I even managed to trip and fall down while proving the impermanence of sound. What frustrated me in particular was the common perception among Tibetans that, in addition to explaining the nature of mind and reality, Buddhism also offered an insight into the workings of the physical world. One of the first definitions that I and my classmates (none of whom had gone to secondary school) were given was of the color white. It went as follows: *white is that which appears white.* I was absolutely dumbfounded. First of all, it was a tautology. Second of all, at the end of the twentieth century, anyone studying color should be at least aware that color is a wavelength. And if one needed a definition, "an electromagnetic vibration whose wavelengths are evenly distributed from 35 to 75 millionths of a centimeter" would have been quite appropriate. (Good luck to anyone attempting to translate "electromagnetic vibration" or "wavelength" into Tibetan.)

My first real debate—after weeks of reciting memorized arguments—took place on the balcony of the Main Temple, where all the monks from the Institute of Buddhist Dialectics had gathered to escape the rain. My opponent was an eighteen-year-old monk who through some weird machination had been given the title "Rinpoche"—a reincarnate Buddhist teacher—and as a consequence enjoyed money, servants, private tutoring, respect, and other privileges befitting a boy-king. He didn't like me very much, since I treated him like any other confused and pimpled teenager, and was eager to crush me in the opening moves. He was standing up, ready to attack. I was sitting cross-legged, wrapped up in my *zen.*

"Give me the definition of space," he shouted, snapping his fingers under my nose—a small, contemptuous gesture that was meant to establish his superiority right from the start.

"An absence of obstruction," I replied confidently.

The monk stepped back, raised his right hand while simultaneously pulling a rosary up his left arm (a lot like an archer pulling back a bowstring), and then rushed toward me to deliver his claim: "It follows that you can't see space directly." (Hands clapping.)

"Why?" I demanded. Why was one of the four standard answers available to a defendant. It prompted the attacking opponent to state his reasoning.

"Because space is a negation," the monk declared.

At this point I had three options: to say "Do," which in Tibetan means "I agree"; to say, "The reason is not established," which would prompt my opponent to prove that space is a negation, not a positive phenomenon; or finally to say, "It doesn't follow" (meaning that the reciprocity between the terms— negation and direct perception—isn't proven), which would call for further reasoning demonstrating that if something is a negation, it can never be perceived directly. Unhappy with the lines of argument that these three answers were certain to bring, I opted for something entirely different: an illegal move.

"I see it," I announced finally, shrugging my shoulders. This kind of thing was absolutely verboten. It was like taking your king during a chess game and moving him slowly to the edge of the table and then onto the floor.

"What did you say?" the monk asked, looking confused. Maybe he hadn't heard me correctly. After all, I was just an Engie. Tibetan wasn't my native language.

"Turn around," I ordered him. (The monk obeyed.) "Look at all that empty space behind you!"

Dumbfounded, my opponent stared at the open space enclosed by a wall of mountains and capped by a dome of melting gray clouds. The other monks also stopped their debates to examine the sky. Everyone looked like they'd taken acid and were experiencing massive hallucinations.

Regaining his composure, my opponent took a step back and delivered his next verdict: "It follows that you can't see emptiness directly. Because it's a negation, just like space." (Hands clapping.)

Now I got it. He'd hoped that I would say that space wasn't an object of direct perception so that he could transfer the argument to emptiness. And, of course, I couldn't claim that emptiness isn't perceived directly, because that would mean that Enlightenment isn't achievable.

"But I *can* see space directly," I insisted, refusing to follow the debate protocol for a second time. "It's very easy. Look over there, all that beautiful empty space!"

Again, everyone stopped to look at me and then at the empty space. Now the debate digressed into a conversation, with all the monks nearby begging me to come to my senses.

"Come on, Lodro, you can't say that you can see space!"

"Why not?"

"Because there's nothing there! No one can see nothing!"

"But I love nothing! I'm looking at it, and it's breathtaking. It fills my eyes."

"But you can't see the absence of something!"

"Everything is an absence of what it is not," I countered.

"And what about direct perception?"

"There's no direct perception."

Granted, I wasn't a good debater, but at least I managed to get everyone totally confused. You could always count on an Eastern European to play against the rules.

MY REBELLIOUS ATTITUDE at the debating ground and my utter refusal to accept the definitions of color, taste, smell, space, direct perception, and matter—among other things—soon put me in the group of the least intelligent students who pretended to debate (to keep the ge kul, or supervisor, away), stomping their feet and clapping their hands, but in reality talked about momos and Bollywood movies, or didn't talk at all. This, apparently, mattered very little to Ani Dawa, who was extremely proud of me (her son, in a way) and came every afternoon to watch me, goggle-eyed, as I did all the ballet moves and shouted, *"Win par tal!"*—It follows!—and *"Ma win par tal!"*—It doesn't follow! Even Ama-la, Ani Dawa's mother, was impressed with my sudden, and certainly unexpected, ascent up the theological ladder and frequently pointed me out to her octogenarian friends.

There were other important things that happened in March: Tsar left town without warning, and I met Merry Anne, a Bulgarian student in philosophy who had recently arrived in Dharamsala to write a paper on Buddhism. Merry Anne (this wasn't his real name, but all Tibetans, starting with Ani Dawa, insisted on calling him Merry Anne) was the quiet, perpetually spaced-out type, who walked slowly, dragging his feet, asked bizarre questions, and lived his life according to the Chinese moon calendar. He had brought two books to India: the *I Ching*, with a commentary, and a book in Russian titled *The Mysterious and Completely Unfathomable Nature of Female Creatures*. Merry Anne read both books obsessively, at times entering deep meditative states, prompted by lengthy ruminations on matters such as women's secret source of wisdom and the purifying aspect of karmic obstacles. Tall, green-eyed, with copper-colored hair, thick lips, dark rings under his eyes, and an expression of extreme fatigue, Merry Anne looked like a Slavic mystic lost in the Negev desert in search of the Holy Grail.

It so happened that at the time I met Merry Anne I had just moved to a shanty that I couldn't really afford. The location of the shanty was excellent—a one-minute walk from the Institute of Buddhist Dialectics and no more than two hundred yards from the Dalai Lama's residence—but seven hundred rupees a month was twice the going rate of a small room in the village down by the river, not to mention that the gaps between the boards were wide enough to see the faces of people passing by. The shanty belonged to one of Ani Dawa's aunts (apparently, she had many) and Ani Dawa never missed an opportunity to remind me how difficult it had been for her to convince her aunt to rent the room to a foreigner. At first I thought that I was taking the space intended for Ani Dawa's homeless relatives. It wasn't until later that I realized that Ani Dawa's aunt's reluctance stemmed from the uniquely Tibetan belief that letting a foreigner or an outlaw live near the Dalai Lama was equivalent to allowing a mass murderer to enter heaven.

So I was low on money, and Merry Anne was looking for a cheap place to stay. I was a little weary of entering into a roommate situation with someone who was clearly a pothead, but I needed help with the rent and, in a way, Merry Anne was the perfect roommate: he was self-entertained, nonconfrontational, and talked very rarely, if at all. He had also assured me that he was done with the ganja and was on the road to recovery, his short-term memory and attention span swelling by the day.

One of the first things that Merry Anne decided to do in town was to sign up for an audience with the Dalai Lama. I took him to Dalai Lama's private office and spoke to the clerk there on his behalf. Merry Anne was lucky: there was an audience scheduled for three o'clock later that day and there were still spots available. We put our names down and agreed to meet at our house at quarter to, right after I finished with debate. Then I went to class.

At quarter to three I returned to our shanty and found Merry Anne sitting on the edge of the street, smoking and talking to a leper wrapped up in blankets.

"Are we still going?" I asked him.

Merry Anne nodded solemnly and continued to smoke in slow motion.

"We don't have to go," I told him. "I actually have other things to do."

"But we *have* to go!" Merry Anne replied boldly, as if now we were dealing with an evil force that was trying to stop us from going. "This is the most exciting day in my life!"

I looked at his face again, expecting to see a hint of excitement, but his expression remained uniformly gloomy, his eyes closing for three or four seconds at a time, as if he were struggling to stay awake. He took one last drag from his cigarette and rose to his feet.

"Have a great day and see you, uh, later!" Merry Anne told the beggar with a sudden burst of energy, tapping him gently on his back.

We were already running late but Merry Anne insisted on taking the *kora* path through the forest, which made a wide loop around Dalai Lama's residence.

"He is a Gemini," Merry Anne observed.

I gathered that he was talking about the Dalai Lama. "So?"

"It explains everything . . . you know . . . how he could be both human and nonhuman."

"Why do you think the Dalai Lama isn't human?" I asked.

"I don't know."

A few hundred yards down the path, Merry Anne squatted and picked up a hook-shaped piece of metal wire. He examined it closely and shoved it in the pocket of his military-style dark green pants.

"Today is a very special day," Merry Anne confided, quickening his pace. "This is clearly a sign. It must mean something."

"What is a sign?" I asked him.

"This!" Merry Anne pulled the hook-shaped wire out of his pocket and held it out. "See? It's a question mark."

"It's a broken coat hanger," I objected.

"Yes, but when I found it on the street it looked like a question mark. It is a question mark! Someone is trying to tell me something!"

Merry Anne started walking faster and faster, and I noticed that he was smiling. It was the first time I had seen him truly excited.

"The question is what is the question," Merry Anne shouted as he broke into a run. I tried to keep up with him, but every twenty feet or so my flip-flops flew off and I had to go back to retrieve them.

"You should just go in by yourself!" I yelled after him, exasperated.

Merry Anne kept on running, zooming past wandering cows and old Tibetan men and ladies with rosaries. Then, all of a sudden, he swerved off the road and tumbled down the slope. Worried, I rushed to the spot and started making my way through the dense thornbushes. In the end, I spotted the back of Merry Anne's head sticking out from behind a squat rhododendron tree.

"Merry Anne?" I asked. No answer. "What's going on?"

"I'm shitting," he replied with irritation.

TEN MINUTES LATER, we were standing at the gate of Dalai Lama's residence, surrounded by ragged backpackers and jolly New Agers enveloped in pashmina scarves. Merry Anne looked pale; his pants were covered with mud. He wiped the cold perspiration off his forehead and glanced nervously at the Tibetan bodyguard, who held a list with the names of all the foreigners who had signed up for the audience. "Merry Anne?" the bodyguard read and looked around. Merry Anne raised his hand and took a step forward with the stiffness and obedience of a soldier. "Go in," the bodyguard ordered him. Cautiously, Merry Anne took another step forward, then turned around and ran like hell in the opposite direction. The bodyguard called the other bodyguards nearby and explained to them what had happened. Everyone looked very concerned.

I went back home and found Merry Anne in bed, shivering. The hooklike wire he had picked up from the street lay on the table in the middle of the room.

"I guess I'm not supposed to meet the Dalai Lama," Merry Anne said with morbid resignation. "The question is why."

"How about you've got diarrhea," I offered.

"But, but why? Why did I get diarrhea on the way to see the Dalai Lama? And then, then, there's the question mark. It must mean something!"

Merry Anne sat up in bed and looked out the window. Om Giridi, the Shiva priest, was walking up the stone steps leading to our shanty. Now that I lived fifty yards away from the Shiva temple, he visited me every day.

"*Namaste*, Guru-ji!" Om Giridi greeted me in his deep voice, which sounded like a sigh. "May I come in?"

I removed the Tibetan books scattered across my bed and gestured for Om Giridi to take a seat.

"Your friend sick?" Om Giridi asked.

"Diarrhea," I explained.

Om Giridi stood up and tied a red string on the shelf above Merry Anne's bed. Then he mumbled something in Sanskrit and dumped a handful of seedpods on the table.

"Boil some water, put these inside, then drink," he told Merry Anne.

I transferred the seedpods into an empty cup and went into the kitchen to start the kerosene stove. When I returned, Om Giridi was sitting next to Merry Anne, enveloped in thick hashish smoke.

"I see big work," Om Giridi told Merry Anne as he studied the palm of his hand.

"Very big?" Merry Anne inquired.

Om Giridi nodded and turned to me. "Your friend Tsar came to the temple. He was looking for you."

I jumped. "When?"

Om Giridi searched his pockets, then his bag, and handed me a piece of paper. It was a note from Tsar: "Come to Durga Nivas at 8. We are having a *momo* party."

"Did he say anything?" I asked.

"He asked, 'Where is Guru-ji?' then he went. There was a lady with him."

A lady? I said good-bye to Merry Anne and Om Giridi, threw my *zen* over my shoulders, and ran out of the house. I was desperate to find out what had happened to Tsar. Did the police track him down again? Did Kaila, his Israeli girlfriend, come back to India to save him? And why didn't he tell me that he was planning to leave town?

I went to the post office and asked the lady if she'd seen Tsar. She responded with a negative head wobble. I rushed to Tsonka Restaurant and climbed on the roof, which had outdoor seating. This was the best observation post in town. I scanned the street with the vegetable market, then walked to the opposite end of the roof and examined all the places that Tsar liked to visit: the phone booth across from the prayer wheel, the samosa joints, the barbershop, the tiny Tibetan kitchen that offered cheap soup. A group of people emerged from a narrow alley between two buildings and I spotted a familiar rucksack. "Vinnie!" I shouted as loud as I could. Vinnie waved and started moving toward me. Stepping onto the roof of the restaurant, he walked to the nearest table, took the paper chessboard from his rucksack, and began arranging the black pieces. I admired his long, flaming red hair for a moment, then sat opposite him and swept all the white pieces to my side of the table.

"Are you going at eight?" I asked him.

Vinnie nodded and turned the board around. "I played black last time."

"So do you know what happened?"

"It's all over," Vinnie announced. "Tsar is leaving India."

"How?" I asked.

"He's getting married. To an American."

Vinnie waited for the news to sink in, then moved his pawn to b4 and got up to order lemon tea.

"You're going to lose, man," I teased him as he went down the stairs. "Every time you play the Orangutan, you lose disastrously."

"I played it against Erick and I won twice," Vinnie answered with a deadpan expression.

It occurred to me that one day my life in Dharamsala would certainly end—Tsar would be gone, I would move to South India or some other place—but the image of Vinnie telling me, in all seriousness, that he had employed the Orangutan opening against Erick and won would remain perfectly intact in the back of my mind for a very long time. It was a great image—Vinnie's head sticking out past the edge of the flat roof as he went downstairs, as if cut off and miraculously suspended in midair, and the bustling of the street down below—Rajasthani merchants selling cages with green parrots, professional ear cleaners with knitting needles and balls of cotton offering their service for five rupees per ear, a Tibetan lady hanging laundry on a clothesline, the orange sun reflected in the windows of the room of the prettiest prostitute in town. In the distance were rectangular rice paddies, the glistening slate roofs of village houses, and the Himalayan pinnacles shooting straight up like a colossal granite geyser. Somehow, Vinnie's comment about the Orangutan opening had a lot more to do with Tsar leaving India than with anything else. Somehow, Vinnie and I played chess and talked about end-game positions, but what we were really discussing was meaning, the meaning of waking up every day to the smell of cow-dung-plastered walls, the meaning of believing—despite all facts pointing to the contrary—that the little bubble of reality that we had created around us would hold off change forever.

THE MOMO PARTY WAS HOSTED by an Amdo monk who used to be Tsar's neighbor back in the days when Tsar first moved to Durga Nivas. Lobsang and Purba were both in the kitchen, pounding small balls of dough into paper-thin round pieces, which the Amdo monk then stuffed with boiled potatoes or lemongrass and sealed with a fork. There were two whole tables covered with dumplings ready to be steamed. I cut some onions and chilies for the hot sauce and walked out to the patio to see if Tsar had finally arrived. I listened to Vinnie as he explained to a young Australian girl the different stages of adaptation that a Westerner living in India goes through: during your first year, you extract the cooked flies in your *aloo gobi* and continue eating; during your second year, you suck the juice out of the cooked flies and spit them out; at the end of your third year in India you just eat and drink everything—flies, spiders, mosquitoes, and so on. Then I went and sat out on the grass, away from the blond Australian lad who had produced an acoustic guitar and was threatening to sing. Just by the look of him, I knew it was going to be either Bob Dylan or Leonard Cohen. There was always someone who played guitar, or juggled, or did both.

The thought of answering the inevitable "Why did you become a Buddhist monk?" question one more time made me ill. Most of the Westerners attending the party were just tourists passing through on their way to Manali, or Rajasthan, or New Delhi, and it was impossible for them to see that I hadn't dressed up as a monk that day just to be different. Being a monk was inseparable from who I was; *why* and *how* implied that I could somehow step out of my identity and examine myself from the point of view of someone who no longer existed. A caterpillar thinks "I am a caterpillar." A butterfly thinks "I am a butterfly."

Tsar showed up at nine o'clock and immediately went for the *momos*. He was wearing a black T-shirt, jeans, and a large wool sweater wrapped around his shoulders like a scarf.

"So," I began as he came closer.

"*Choveche*, I don't know how people survive here," he interrupted me, looking at the mountains. "The Himalayas are so fucking unfriendly, they crush you. I mean, it's no wonder people here look like they're dead. I was in Goa for how long, two weeks? By the way, I was lying on the beach with Samantha—she's going to be here any minute, I'll introduce you to her—and I thought of you up here in the fog and the rain. I just thought, this kid has to get away from the mountains before they kill him. *Choveche*, it never occurred to me before that the sun is as important to us as water. Spending two hours in the sun made me so happy I didn't have to think for three days straight. Seriously. Not a thought crossed my mind. It was more sun than I'd gotten in the last two and a half years since I came to Dharamsala."

"So are you really getting married and leaving India?" I asked him.

"It's time," Tsar said, lighting up a cigarette. "I'll probably come back one day, when I have a passport and some money. But if I don't leave now, I might never get out of here alive."

"What about your documents? How are you going to apply for an American visa if you don't have a passport?"

"Samantha and I already went to the American embassy in New Delhi and got all the necessary papers that we have to fill out. The immigration officer we spoke to said there shouldn't be a problem. We're going to get married, then Samantha is going to fly back and hire an immigration lawyer who's going to take care of everything. That's the plan."

"Where is she from?"

"Hawaii," Tsar answered, giggling.

"Of all places . . ."

Just then, two women emerged from behind the house and one of them waved at us excitedly.

"She is very nice," I commented. "And pretty."

"A blind hen also finds a grain of barley every once in a while," Tsar replied and stroked his three-day beard.

I knew that this was a Serbian proverb but I still found it strange that Tsar would identify himself, subconsciously, with the archetype of the blind hen. It was a perfect illustration of Eastern European fatalism, the sense that you come into this world deprived and destined to end up in the gutter, and that whatever good happens to you is always the result of chance or some wild statistical aberration.

I didn't get to talk to Tsar much for the rest of the night, but I noticed that he looked rather sad for someone who had just stumbled upon a grain of barley. Standing quietly in the corner, he was saying good-bye to his life in India—his first room where he'd lived as a monk; his two sets of monastic robes, folded and locked up in a rusted metal trunk; his second room up the hill, where he and I had lived together during the monsoons; the river, where he had bathed with Kaila; the whisper of the mountains at night; the twinkling lights down in the valley; the long hours he had spent playing chess with Vinnie in the Last Cow Chai Shop; the melancholy Shiva hymns blasted at sunset through the loudspeaker on the roof of the temple across the river.

Sixteen

I should've attended Tsar's marriage ceremony. That's what any real friend would've done. We would've walked into the courtroom together, Ani Dawa, Vinnie, Tsar, Samantha, and I, and I would've stood on Tsar's right side because I would've been his best man. Then the government clerk would've entered into the courtroom, followed by the typist on duty—carrying an ancient typewriter strapped to his neck—and when the clerk had looked us up and down with a sinister government expression, Vinnie would've said, "We can't start without Mendelssohn," and the typist would've written it down, and when the clerk had asked, "Mendelssohn who?" Vinnie would've answered, "Jakob Ludwig Felix," and we would've all told him to shut up. Tsar's breath would've smelled of tobacco, booze, and bubble gum, and his hair would've been combed back and thickened with brilliantine, and he would've winked at me and cursed all of human civilization, and the marriage institution, and God in Serbian, and when Samantha asked me to translate what Tsar had said, I would've replied that it's just something that Serbians say when they are getting married—something along the lines of "cheers" and "gesundheit." There would've been stacks of birth, marriage, and death certificates touching the ceiling, and I would've commented on how funny the whole thing was: getting born and dying and signing papers and court settlements, and how everything happens simultaneously, only you don't realize it until the very end, and Ani Dawa would've scolded me for acting inappropriate, and the typist would've typed it down, and the government clerk would've stood on tiptoe to stress the importance of the situation, and his comb-over would've collapsed, leaving his egg-shaped skull exposed to the brutal elements. Then Samantha would've spotted a cat-size rat chewing on somebody's death certificate, and Vinnie would've advised us against disturbing the rat because rats are known to bear grudges and they might follow us home and shit in our flour and punch holes through our socks, and then the government clerk would've coughed and recited, "I shall now pronounce the undersigned unless otherwise stated having acquired prior approval under the provision of the Foreigners Act of 1946 as per the above particulars be liable to prosecution for contravention without any further notice in the event that the abovementioned parties unless he or she has obtained the permission of the Central Government to enter into a marriage union subject to consideration by the latter Government granting full discretion to withhold any application unless previously stated and shall hereafter assume full responsibility as indicated in other particulars or other forms of identity until further notice and therefore pronounce you husband and wife," and Tsar would've kissed Samantha and Ani Dawa would've looked away because the Buddha had allegedly said that body touching is a dirty business and that it is better for a man to stick his member into a snake's mouth than into a woman's womb. Then we would've left the court building and the photographer standing outside would've taken a group photo of us, and years later I would've pulled the photograph out of my trunk of Indian memorabilia, and, looking closely at Tsar's smile and at the corners of his eyes, I would've noticed tiny sparks of sarcasm betraying the festive spirit of the occasion. It would've been all documented: Ani Dawa, with her red umbrella and natural smile; Vinnie, with the chessboard sticking out of his rucksack and an expression obscured by his enormous Bavarian mustache;

me, looking trustworthy and concerned, like someone who had just adopted a dozen orphaned Tibetan children; the bride, happy but slightly stunned by the new direction that her Indian adventure had taken; and the groom just being himself—a con artist putting on a new act, a metaphysical clown posing for the grand show of existence.

But I didn't go to Tsar's wedding. When Ani Dawa knocked on my door at eight-thirty in the morning, shouting that I should hurry up, I suddenly felt that I had to make a choice: to attend the morning debates and my lesson with Geshe Yama Tseten, or go with Tsar and watch him perform his latest stunt. The truth was, I knew that Tsar wasn't in love. He'd told me that himself. How was I supposed to respect his decision to marry someone he'd met just a few weeks before? He was taking the easy way out of India, and that was not like him. What had happened to his fiery spirit and his grand metaphysical pronouncements? Was he really going to settle in the U.S. and become an ordinary family man?

"Are you coming?" Ani Dawa asked me, a flower bouquet in hand. I was surprised to see her so excited. She didn't even like Tsar. Why was she going to his wedding, then? Perhaps she thought that she was just carrying out one of her saintly deeds, like cooking food for the sick and donating clothes to the poor. Or maybe she was friends with the bride.

"Come on, Nikola," Tsar called out to me from the front of the taxi minivan. "We have an appointment at the courthouse in Lower Dharamsala."

Vinnie and Samantha waved at me from the back of the car. Samantha was wearing a colorful *chuba*, a traditional Tibetan dress.

"I'm sorry, guys, but I can't miss class today," I told them. "I'll catch up with you later."

If Tsar was upset with me for not going, he didn't show it. He shrugged his shoulders, adjusted his sunglasses, and gestured at Ani Dawa to get back in the minivan.

·　·　·

A FEW WEEKS WENT BY, and Samantha left for the States to hire a lawyer and work on getting Tsar's papers. One night there was a knock on the door; in came Tsar and Vinnie, both drunk and laughing and leaning on each other.

"That was the best part," Vinnie said, bending over and slapping his knees. "'Good-bye, Argentina!' Or no, it was, 'Don't cry for me' . . ."

Tsar climbed on Merry Anne's bed with his shoes on, and pretended to open a window and look down at a gathering of people. "Don't cry for me, Argentina!" he sang with a tragic face, his voice reaching a glass-shattering, operatic vibrato on *Ar-gen-tiii-na!* Then he slipped and fell to the floor, bumping his head against the table.

Merry Anne had never seen Tsar in action before but his reaction wasn't one of surprise: he smiled forgivingly, like an old man passing a group of rowdy teenagers, and continued reading the *I Ching*.

"You've done it twice now," Vinnie observed, sitting at the edge of my bed. "When the scene with Madonna on the balcony came up, Tsar fell off his chair and hit the floor."

"*Choveche*," Tsar said, climbing up from under the table, "forget about Woody Allen and the Monty Pythons. This is the funniest movie that has ever been made."

"I think it's meant as a tragedy," Vinnie noted soberly.

"Bullshit," Tsar bellowed. "It was obvious from the start that they were making fun of everyone. Who in their right mind would produce a serious movie about Evita and her dictator husband?"

"Eva Perón?" Merry Anne asked, putting his book down. When it came to the subject of women, Merry Anne never missed an opportunity to demonstrate his great expertise.

"You know her?" Tsar asked.

"Of course," Merry Anne answered, tossing his hands in search of the right words to describe Evita. "She was . . . uh . . . great . . . wise, yes, wise, and she made . . ."

"She was a fascist whore," Tsar concluded and stuck a cigarette in his mouth.

"They weren't really fascist," Vinnie objected.

"What do you call people who shelter Nazis?" Tsar exploded. "They invited all the German fucking Nazis and gave them houses and pensions."

Vinnie gave a forced laugh, trying to conceal his anger. "They didn't give them pensions."

"How do you know?" Tsar pressed on. "Did your father go to Argentina?"

"You don't know my father," Vinnie replied and touched the side of his face with trembling fingers.

I looked at Merry Anne, thinking that maybe I could ask him about the moon calendar and change the subject, but he was sound asleep, his chin pressed against his chest.

"During the war, your father worked at the German embassy in Tehran," Tsar said and smiled sarcastically. "But I guess that doesn't tell us a lot about who he was as a person."

"You need to apologize!" Vinnie demanded, standing up. "If you don't, I'm leaving!"

They looked at each other for a minute—Vinnie, panting and clenching his fists, and Tsar, smiling and smoking nonchalantly—and then Vinnie stormed out, slamming the door and sending the rats hiding between the roof beams running for their lives, the *tick-tick-tick*ing sound of their nails digging into wood building up to a dramatic drum-solo climax.

"Ah?" Merry Anne said, waking up to a dense cloud of dust descending from the roof.

"We were just talking about the earthquake," Tsar offered.

"Earthquake?" Merry Anne repeated, confused.

Tsar shook his head, as if to chase away a stupid thought, and poured himself a cup of black tea from the thermos. "I don't know what's wrong with people. I don't need to apologize for his father! His father was a fucking Nazi."

"Vinnie's had a hard life," I said. "He's been wandering around Asia practically since the end of the war. That's a long time. And he's recovering from throat cancer."

"That's fine," Tsar replied. "I mean, I like the guy. But he gets drunk and starts acting aggressive."

Without asking, Tsar took Merry Anne's pillow and placed it behind his back. "This room has a lot of potential," he noted, studying the walls and the ceiling. "If you put some work into it, it'd look great. And the location is great, too—you can get to the post office in five minutes. I'm thinking of leaving Gamru village and moving closer to McLeod Ganj. It takes me an hour of walking just to make a phone call or meet someone at a restaurant. I'm so tired of walking up and down these mountains, *choveche*, I want to shoot myself. It's like a nightmare: every morning I have to conquer the same hill, starting from the bottom."

"What about your bread business?" I asked. "Isn't it more convenient for you to live near the library?"

"I'm done with bread," Tsar announced. "Waking up at four o'clock in the morning and going to bed when the sun goes down—that's not a life. All these months I've been working like a slave and I haven't saved a penny. I'm totally broke. By the way, my life in India is coming to an end: Samantha has hired a lawyer and, really, it's probably just a matter of days. I could wake up tomorrow and find all the documents waiting for me in the post office. I just need to survive for a few weeks, that's all."

"We have an extra bed," I said, turning to Merry Anne for approval.

"Yeah," Merry Anne consented, straining to keep his eyes open. "You could take my bed if you want—I mean, if you don't like the one you're sitting on."

Tsar seemed pleased: he put out his cigarette, took his shoes off by the door, and slipped under the moldy afghan covering the empty bed. "I'll bring my stuff tomorrow," he mumbled, his head buried in Merry Anne's pillow.

When I came home from class the next day, the room had been completely transformed: the roof was insulated with a sheet of blue plastic; the walls were covered with thin linoleum—black, with white and yellow flowers—originally intended as a tablecloth; the only lightbulb in the house had been moved from its place above the door and now hung over the table in the middle of the room. The floor was carpeted, the windows were adorned with Tsar's monastic robes, and on the wall above Tsar's bed hung the sign that made Tsar famous: "Bosnian bread! Try it! Only five rupees!"

I looked through the pile of books lying on Tsar's night table and was just about to open his drawing pad when suddenly my eyes started burning and I felt as if the air from my lungs had been sucked out. Crying and choking, I went into the kitchen, where Tsar was stooped over the pressure cooker making his signature dish—beans with chilies, tomatoes, potatoes, and lots of masala. "Good god!" I cried opening the outside door to get some fresh air. "How many chilies did you drop in the pot?"

"Less than half a kilogram," Tsar answered matter-of-factly.

An hour later, Merry Anne returned from the market with a bag of sugar for the tea and the three of us sat down to eat lunch, sweating, cursing, and gasping for breath. I imagined myself with a bleeding ulcer on the way to the hospital in Chandigarh. I imagined how the Indian doctors would explain to me that the acid from the chilies had melted my intestines. "It happens quite often," they would say with a friendly head wobble.

There was a knock on the door and Tsar lifted his hands in the air as if to say *No one moves or says a word!*

"It's probably Lobsang or Purba," he whispered. "They're going to eat everything that's left and we'd have to cook again tonight."

"You can't leave someone, uh, on the street, hungry!" Merry Anne protested and got up to open the door.

Tsar looked at me and shook his head. He couldn't stand philanthropists.

"Here you are!" said Ani Dawa, peeking into the room. "I was waiting for you by the gates of the institute. Where did you go?"

"I must've walked past you," I replied. "I went to class and then came home."

"Ama!" Ani Dawa exclaimed, looking at the walls and the ceiling. "Scary!"

"Why scary?" Tsar asked.

"It just looks strange, all the plastic and the robes hanging over the windows," she explained. "Have you heard from Samantha?"

"I talked to her a few days ago," Tsar said. "She said my documents are almost ready."

Merry Anne brought the plates into the kitchen, tripping repeatedly on the wrinkled carpet, then returned, an apple in hand, and paused to examine the clothesline stretching from the door to the opposite corner of the room. He had the astonishing gift of appearing lost and disoriented even when he was doing something as simple as opening a window, walking to the kitchen and back, or picking up a book. I noticed that Ani Dawa was looking at the metal trunk under Tsar's bed and the "Bosnian bread" sign hanging on the wall. Her face had lost its color and her eyes seemed cold and tired—a clear sign that she was angry about something. Sensing the tension in the air, Tsar placed an empty cup on the table in front of her and offered to pour some tea. Ani Dawa covered the cup with her hand and attempted a smile.

"Is he staying here now?" she asked me in Tibetan.

"Why?" I asked in turn. "Is that a problem?"

"I promised my aunt that I'd take care of things," Ani Dawa said sternly. "This is my responsibility and I can't let it happen. If my aunt found out, it would all be my fault."

"I don't understand what you're talking about," I said. "Is your aunt going to be upset because there are three people living in her house instead of two?"

"That's not it," she replied. "It's him. He can't stay here. He is . . ."

"Are you talking about me?" Tsar interrupted her in English. "Because if you are, I'm right here. It's not very polite to talk about people in their presence."

Tsar placed a cigarette behind his ear and started playing with his lighter, clicking it on and off and adjusting the height of the flame. He hadn't had his after-lunch cigarette and he was waiting for Ani Dawa to leave so that he could light up.

"I was telling Lodro that you can't stay here," Ani Dawa confronted him. "You have to find another room. My aunt made an exception for Lodro because he is studying at the Institute of Buddhist Dialectics and he needs to attend all the debates. Don't get mad. That's just how it is."

"Don't get mad!" Tsar repeated laughing. "Merry Anne is allowed to live in your aunt's house, but I'm not? What do you have against me? What have I done wrong?"

"It's Tibetan culture," Ani Dawa replied, struggling to calm her voice. "This is a very special house. Dalai Lama's residence is next door."

"What does Dalai Lama have to do with it?" Tsar asked, incredulous. "Are you afraid I'm going to jump over the fence and knock on his window?"

Ani Dawa got up, flung her *zen* over her shoulders, and grabbed her bag. "We've known each other for a while. You've made a choice and your life is your life."

"I wish I could understand what you're saying," Tsar told her and stretched his legs so that the soles of his feet pointed at Ani Dawa. Showing the soles of your feet to a Tibetan was a grave offense, on par with placing your shoes on top of a Buddha statue or peeing on a stupa, and Tsar was perfectly aware of that fact.

"One is this one," Ani Dawa announced and took a step back.

Tsar looked at me, expecting that I would intervene on his behalf, but I pretended that I didn't notice and looked away. I didn't want to be caught in the middle of a war between Tsar and Ani Dawa, and so I thought that the best thing for me to do was to sit quietly and look remorseful. I was certain that, in the end, Ani Dawa would calm down and let Tsar stay. The whole thing with Ani Dawa talking in circles and saying things like "One is this one" was—I thought—a way for her to show Tsar that she was in charge and doing him a big favor.

"I'm very curious to hear what you really think about me, Ani-la," Tsar said. "A few weeks ago, you came with me when I was getting married, and you were smiling and laughing and everything was fine. Now I'm not good enough to be in a two-hundred-meter radius of the Dalai Lama."

"People would say things," Ani Dawa replied. "If you got drunk and caused trouble, it would be my fault."

Tsar snickered and rolled his eyes. "Nikola, did you hear this? I love Tibetan logic. It's a good thing they're praying for everyone's Enlightenment."

"I'm going to come back tomorrow," Ani Dawa said and walked to the door. "You should pack your things and look for a new room tonight."

I jumped from my bed and ran after her. She was standing by the side of the road, apparently waiting for me.

"Ani-la, please don't do this. You can't kick Tsar out on the street. He doesn't have anywhere to go."

"You should've asked me if it's okay for Tsar to move in. I'm very disappointed."

"I've never had a problem with my previous landlords. They never cared how many people lived in their rooms. Besides, it's not like we are staying at a hotel. Look at these houses!" I pointed at the lopsided tin-roof shanties lining the narrow pathway that connected Namgyal Monastery to Jogibara Road. "We have to carry water from the Main Temple. The electricity works only two hours at a time. And you should see the rats."

"If Tsar doesn't leave by tomorrow, you and Merry Ann will have to look for another room. That's my final word."

I watched Ani Dawa walk away, unable to find the right words to defend myself. What's the Tibetan word for "ultimatum"? Most probably, there wasn't one. Shaking with anger, I walked back into the house and found Tsar pulling down the blue plastic from the ceiling. Merry Anne was sitting cross-legged on the floor smoking a joint.

"Merry Anne!" I exploded. "You told me you've quit that shit!"

"I just wanted to see what Himalayan hash tastes like," Merry Anne replied with an innocent smile. "Om Giridi gave it to me."

"It's all because she's jealous," Tsar noted as he extracted a nail with a fork. "She just wants you all for herself."

"That's bullshit," I said. "Ani Dawa is like a mother to me."

"Come on, Nikola!" Tsar bellowed. "Grow up! Ani Dawa is just a horny forty-year-old woman who can't get laid, can't marry, and can't have children. So, instead, she builds these obsessive relationships with young monks where she's the mother, and the monks are helpless boys who need someone to take care of them. Before you came, she was taking care of a British monk, what's his name . . ."

"Maybe she's a bodhisattva," Merry Anne suggested.

"Even if you're right about her—and you probably are, to some extent—that doesn't explain why she wants to kick you out," I said to Tsar. "She doesn't seem to care about Merry Anne."

"It's simple," Tsar explained. "In her mind, I'm the devil and I'm going to make you disrobe. And if you disrobe, she'll lose you forever. Think about it: how's she going to compete for your attention if you are screwing two Norwegian chicks at the same time?"

"Why Norwegian, and why two?" Merry Anne inquired, blinking attentively.

I put my money belt in my bag, adjusted my *shanthab*, and grabbed the umbrella propped up by the door. "Don't pull everything down," I told Tsar. "I'm going to go over to Ani Dawa's house and talk to her one more time."

Ani Dawa no longer lived by the Jogibara laundry. She had moved to a windowless fifteen-by-fifteen-foot cell on the ground floor of a newly constructed building above McLeod Ganj. From the outside, the building looked like something that had emerged as a result of a massive excavation project:

the ground floor was buried in mud and rubble, the walls were bare and chipped, and twisted metal rods poked out of the concrete. Monkeys played on the branches of a giant tree whose trunk was integrated into the structure and served as a supporting beam.

I walked through the doorless entrance and immediately got lost. There were many doors, all identical. Then I heard a familiar voice: "Dawa! Dawa, come!" I located the door where the voice was coming from and knocked. "Who is it?" asked Ama-la. "It's Lodro," I replied. "The door won't open," Ama-la said. "I've pushed and pushed."

She was right: the door was stuck. "Are you sure it's not locked from the inside?" I asked her. "It's not locked," Ama-la replied confidently. I put one foot on the wall and pulled as hard as I could. The door snapped open with a loud bang. I had completely destroyed the locking mechanism.

"Is Ani Dawa home?" I asked her. Ama-la came out of what turned out to be the bathroom and toddled down the corridor. "I don't know where Dawa is," she mumbled. "She was home, then she wasn't."

I followed Ama-la to her room and sneaked in behind her. Ani Dawa was standing by the gas stove, sautéing onions and ginger. "Come in!" she told me. "You should stay and have dinner with us."

I slumped in the fold-up chair for guests and looked around the room. There were hardly any changes in the way that everything had been arranged: the two beds met at an angle, separated by a shrine stall; the square table stood in the center of the room; the gas stove, the tub with dirty dishes, and the chopping board were placed on the floor; the frying pans, the ladles, and the long knives hung on the wall; the butter tea mixer collected dust in a corner.

"You never told me why you left your place on Jogibara Road," I said. "The view of the valley was spectacular."

"Mother is getting weaker and weaker," Ani Dawa replied, pouring freshly brewed tea in the thermos. "Here at least we have a bathroom. That's very important for old people."

"True," I agreed.

"You've committed a very big sin, letting your friend Tsar stay in your room," Ama-la interjected, shaking her glass rosary. "He has to get out of there right now."

"Mother, don't," Ani Dawa pleaded. "Lodro knows what to do."

"He's just ungrateful," Ama-la went on. "When have you seen a Tibetan man act like that? We've fed him—*here's chai for you, here's dinner, you want Tibetan lessons, come over tomorrow, you don't need to pay anything*—and this is what we get: he invites that scoundrel Tsar. They are all going straight to hell."

"We'll discuss this later," Ani Dawa told her angrily.

Ama-la got off her bed and opened the trunk where she kept all of her clothes. "I'm telling you, Dawa, it's all going to be your fault in the end, when Tsar does something embarrassing. He has no business living near the Dalai Lama. You can't let a vow breaker live in a temple—he's an evil spirit, and he'll show his face soon, you'll see."

"Evil spirit!" I snickered. "This is all very nice."

"Mother is right," Ani Dawa said, lowering her voice. "Tsar has to move out tonight."

"You can't ask me to kick him out on the street!" I protested. "He doesn't have money for a hotel and there are probably no rooms available. He'll just have to stay until we find a new room for him. Besides, I just paid my next month's rent."

"Then you all have to move out," Ama-la said. "You have no place being near Gyalwa Rinpoche. I know what *Engies* do."

As I sat there, my blood boiling, it occurred to me for the first time that Marx had gotten at least one thing right: religion *was* opium for the people. Religion—as a system of subservience, as a factory spouting hopes, fears, and new, heavier, alter egos—made people stupid. It made them less human.

"This is very strange," I said, turning to Ama-la. "I've seen you recite the prayer about delivering all living beings to Enlightenment, and you care so much about the bugs that you step on while you're out walking around, but when it comes to *Engies*, they are evil spirits and need to be kept away from your precious Dalai Lama. It's good that you're counting your mantras: I'm sure your love and compassion are growing bigger every day. At least the bugs that you squash are going to a better place. That's what Mahayana Buddhism is all about: loving those that you've trampled on."

I paused to gauge the damage that my outburst had caused and concluded, with pleasure, that it was massive. Both Ani Dawa and her mother looked absolutely terrified.

"And I really don't care about your aunt's house," I carried on, shouting. "It's the worst place I've lived in, and it's expensive. I'd much rather live down in the Indian village, with the cows and the donkeys, and the kids running around, far away from the Main Temple and Dalai Lama's residence."

"You should leave now," Ani Dawa said, her lips twitching.

I got up and walked out of the room, glancing at Ama-la with a victorious smile. I was quite proud of myself for defending my dignity and speaking my mind for once. *Fuck the whole two-faced Eastern shit*, I thought. *Fuck religion. Fuck cultural differences and all the fake, petty things that make up people's identities.*

I heard the sound of clapping sandals and turned around: it was Ani Dawa, trying to catch up with me. It made me sad to see her pretty face disfigured by anger and disappointment.

"You should never come to my house again," she yelled. "No one has ever talked to Ama-la like that. No one."

"I'm sorry," I said. "But you are treating Tsar like an animal. How can you pretend that you're Tsar's friend when Samantha is around, and then kick him out—kick all of us out, as a matter of fact. . . ."

"You were like a son to me. I really thought you were special. Now I know: all *Engies* are the same. This is the end between us. Once I make up my mind about something, that's it."

I turned around and walked away. So be it.

"And I want the keys back by five o'clock tonight," she yelled after me. "Or I'm going to come and nail boards over the door."

I kept walking. Kicking stones. Dragging my feet.

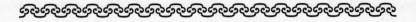

Seventeen

Geshe Yama Tseten opened his eyes and looked out the window. Down in the courtyard an Indian tabla salesman was demonstrating his hand-drumming techniques to a group of monks and Western tourists. The air smelled of rain, burning wood, and potato *tugpa*, the monastery kitchen lunch special.

"So where were we?" Geshe-la asked me, paging through the *pecha* laid out on the table in front of him. "Ishvara? No, we talked about that. What were the twenty-five aspects of knowledge according to the proponents of Ishvara?"

"The One and Only, capacity, pride, the five objects of the senses, the four elements plus space, the five organs—voice, hands, feet, butt, penis . . . and . . . I lost count."

"These people are weird," Geshe-la announced, scrunching his nose. "I've seen them in Varanasi, standing on one leg in the middle of the river."

Geshe-la raised his hands in the air and froze to show me what someone standing on one leg looked like. Then he scooped an imaginary substance from an imaginary bowl and poured it on top of his head, blinking and spitting.

"Human ashes," he explained, as he scooped another handful of the imaginary substance and began applying it to every part of his body. When he finished, he raised his hands again and remained motionless for about two minutes.

"They stand like that for years," Geshe-la went on. "A thousand years from now they are still going to be there, standing on one foot in the middle of the Ganges. They think that if they catch a glimpse of the One, He will get embarrassed and retract all of his apparitions, thus making the universe disappear. This is really crazy. Very crazy."

"Why?" I asked.

"Why! Ha!" Geshe-la jolted backwards and folded his hands over his chest. "Say I am a magician and I just sit around conjuring orange elephants that fly in the sky. One day there is a knock on the door: who is it? It's Lodro. Lodro comes in, drinks all of my butter tea, ruins my floor, and says, 'Geshe-la, I'm tired of looking at your orange elephants floating up there, please take them down right now.' So I take them down"—Geshe-la demonstrated with his hands how a magician retracts his orange elephants—"and then there are no more elephants left. Lodro doesn't see them, Ani Dawa doesn't see them, no one sees them. In the same way, if one saddhu embarrasses the creator deity, and the deity stops doing magic tricks, the world would disappear for everyone, not just for the saddhu. That's very simple."

Geshe Yama Tseten was a master logician with bad knees. He stretched his left leg with a pained expression, and lifted his *shanthab* to show me the swelling around his kneecap.

"I'm going to die soon," he informed me, looking heroic. "My knees are eating me slowly, every day a little . . ." He opened the *pecha* at random and skimmed through the text on the page, squinting. "Yeah, yeah. 'I don't have any quarrels with the world. . . .' This is very profound. Some people went to the Buddha and asked him to resolve their argument. 'I don't argue,' he told them. 'You argue between yourselves; I would side with the winner.'"

"He said that?" I asked, trying to find the page Geshe-la was looking at. "Where is that written?"

Geshe Yama Tseten raised his right arm—in preparation for clapping the palms of his hands in my face—and translated what he'd just said in a debate form: "The subject, Buddha. He doesn't need to argue with the world; all conventional entities exist as mere concepts contrived by an ordinary mind."

"It doesn't follow," I responded mechanically. This was one of the four standard answers in Buddhist debate.

"Bah! It doesn't follow! They taught you a few words at the Institute of Buddhist Dialectics and now you think you can come over and debate with me!"

"It doesn't follow," I repeated belligerently.

"What do you call this?" Geshe-la asked and lifted the metal cap covering his butter tea cup.

"A *momo*," I said, gambling.

"A *momo*, you say? *Kun chog sum*! Get up and open the cooking pot that's on the kerosene stove."

I walked over to the corner of the room and looked inside the pot. It was full of steamed *momos*.

"What's in there?" Geshe-la inquired sarcastically.

"Stones," I said. "Lots of stones."

"You're so . . . so arrogant! Is this how you debate at school? Calling a car a cow, a house a donkey. How will you ever pass your exams?"

"All conventional entities exist as mere concepts contrived by an ordinary mind," I countered, using his argument. "So if I decide that it's a *momo*, it's a *momo*. If I decide it's a stone, it's a stone. You think that Tibet is Tibet. Others think that Tibet is China. No one is right and no one is wrong."

"You think everything is a big joke, and you talk like a fool. One day you're going to wake up"—Geshe-la pretended to wake up, rubbing his eyes and stretching his arms—"and you're going to see them, standing around the room, lying under your bed, hiding in the cupboards."

"See who?" I asked, judging by his facial expression that he was probably talking about the guardians of hell.

"The Chinese," Geshe-la confided with a bitter expression. "They're already here, they're just waiting for the right moment to come out."

"The Chinese? Where would they come from?"

Geshe-la pointed to the floor. "They live under the ground. There are hundreds and hundreds of thousands Chinese people staying under Dalai Lama's residence right now. During the day they sleep. At night they come out and run around the village, stealing chickens and dogs."

Here, Geshe-la transformed himself into a smug Chinese spy. He wiggled out of a hole, inspected the scenery, shielding his eyes from the blinding bright moonlight, and started chasing after what I assumed was a giant chicken. Squeezing the neck of his prey between his fingers, the spy returned to the hole he'd crawled out of and shoved the chicken inside.

"The Chinese don't talk too much," Geshe-la explained. "You go to them: *How are you? How are you. What are you doing?* We're not doing anything. Chinese people are very quiet: they go underground and dig holes. They've dug a hole that begins in Beijing and ends at the gates of Dalai Lama's residence in Dharamsala. They've been digging holes for forty years. The Indians ask them, *Do you want to start a war with us?* We don't want any wars, we want peace. The Indian government is happy: the prime minister lies around, doing nothing. Buses fall off cliffs. Trains crash. Planes crash. Trucks crash. Rickshaws crash. Pregnant Rajasthani women carry bricks and build hotels and tall buildings. Drunk Rajasthani men sit around and play with balloons. Kids run naked and eat stones: everyone's happy. One day you see two Indian soldiers sitting outside a chai shop by the bus station. They talk: *It's pleasant.* It is. *It rains all the time.* It rained yesterday as well. *My wife is fat.* My wife is fat, too. Suddenly, they notice something strange: everywhere they look, the streets are filled with Chinese people. Hundreds and hundreds of thousands. The soldiers stand up and wave their hands: *What are you doing here? This is not your country!* The Chinese say nothing: they go about their business."

Geshe Yama Tseten went on like this for another half an hour. He told me about the time when the Dalai Lama had crossed from Tibet into India, trailed by a dozen donkeys carrying all of Tibet's gold and diamonds. He claimed that in Tibet there were people who could make special amulets that had the power to stop bullets. He said that if you wore such an amulet and the Chinese started shooting at you, you'd be able to see the bullets dropping by, making a *ding-ding* sound. I asked him if he'd worn an amulet when he'd crossed the Chinese-Indian border thirty years ago; he looked at me like I was out of my mind and said, "Of course." In fact, he'd worn two amulets: one that had offered protection from bullets, and one that had been designed to pacify Himalayan bears. Unfortunately, the anti-bear amulet hadn't been of much use because instead of bears Geshe-la had encountered another, significantly more vicious animal equipped with large teeth, sharp claws, and a long tail. Geshe-la couldn't remember the name of the beast, but he was certain that it wasn't a leopard, a snow lion, a vulture, a snake, a cat, a dog, or a crocodile. Determined to identify the animal that had attacked him eight thousand feet above sea level, he pulled down the large, illustrated encyclopedia of marine life from the bookshelf next to his bed, opening it in the middle. Aside from being his only source of information on animals and the diversity of species, the encyclopedia of marine life was also Geshe-la's most treasured book. Some days he spent hours staring at the glossy photos of sea turtles, bloated porcupine fish, and bright-colored sea anemones. He had never seen the ocean.

"I don't think we're going to find the animal that you're thinking of in this book," I observed, blinking politely.

"What does this say?" Geshe-la asked, pointing at the caption under a photograph of a manatee.

"*Trichechus manatus,*" I mumbled.

"What does it mean?"

"I don't know," I told him. "It's in Latin. Latin is an old language."

"So you don't know English," Geshe Yama Tseten concluded with disappointment. "You don't know Tibetan, and you don't know English."

I didn't argue with him. It was time for me to go.

"What was her name, the nun who taught you Tibetan?" Geshe-la asked me as I opened the door.

"Ani Dawa," I said.

Geshe-la grimaced and shook his head. "What happened between the two of you?"

"We had a fight," I explained. "She didn't let my friend, the Bosnian guy, stay at the room that I had rented from her aunt. So we all moved out."

"I heard," he said, digging out his wooden hand for back-scratching from under his pillow. Looking out the window fiercely, he rubbed the middle of his spine and then turned to me, piercing my eyes with all his metaphysical might. Standing paralyzed in the door frame, I waited to be crushed. There was nothing that I could say in my defense. I had crossed the line and had acted disrespectfully. I was an arrogant *Engie* who deserved a cruel punishment. I had to return to *Engie* Land, where everyone was monkey-smart and only cared about external things.

"She's weird," Geshe-la said after a long silence. "Really weird."

Eighteen

It had been raining nonstop for nine days. Our bedsheets smelled of fungus, and the mud surface of the northern wall had started to get soft. We imagined that by the end of the monsoons, our new home—a two-room mud structure on Jogibara Road that we had rented, reluctantly, the day after Ani Dawa had ordered us out of her aunt's house—would turn into a pile of Play-Doh and we'd be able to reshape it into a pyramid or a spaceship, depending on our mood. Not for the first time, I had to evacuate Mona Lisa—a nine-foot nacreous green snake that lived in a secret location around our kitchen and was in the habit of venturing boldly through the house, in search of rats and lizards. This time, I almost got killed. Merry Anne kept running back and forth between the kitchen and the bedroom with a bundle of garlic, and when I finally lost it and yelled at him to sit on his stupid ass, Mona Lisa coiled up and sprang forth, whereupon I dropped both umbrellas and ran out of the house, slamming my head against the door's upper threshold, which was how I ended up with an orange-size swelling above my forehead. And, just as usual, Tsar did absolutely nothing to help the situation. He remained comfortably seated on his bed, playing solitaire, smoking, and cursing his Bosnian luck.

"Tsar," I said to him, "Mona Lisa is in the kitchen again. We can't make dinner and we can't boil water for chai."

"Snakes don't bite people," Tsar replied in the tone of someone who had watched a lot of shows on *Animal Planet*. "That's common knowledge. And, by the way, someone has to go next door and borrow a cup of sugar."

The three of us had very different ideas about what we should do with Mona Lisa. Tsar's approach was: let's not do anything about it and pretend it's not there. Merry Anne agreed with Tsar about leaving the snake alone, but believed that we had to exercise caution and protect ourselves—hence, the bundles of garlic and the Sanskrit spells hidden in the wall crevices near his bed. My approach was openly xenophobic. Upon spotting Mona Lisa, I would rush in with two long umbrellas, lift her tail with the tip of one umbrella and her head with the tip of the second umbrella, drop her into a bucket, and then carry the bucket outside—using the umbrellas again to keep the bucket away from my face. This evacuation technique, while relatively safe and easy to execute, had two flaws: one, Mona Lisa always returned, and two, every time I kicked her out of the house, I only increased my chances of getting bitten when I was asleep. Consequently, I had a recurrent nightmare where I'd dream of waking up to the cold caress of the green snake as it slithered across my naked stomach. Realizing that it was too late to run, I'd lie still, holding my breath, for what seemed like hours.

There was a second snake, a small gray one, but we saw it only once a week or so, and we didn't count it as one of the permanent members of the household. The snakes, of course, were primarily interested in rats, and the house that we had rented on Jogibara Road happened to be one of the most populous rat shelters in the entire village. This was perhaps due to the fact that the previous tenant of the house, an old Tibetan man from Kham, had insulated the bare slate roof tiles with a sheet of tarpaulin, thus creating a cozy cavity where the rats bred, ran wild, and planned raids on the food supplies in the kitchen. The most prominent, and certainly fattest, member of the rat society was a cat-size elder who would often descend through a slit in the tarpaulin at around nine o'clock at night and venture through the bedroom for no other reason than to see how we, the humans, were holding up. One night, we had just turned the light off and begun to doze when we heard a loud screech, followed by what sounded like a cat descending a wall. Suddenly, the light was on again, and Tsar and I were up, staring at the rat elder, who was staring back at us from the small table next to the light switch across the room. Merry Anne didn't witness the miracle. He had fallen asleep much earlier, right after Tsar had decided to share with us his theory on the space travels of the second-century Indian alchemist and logician Nagarjuna.

"Yebem li te," Tsar greeted the rat elder and threw his shoe at it. It was a close shot, but the rat looked unperturbed. "Who is this guy?" I asked, rhetorically, and Tsar replied, "Thomas Edison." So it was decided. Being a lover of electricity, Thomas Edison successfully chewed through the cable powering the lightbulb in the kitchen, which prompted Tsar to install a new, thicker cable that ran along the wall for easier maintenance. Slowly, we grew fond of Thomas Edison and began to worry that sooner or later Mona Lisa would get to him and we'd never see his fearless pink eyes again. We watched the long snake slide above our heads, its body drawing spirals and wavy lines in the tarpaulin. We cringed as dozens of tiny rat feet in groups of four scattered to the corners of the room, leaving the snake in the middle. We knew what happened next: there was a jump, a short scuffle, and a near-ultrasonic yelp signaling the beginning of the end. We imagined Thomas Edison's ass sticking out of Mona Lisa's mouth. It was too much for us. Taking into account the strategic importance of the tarpaulin sheet, we decided that our best tactic for saving the lives of Thomas Edison and the members of his extended family was to make it impossible for Mona Lisa to launch a surprise attack. All we had to do was pound a few times on the tarpaulin sheet and, if necessary, give Mona Lisa a slap from below. After some practice, we developed a kind of volleyball where Tsar would push Mona Lisa back toward the kitchen with light punches and I would toss the rats in the opposite direction. Merry Anne, for his part, would supervise the action from his bed and offer

directions: "To the left! Right behind you! She's coming down the left flank!" Once, Tsar punched Mona Lisa a little too hard and she flew over the wall and landed all the way into the kitchen, right above the kerosene stove. We poked her through the tarpaulin, to make sure she was okay, and then watched as she reluctantly exited the house. Our tactics were working. We were going to teach Mona Lisa nonviolence. We'd make her a vegetarian.

In addition to the rats, snakes, and lizards, our house was also a home to praying mantises, crabs who'd scurry sideways and then freeze, as if struck by a major realization, kamikaze beetles who'd dive into your plate of dal with the ascending roar of a crashing fighter jet, moths big enough to cover a light-bulb, glowworms, woodworms, fireflies, bedbugs, earwigs, book lice, red ants, black ants, grasshoppers, flies, fleas, and five-, six-, seven-, and eight-legged fist-size spiders with fluorescent eyes, who'd eat each other and hide cotton balls filled with baby arachnids in the cracks of the walls. One time, Tsar knocked one cocoon down by accident and Merry Anne spent the entire day chasing after the microscopic things with a cotton-stuffed matchbox in hand and a Mother Teresa look on his face. Scorpions were also a frequent nag, but they were easy to catch and looked quite benevolent once dropped in a pot filled with water.

As it happened, our new room was located right next door to Ani Dawa's old house, and I often found myself climbing the three stairs and pulling at the small, rusty padlock. I felt that if I could somehow get the padlock to open, I would walk into the house and find everything the way it had been two and a half years ago, when I had met Ani Dawa for the first time. I would see Ama-la sitting cross-legged on her bed, holding a teacup in one hand and a glass rosary in the other. An oil lamp would light the back left corner and cast elongated shadows on the uneven mud wall, illuminating Manjushri's sword of discrimination, a cone, a flower. I would take my sandals off and feel the cold earthen floor. Passing by the rack of spices, I would notice an old photograph of Ani Dawa from the time when she'd still lived in a nunnery. One of Mr. Chandradas's grandkids would start crying outside and I would turn around and look at the small shrine at the far end of the courtyard, where the orange clay statues of Shiva, Wife, and Son—defaced by the incessant rains and garnished with dried-up dandelions—marked the burial place of a now forgotten nineteenth-century Hindu saint. And somewhere in the middle of taking in the strong smell of cinnamon and cumin, and hearing the child's cry, I would slump into the fold-up chair and feel like I had come home.

I found it disconcerting that Ani Dawa had taken the door curtain with her when she'd moved to the new building in McLeod Ganj. Without it, her old house seemed incomplete, as if it were missing a roof. Through the tiny barred window, the space inside appeared even smaller than during the time when it had been crammed with furniture and cooking paraphernalia. How could such an uninviting and miserable den once have been so full of life?

A lot had happened in two and a half years. I was no longer the naïve novice monk who thought that the key that unlocked the absolute was hidden in an old Tibetan book half-eaten by book lice and buried in somebody's basement. It had taken me some time to realize that one didn't have to be particularly bright to memorize texts and debate emptiness. It had also taken me a while to see that if there was a truth square enough to support the sprawling edifice of a particular doctrine, then it probably wasn't a truth at all. I had begun to notice the ramparts and fortifications of man-made dogma, at first elusive and obfuscated by abstract nouns and promises of transcendental states of perception, and then increasingly more visible and familiar. With so many people claiming ownership of the truth, it wasn't hard to conclude that it wasn't the truth being a plurality; rather, it was the human factor, the archetype of appropriation that was responsible for turning every piece of knowledge—profound or mundane—into a chewable, easily digestible entity that could be distributed to others like a pharmaceutical drug, with a price tag and a dizzying array of side effects. That said, I was convinced that a trace of the Absolute, unspoiled by rules and categories, still remained out there, lurking in the background like an aftertaste from a distant memory without a shape, color, or any descriptive characteristics. I noticed it when I sat next to the bespectacled leper begging outside the sandalwood shop behind the bus stop. There was something about his smile and the way he bowed down to every person going down the street—lowering his head, closing his eyes, and touching his forehead with his fingerless hand. I noticed it when I saw the prettiest Tibetan prostitute walk out of a hotel room holding a flower. I noticed it when Geshe Yama Tseten lost his train of thought and started talking about the wondrous life of sea turtles (did I know that the Buddha had turtle feet?) and when Tsar expounded his theories on thermodynamics and claimed, among other things, that the moon was invented by the Chinese for the sake of setting up the moon calendar and that the camel was invented by the Egyptians in 1502 B.C. I noticed it when I walked hand in hand with the Blind Man, a former engineer from New Delhi with a noble face and a dignified stride who had unexpectedly turned completely blind at forty and had decided to move to Dharamsala to attend the Buddhist lectures offered year-round. He would stand at a corner, holding out his right hand as if waiting to introduce himself, and repeat the name of his destination—quietly, and with no urgency. "Post office. Post office." Whenever I had a chance, I'd take his hand and we would begin a slow journey through the crowded streets, stepping aside to let cows, rickshaws, and Tata Motors trucks pass by. Our conversation was exactly the same every single time. "The weather," the Blind Man would begin, "what is it like?" "Dark gray cumulous clouds stretching to the horizon," I would answer, trying to be somewhat descriptive. "I see," he would say. Long pause. "Have we walked together before?" he would inquire. "Yes. I'm the Western monk." "I see." Long pause. "The dharma," he would say, "I listen to a lot of dharma talks. It is strange." "It is," I'd agree. "Do you understand it?" he'd ask, wearily. "No," I'd confess. "Except when they talk about emptiness," he'd go on. "I can't see anything as it is." Long pause. "It is strange, going somewhere," he'd observe. "It is," I'd agree. He'd clutch my hand eagerly, like a child. I'd leave him in front of the post office. He wouldn't go in; he'd wait for me to go away, then catch another ride and wait somewhere else.

· · ·

IT WAS JUNE, and I was sitting in Om Restaurant watching Tsar slaughter Vinnie in a fifth consecutive game of chess. Vinnie's face and neck were red, and he was having a hard time moving his pieces without knocking Tsar's down. "*Scheisse!*" he exploded and threw his king on the floor. Tsar extended his hand, but Vinnie ignored him and covered his face. "Why do you have to throw your pieces all over the restaurant every time you lose?" Tsar asked playfully. Panting and cursing in German, Vinnie turned around and waved at the Tibetan waitress. "Lemon-ginger-honey tea," he ordered and crawled under the nearby table to retrieve his king. Realizing that while reaching for the king, he'd managed to stick his head between a woman's knees, Vinnie stood up abruptly, banging his head on the table, and held the chess piece to prevent a possible misunderstanding. "What on earth were you doing down there?" shouted the assailed woman, presumably British. Vinnie stared at her for a moment, then turned to Tsar and me and gestured uncontrollably at the fogged-up windows. "Everyone's mad!" he roared. "Everyone is *ma-a-a-ad!*"

Game number six began, and for the third time that day Tsar opened up with the King's Gambit.

Vinnie was fuming. "I can't stand this opening," he said. "It's just the ugliest position on the board, aesthetically speaking."

"There's nothing aesthetic about chess," Tsar countered. "It's war."

"Even at war, there are aesthetic considerations to be made," Vinnie observed, and both Tsar and I looked at him, demanding an explanation.

At that moment Kamal, the STD owner, walked in and beckoned for Tsar to follow him. "My wife is calling," Tsar announced smugly, and left the table. I sat in his chair and studied the position on the board. Vinnie had two hanging pieces and was certain to lose both of them in the next few moves.

"Tsar seems to think that he could leave India," Vinnie noted somberly. "But he's wrong! None of us will ever leave this place. Other people, tourists, they will come and go." He looked at the British woman who had yelled at him, and nodded. "You and I and Tsar, we are going to be here till the end. I've tried to escape before. Many times. I was in Singapore. I went back to Germany. And now I'm here again, and this time I'm going to stay until I die. Hopefully, I will expire in the bathtub while showing my secret moves to a young frau with golden hair. Don't cry for me, Argentina!"

Vinnie laughed and stomped his feet, jolting backwards and forward with great force. He knew other people were watching him, and whenever that happened, he invariably started acting as if he were onstage and everyone had paid to see his incredible performance.

"You don't even have a bathtub," I reminded him. "And you should really calm down. Do you know that the Tibetans call you Pala Nyumba, the Crazy Grandfather?"

"Grossvater? After initiating their daughters in the great French oral tradition, they dare call me Grossvater?"

Pretending to be profoundly saddened by this news, Vinnie sighed and turned to the British woman, as if to seek reassurance. He shaped his hand into a spider, placed it at the very back of his head, and began moving his fingers forward—creating the impression of a spider who was groping around, examining its environment. A minute passed, and Vinnie stared, transfixed, at the British woman, seemingly oblivious of the hand-spider that was crawling on top of his head and probing his ears. Suddenly, the hand-spider began inching down his forehead and then moved over his eyes, at which point Vinnie gave a horrified shout, swept all the chess pieces on the floor, and placed his hands over his chest. Now he was experiencing a cardiac arrest and choking, and so I pulled a Tibetan book out of my bag and pretended to read. I knew from experience that the more attention you paid to him, the more he invested in his performance. "Lodro!" he called out. "*Lod . . . hr-r-r-r. Ro . . . hr-r-r-r.*" I looked at him: he was clearly suffocating. His face was blue, his tongue was hanging down his chin, and his eyes were rolled up in his head. "*Hr-r-r-r . . . kh-kh-kh.*" I squinted harder at the Tibetan words. I just had to act as if I wasn't with him. The British woman and her companions got up

and left. The guests sitting at the table behind us followed suit. "I shall hear
again in heaven!" Vinnie shouted after them and continued to die. Out of
the corner of my eye I noticed a group of monks sitting at the opposite end of
the dining room. One of them was a senior teacher at the Institute of Buddhist Dialectics. I was just planning to run out when I saw Tsar walking back
into the restaurant, pushing the door open with his umbrella. He slumped
heavily in the chair next to me and tossed his smoldering cigarette into the
ashtray. "When he was dying," Vinnie said with a cheerful expression,
"Beethoven turned to his friends and assured them that he would hear
again in heaven. He had written and performed all of his late works completely deaf."

Tsar put a new cigarette in his mouth and froze, just as he was about to
slide the matchstick across the striking surface. "I don't know what's wrong
with everyone. What does it mean when a woman says to you, 'We should
start seeing other people'?"

"It means that she wants to have sex with many different people and she
wants you to do the same so that she doesn't feel bad about it," Vinnie
explained with the authority of a relationship expert.

"I know what it means," Tsar snapped. "What I don't understand is the
politeness. *I really love you, and I always will, but I'm going to see other people
because you're in India and I'm in Hawaii.* Why not say, 'This was a huge disaster. Good-bye.'"

"What's going on?" I asked him.

"I just told you," Tsar replied. "Everything went to Pichku Materinu."

Vinnie nodded with understanding. "Would you like to play another
game?"

Tsar didn't respond. He lit his cigarette and looked out the window,
squinting. His eyes were dark and dry, his faced puffed up, and the movements of his right hand—flicking the ashes in the ashtray, spinning the
matchbox, aligning the pack of India Kings with the corners of the table—
seemed almost artificially precise. He was calculating his next moves. He

didn't have money. He didn't have a passport. His American wife had dumped him. His country had been erased from the map and his relatives had fought on opposite sides in the war. He was nearing forty and he was stuck in the Himalayas, playing chess and passing time with a German and two Eastern Europeans. What was he going to do?

"I thought she was working on getting your papers ready," I said after a while.

"Her lawyer told her that my case is hopeless," Tsar explained. "That's why she's thinking about *other people*. She's just practical."

"So how did your conversation end?" I asked.

Tsar put out his cigarette and shrugged his shoulders. "I hung up."

"On the bright side," Vinnie observed, "she will never be able to remarry. She'll have to come back to India, file for a divorce, explain to the judge how she'd gotten married to someone whose passport had expired prior to the date on the marriage certificate, then the police will open an investigation into a possible bribery of a government official, and once the case has been transferred to a higher court, she'll have to wait ten years before she hears anything about it."

Tsar got up and left the restaurant without saying a word. I ran after him, leaving Vinnie to pick up the scattered chess pieces from the floor by himself. Outside it was pouring so hard that the open sewers had overflowed and a powerful, ankle-deep stream ran down the main street, cascading over ossified heaps of rubbish, sacks of vegetables, and toppled carts. Tsar and I huddled under one umbrella, our feet covered with water, and watched as a group of bewildered backpackers descended from a government bus and started wading upstream.

"Two and a half years ago," Tsar reminisced, "I stepped off this same bus and thought that I'd finally arrived home. I imagined myself sitting in a cozy room in some monastery and thinking all day about the origin of things. Then I found out that the Tibetans don't let Western monks stay at their monasteries for free, and I was broke. If I had known what I know now, I would've made a quick loop around town and jumped back on the bus."

"And gone where?" I asked.

"That's a good point," Tsar admitted. "I had nowhere to go."

WE DRANK HOT APPLE CIDER in the restaurant overlooking the bus stop, expecting that eventually Vinnie would find us. He didn't. After the rain had subsided, we went to the nearest movie shack and walked into a screening of *Evita*. We laughed hysterically for an hour, then the videotape jammed and the Video Operator kicked us out, telling us that we had ruined the movie for everyone—meaning the other two people who'd attended the screening. Walking past the post office on our way home, Tsar stopped and smiled deviously. He asked me to lend him some money, and I did. He said that he was going to let his white horses run loose tonight. I gathered he was going to the whorehouse.

Nineteen

In a time of crisis, people often sit down and write long letters to their benefactors and to certain individuals in a position of power. Facing a life term in India and realizing that we were on the verge of total financial collapse, Tsar decided to compose a series of letters that would inform the outside world of his dire situation. Sitting cross-legged on his bed, and armed with a tattered edition of Omar Khayyám's *Rubaiyat* and a copy of Steven Hawking's *A Brief History of Time*, which appeared to have been left out in the rain for at least a month, Tsar dictated the text of his letters, speaking in a low, authoritative voice and taking long pauses to relight his *biddie*. I sat on the bed opposite his, pad and pen in hand, and wrote everything down. (Tsars and kings seldom write their own letters; they have scribes.) Merry Anne, for his part, occupied the middle bed, tossed I Ching coins, and announced the key characteristics of the resultant hexagrams.

The first letter that Tsar started working on was addressed to Kaila, his Israeli ex-girlfriend. Here's how the letter began:

"Dear Kaila. The tiger sleeps in the forest bereft of valediction."

After vociferous protests on my part, Tsar consulted Omar Khayyám, looked up a word in his pocket Serbian-English dictionary, and offered a correction: *"The tiger sleeps in the forest*—comma—*bereft and full of valediction."*

Reluctantly, I wrote it down. It was his letter, not mine.

"On top of the mountains, under the sky," Tsar went on, tossing his hair backwards, *"white horses venture unconcerned.* Nikola, leave some empty space and start below. By the way, this is called an exposition. Now write: *How long has it been since the tiger slept in your bracelet arms? How long since I let my white horses run over your fevered body? Sitting here in this darkened room I see the walls of old Jerusalem. I don't know the way henceforth. The white horses are taking me to you, leaping with the strength of a hundred thirsty elephants. I climb the Wall of Tears and look down at the artifacts. Where is your long hair? Where are your notable spheres? The white horses know. I gallop without a rest. I am a lone tiger, splendid with stupefaction. More rocks. More houses. It is getting dark. Is this your window? I look inside. By the way, I found a book about time. It is very interesting because the author doesn't know anything about time. He just sat down and wrote whatever came to his mind—black holes, quarks, quantum fluff, all kinds of fantagorisms. It is obvious to me that the Past, the Present, and the Future exist simultaneously. Everything has already happened, and everything is yet to happen—how is that difficult to understand?"* Tsar took a long drag and opened *The Rubaiyat* at random. *"But my white horses are treading a road of darkness. The tiger is scrunching his whiskers. The black hole is closing. Nikola and I live together now. We haven't eaten anything in three days because we ran out of money due to inexplicable circumstances. Do you remember Norbulingka? There was a storm and my white horses jumped out, ripping my monastic robes to little strings. And then we rode together and the tiger roared—semantically speaking.* Nikola, why are you looking at me like that?"

"Well," I said, "I just wonder what Kaila is going to think when she gets this letter. All the stuff about tigers and white horses—it's a little too much."

"It's called poetry," Tsar explained. "Poetry means metaphor. Everybody knows that. Leave some empty space and write: *P.S. Are you still working for the humanitarian organization?"*

I handed Tsar the notepad and he read the letter out loud, laughing at his own wit. "Notable spheres! Kaila is going to like that."

He folded the letter, placed it in an envelope, and licked the envelope sealed: letter number one was ready to go. We took a break and made a fresh pot of Darjeeling, even though it was two o'clock in the morning and we'd consumed enough caffeine to last us for three days. Wrapped up in our afghans, we sipped the tea and listened to Yanki—an adorable three-year-old Tibetan girl who lived next door with her grandparents—cough with the ferocity of someone who has been administered poison gas. She coughed all night, every night, and Tsar and I were worried that she was entering an advanced stage of tuberculosis. Her grandparents refused to take her to the hospital for tests and insisted on treating her with traditional Tibetan medicine.

IT WAS RAINING, but we could still see the full moon through our tiny skylight—a paradox that Tsar attributed to the peculiar behavior of the autonomous, low-flying Himalayan clouds. (Our skylight, I should mention, consisted of a jagged piece of Plexiglas that Tsar had inserted in the place of a broken slate tile, after cutting a small opening into the overhanging tarpaulin sheet.) Having finished writing down the last set of hexagrams, Merry Anne put away his Chinese coins in a green silk purse and paged through the *I Ching*. "Six in the fourth place," he read, bewildered by the profound prophecy that followed, "means that you will find a . . . friend. He plays the drum, then he doesn't. He cries. He sings."

"*Choveche*, you're really going to kill me!" Tsar shouted and burst out laughing. "You toss coins all night just to read some nonsense from a book that no one understands. *He plays the drum, then he doesn't*. Leave the Chinese alone. If you want to know the future, you should ask me: I'll tell you everything."

Offended by Tsar's lack of appreciation for the coded writings of Lao-tzu,

Merry Anne got off his bed, slipped his hand under his mattress—as if to search for the origin of an annoying bump—and drifted in the direction of the door, a misunderstood mystic leaving the world of ordinary beings.

"Have you noticed that every time Merry Anne decides to go pee, he takes something from under his mattress?" Tsar asked, as we listened to Merry Anne jumping over puddles out in the courtyard. Propelled by a sudden realization, Tsar pushed the table to the middle of the room and lifted Merry Anne's mattress. Underneath, covering the entire surface of the bed frame, lay flattened bundles of ganja shoots—some noticeably drier than others. "This explains why our room smells like a tomb full of mummies," Tsar observed. "For a long time I thought that there were dead rats rotting on the roof."

When Merry Anne returned from his midnight stroll fifteen minutes later—wet, bright-eyed, and with a touch of unusual swiftness in his movements—Tsar and I said nothing of our discovery. Instead, we started questioning him about the progress of his thesis on the Madhyamaka school of thought.

"I haven't started writing anything yet," Merry Anne confessed, "but I've found a book—a big one, it's in the Tibetan Library."

"You know," Tsar said with a conspiratorial look on his face, "a Tibetan master once told me that if you layer fifty kilograms of ganja under your mattress, Nagarjuna will visit you in your dreams and explain everything that you need to know about Madhyamaka."

"Really?" Merry Anne cried out and looked at both Tsar and me with a newfound understanding of the world.

Tsar and I nodded. Really.

It started raining harder and the massive water bubble that had formed in the center of the tarpaulin sheet began to drip. Tsar went into the kitchen and returned with an empty bucket. We endured the sound of raindrops hitting the bottom of the bucket for about two minutes, then decided that it was too depressing and put the bucket away. The carpet was already wet and reeked of mold. I stacked up the looseleaf Tibetan books that I had spread out on the table earlier in the night, removed the tablecloth, and placed everything in a shrine-size wall cavity that was relatively dry. Tsar, for his part, yanked the thumbtacks holding the four corners of the large world atlas covering the wall above his bed, folded the atlas, and wiped the black fungus that had grown on the wall's surface with a rag. It was two months after we had first moved in, and the dark blue paint that had originally covered the walls was now completely washed out and replaced by stains of water seepage.

Mona Lisa was out hunting again, and Tsar quickly pushed her back into the kitchen, punching the soaked tarpaulin sheet and cursing the snake's relatives in Serbian. In five hours I was going to be sitting in class at the institute and Tsar and I still had a lot of work to do before we could go to sleep. I pumped the kerosene stove, placed a fresh pot of water to boil, and went out in the rain to pee. Standing no more than a foot past the front door, I tried to make out the silhouette of the mountains across the river. Dipped in the phosphorescent monsoon fog, the objects of the material world seemed less tangible, less coherent. At night the Himalayas appeared somehow smaller and ethereal, almost fake. I imagined hiking to the highest ridge and taking a peek at what lay on the other side: I'd see a decrepit stage set with a few projectors, steps leading nowhere, and some hollow ramps. A half-naked demiurge smeared in human ashes would lie asleep on the ground, hugging a script and a rusty trident.

Back in the kitchen to strain the tea, I spotted a translucent cylindrical coil stretching across the middle of the room. Mona Lisa had left us her skin. "We forced her to become vegetarian and she died," Merry Anne concluded, straining to keep his eyes open, and dropped the snake skin in the trash can. We filled our cups with tea and returned to our beds.

"Top right corner: *To the attention of the Secretary of the Indian Ministry of Home Affairs*." Tsar lit a *biddie* and stared at the ceiling. In the month since he had broken up with Samantha, his hair and his beard had turned almost entirely gray and the wrinkles around his eyes had deepened. He played chess only once or twice a week and spent most of his time wandering through town and reading books that he found lying around chai shops and restaurants.

"Leave some space and begin in the middle of the page: *Dear sir! Unmistakenly, and without a reasonable doubt, for you this is just another busy morning in the Great City of New Delhi. The old Indian sun hangs above the Red Fort like a maggot. Fantagorismic, rainbow bubbles hatch from the yellow waters of the mighty Yamuna river and fling into the sky. Connaught Place is bustling with vendors who sell toy boats that can turn into flashlights, screwdrivers, knives, cooling fans, and umbrellas. Some citizens ride on scooters. Others lie frozen on the sidewalk. This is the edge of the Rajasthani desert, and the nights are cold and unflinching.* New paragraph: *You may begin to wonder why I have thus decided to acquaint you with my problems. My story is like a one-trick horse. I left my home town Sarajevo a few days before the outbreak of the Bosnian war and traveled to Germany, where I spent a year studying German in a refugee camp. After the German government denied my asylum petition, I went to the Netherlands, where I spent another year in a refugee camp. That time I studied Dutch and English. After leaving the Netherlands, I disembarked in Nepal and then came to India to become a Buddhist monk. This is most straightforward.*" Tsar threw a pencil at Merry Anne to make him stop snoring, lit a new *biddie*, and consulted Stephen Hawking's book on time. "*Unwarranted circumstances such as thieves and abrupt conjunctivitis prevented me from keeping my passport and now I reside in the Great Bharat illegally. You may wonder why you need to help a person who isn't your friend or relative. I offer a few reasons. Recent findings in genetics, plate tectonics, and quantum physics have provided tantalizing facts that no living organism on this planet can ignore any longer. First, it is now known that all human beings have descended from a single deranged female ape affected with bipedalism who had lived in South Africa ten million years ago. Second, all continents and islands have once been part of a single blemish of hardened lava. And third, all the planets, stars, and black holes in our universe have emerged from a single quark invented by a mathematician living in a parallel universe. In other words, we are all brothers and sisters who have been born in the same country and live a life which is an optical illusion.*"

Tsar went on to describe his life in India—making omelets for his first landlord, selling Bosnian bread in front of the Tibetan library, and studying the writings of the Great Bharatian sage Nagarjuna—and ended the letter with a plea to be granted Indian citizenship.

"What are my chances?" he asked me after he'd read the entire letter out loud for the second time.

"Zero," I admitted. "Then again, this is India. Miracles do happen."

I told him a story I'd once heard about a Westerner who'd saved the life of a high-ranking Indian government official and had received an Indian passport as a gift, and Tsar scribbled something in his notebook and announced that this was something we should look into. "You're still very young," Tsar informed me, squinting and pushing the smoke from his *biddie* away from his eyes, "but sooner or later you'll realize that you can make people do anything for you—you just need to know which string to pull. Like that Western guy who'd gotten a brand-new passport. We need to find the name and the address of the governor of Himachal Pradesh. What are his habits? What does he read? How does he like his samosa? These are the things we should be thinking about."

We played Battleship until five o'clock in the morning, and when we finally decided to go to sleep, our landlord turned on his tofu-making apparatus and awoke the entire neighborhood. Tsar and I had never seen the tofu-making apparatus, but judging by the puffing and banging sounds and the tremors it caused within a fifty-foot radius, we'd concluded that it was most likely powered by a steam engine.

I dreamed that I'd been sent to the Red Fort in New Delhi to prove to a gathering of high-ranking government officials that Tsar deserved to be granted Indian citizenship. Everything happens simultaneously, I argued. Therefore, Tsar needs to receive an Indian passport. Remembering that I was a Buddhist monk skilled in the art of logic, I rephrased my thesis in a debate format: given the subjects past, present, and future, it follows that they exist simultaneously, because outside the realm of perception, there's no such thing as slow and fast. I elaborated: without the mind watching, would the world wait before it unwinds to the end of all ends? If it doesn't wait, would it unwind slow or fast? If it doesn't unwind slow or fast, and it doesn't wait, then where would the world be? In the past, the present, or the future? The high-ranking government officials weren't getting it and so I resorted to a more colloquial style of rhetoric. How can you explain the fact that the camel was invented by the Egyptians in 1502 B.C.? They couldn't. I concluded our discussion by performing Chopin's Ballad No.2 in F major on a grand piano the size of an accordion, and as I raced through the final section, where both hands start at opposite ends of the keyboard and converge in the middle, my *zen* collapsed, and I had to finish off abruptly, with an improvised cadenza.

The alarm clock went off at eight-thirty, and when I opened my eyes I saw Merry Anne standing by the door, trying to hang the small mirror we all used for shaving back on the wall. Lifting both of his feet in the air, Tsar flew off his bed, grabbed the razor from the metal cup where he kept his pens and pencils, took the shaving mirror off the wall, and stormed out of the room, spitting and singing "Don't cry for me, Argentina!" I put on my *shanthab* and joined Tsar at the communal spout up the street. He shaved, I brushed my teeth.

"See you, guys," Merry Anne said as he walked by, hands in his pockets, a beaded cylindrical rucksack strapped to his shoulders.

"Are you going to attend the Introduction to Buddhist Hells at the Tibetan Library?" Tsar shouted after him.

"Actually . . ." Merry Anne turned around, for a moment seeming as if he was on the verge of having an epiphany. "Yeah."

"What are you doing up so early?" I asked Tsar.

He made a few last touches to his sideburns and rinsed his razor. "I'm going to take a stroll, look at the nuns, meet some new people. Go to the post office—that's what I'm going to do first. New day, new luck, as they say back where I come from."

"You're not seriously going to send those two letters, are you?"

Tsar looked deeply offended. "Why shouldn't I? They're perfect!"

"Maybe we should look at them one more time," I suggested. "I'm still not very sure about the white horses, the tigers, the apes, and the quarks."

"Look at you," Tsar said and placed his hands on his hips. He was wearing a white undershirt and black sweatpants. "Where's your imagination? In this life, you need to have some imagination, Nikola. People without imagination are called dead people."

Twenty

S tudying Buddhist metaphysics at a Tibetan monastery is all about walking. As entry-level students, my classmates and I used every opportunity to practice our metaphysical gait. We walked from the main
monastery compound to our classroom and back. We walked to McLeod
Ganj. We walked to the library. On Fridays, we walked all the way to Baksunat to wash our robes in the river. Being entry-level students, we knew a lot
about dividing and classifying. We divided and classified everything that we
saw, heard, or thought of. For example, if we passed a pretty nun on the street,
we'd think: nuns are girls, and girls are humans, and humans have five aggre-
gates, which are divided into two types, and of those two, the mind is divided
into seven, and the seven are classified as being two kinds, and of those two,
valid perception is divided into three, and those three are divided into two
types, and of those two types, the latter is divided into three and the former
into two, and of those two, the first is divided into six, and of those six, visual
valid direct perception is the type of consciousness one would use to look at a
nun, although this is highly debatable because according to the Mad-
hyamikas, direct perception in ordinary beings isn't valid at all. Moreover—
we'd think, twenty minutes after we'd passed the nun in question—what

kind of category do men and women belong to? They're not identical, they aren't opposites (a hermaphrodite is both), they don't form a threefold associ- ation because one isn't the property of the other, and so they must belong to the category of fourfold associations. There's a case of a man who isn't a woman, there's a case of a woman who isn't a man, there's a case of both, and there's a case of neither.

Thinking along these lines, we'd inevitably reach the pinnacle of Tibetan metaphysical thought, the mighty double opposite, or *dog pa*. The double opposite of a car is a car. This profound discovery is extremely useful when you're pressed to explain the relationship between two very similar phenomena, and you can't. They have the same meaning—you'd say of the two phenomena—but their double opposites are different. In other words, the double opposite allows you to claim that two things can be the same and different at the same time. No one in the history of logic has been able to walk away from an argument with such a statement. Not until the Tibetans kidnapped the double opposite from India and brought it to Lhasa, tied to the back of an emaciated water buffalo. Nobody has been able to defeat the double opposite. Many great logicians have tried, and their bodies still litter the battlefield of Buddhist metaphysics. The double opposite is a truly evil invention, the kind that makes the elderly theologians toss and turn in their cots all night, lost in a maze of threes and twos and sevens and threefold asso- ciations. Let it be said that you can't walk lightly once you know that the double opposite of a nun is a nun. Carrying a double opposite in your mind is like lugging a hundred-pound cannonball chained to your foot. Hence, on a normal day, you'd see us—the entry-level students—pushing our way into town, constrained by the excessive load of metaphysical knowledge that we'd agreed to carry for the benefit of mankind. We'd walk hunched up and fatigued, like Rajasthani construction workers who had just finished their twenty-hour shifts. Afraid of feeling the wrath of our great logical powers, ordinary Tibetan men and women would stand at the side of the road and wait for us to pass, staring stubbornly at their shoes. "*Kaba?*"—Where?—we'd ask a frail octogenarian lugging a barrel of kerosene. "*Ya dro gi yin*"—Going up—the old man would answer with an apologetic smile and speed up the hill. We had authority and people didn't dare mess with us.

Directly above us on the monastic ladder stood the mid-level students, who studied Maitreya's *Abhisamayalamkara,* an eighth-century Mahayana text that was more a collection of numbers than a philosophical treatise and read like an early attempt at abstract algebra. Memorizing the numbers of all the divisions, subdivisions, and sub-subdivisions of every state that one had to pass through on the way to Enlightenment caused the mid-level students' heads to grow bigger, their necks to get thicker, their shoulders to get wider, and their arms to get longer and more muscular. As a result, when mid-level students ventured outside the monastery compound to practice their meta-physical stride, they looked like beefed-up prisoners on a half-hour outing. "*Kaba?*" they'd ask us, ready to pull out their numbers, sub-subdivisions, and double opposites, and beat the crap out of us. "*Dagas*"—Nowhere in particular—we would tell them, trying to appear as reverential as possible.

Above the mid-level students resided the graduate-level students, who studied a text by Chandrakirti that provided logical tools for deconstructing reality. Graduate-level students never asked us "*Kaba?*" and almost never acknowledged the existence of other, lower-level beings. Having arrived at the end of all knowledge, they found everything rather boring, and so they spent their time practicing a kind of gliding walk, combined with a vacuous expression, an upward-pointing chin, and a total absence of shoulder and arm movement. How the graduate-level students managed to create the impres-sion of gliding across the surface of the earth, we, the entry-level students, could not figure out, try as we did. Perhaps it had to do with memorizing Chandrakirti's head-splitting logical formulas, or perhaps it was a skill that came naturally to those who had practiced metaphysical swaggering for a period of seven or eight years.

Above the graduate-level students were the *Geshes*. *Geshes* walked like Jedi knights—humble and poised, but with an unmistakable hint of hidden powers in their eyes. (Geshe Yama Tseten was an exception: he was the undisputed heavyweight champion.) Lobsang Dawa, the thirty-year-old monk appointed to teach all entry-level classes at the Institute of Buddhist Dialectics was a top-seeded Jedi knight. He was short, bespectacled, and walked with the manner of someone who was afraid to occupy more space than he'd been granted by the karmic forces. His smallness, it should be pointed out, was deceiving. Behind his busy and seemingly timid eyes resided power unseen by most ordinary beings. Though young and unassuming, in private he undoubtedly practiced switching the polarity of Jupiter, causing massive earthquakes on Saturn, or moving uninhabited islands in the middle of the Pacific Ocean.

On the day that Tsar decided to send the two letters he had composed with the help of his pocket Serbian-English dictionary, Lobsang Dawa arrived in class looking distressed. He climbed onto the podium, sat on his throne made of stacked-up mats, and began wiping his glasses—a sign that he was planning to suspend the routine debate session and present one of his three-hour lectures on the goodness of good people and the badness of bad people. "It has come to my attention," he said after a long silence, "that there are students in this class who are intent on disrupting the learning process. I will not name them. They know who they are." A wave of coughing, grunting, and ruffling of robes passed through the classroom and, suddenly, I realized that everyone (there were about thirty of us) was staring at me and Samten Gyatso, my only friend in the monastery. Samten was a tall monk from Amdo with matchstick-like arms and legs and an unusually dark complexion for a Tibetan—hence, his nickname Samten Nagpo, or Black Samten.

"I met with the other teachers in the monastery," Lobsang Dawa went on, looking pointedly at the A-students in the first row, "and we agreed that this cannot go on any longer. There is no place for disrespectful students in our school. If you don't want to bow down to me, that's fine. I don't care. But there is an image of the Buddha right behind me—and even if you don't like me and think, *Oh, who is this guy Lobsang Dawa, I don't care about him, he can't teach me anything, I won't bow down to him,* you should at least pay respect to the Buddha. That, I think, is clear."

Samten and I looked at each other and quickly covered our mouths—to avoid bursting out. The whole thing turned out to be about my and Samten's refusal to bow down three times with the other monks at the beginning of each class. Samten and I refused to do prostrations on principle: we both thought that, ultimately, the act of bowing down to someone stemmed from fear, and fear was an impediment, not a positive quality that deserved to be nurtured.

"I have decided," Lobsang Dawa continued, placing his pencil right in the middle of the table, "to give these students—they know who they are— one more chance. If they don't change their behavior, they'll be asked to leave the school."

The Mongolian monk sitting behind me punched me in the back and roared in my ear, "*Chto sluchilas, Tavarish Nikolaevich!*"—What happened, Comrade Nikolaevich? He always teased me in Russian.

Samten opened his notebook and drew an enormous penis. I responded by drawing a twenty-armed Lobsang Dawa facing a pair of giant boobs. In the meantime, Lobsang Dawa discoursed on the importance of being humble: "You may ask, how can I be humble and at the same time want to win every debate? There is no contradiction. Ordinary people think, *Oh, I'm better than him because I'm such a great person,* and so on and so forth. That kind of pride is an affliction. But if you think, *Oh, I'm going to study hard,* and so on and so forth, and *I'm going to beat everyone in debate, and I'm going to prove such and such to so and so because dispelling ignorance is the best thing I can do to help all sentient beings,* and so on and so forth—that is a very different kind of pride. And if someone says, *Oh, so and so is better than you in debate because he studied with so and so and defeated so and so, and he can recite the entire Pramanavarttika with all its commentaries by heart, and last year he was ranked as one of the top five debaters in the three great monasteries* and so on and so forth, do you have to feel bad about it? Of course not. You should think, *Oh, so and so did such and such and so on and so forth, and that's great because I'll learn from him and study harder and next year when I go down south to attend the big debates, I'm going to win every point and I'm going to be ranked as one of the top five debaters, and as a result I'll gain the power to dispel ignorance because*—and this is said again and again in the scriptures, it goes, oh, so and so, son of a noble family, what was it, something-something—*before you can dispel other people's ignorance, you should first dispel your own,* and so on and so forth. Something like that."

"Fuck," Samten said when the class was finally over and we were walking down toward the monastery kitchen. "Fuck" was one of the half-dozen words he knew in English, and he used it regularly, especially during the evening prayers.

"You have to get used to bowing down to the boss," I teased him. "You should practice tonight."

"I guess it's good exercise," he replied. "It can't hurt."

Samten was a classic iconoclast—he rarely spent a day without spreading heretical views and starting major theological brawls. I admired him for his audacity in questioning even the most fundamental Buddhist tenets and always backed him up when fifteen or twenty monks suddenly converged upon him on the way to the monastery kitchen and forced him to defend his philosophical views. Samten was a brilliant debater, with extraordinary imagination and a penchant for the unconventional. I always enjoyed seeing him come up with answers and definitions that left his opponents silent and completely confused. Sitting next to Samten in class or at the debating ground made me feel protected: I was no longer the only outsider. Samten's interpretations of the ontological concepts that Lobsang Dawa introduced in class broadened my horizons and inspired me to think independently. As a result, the official dogma never appeared to me as something final and unalterable. Rather, I saw it as one of the thousands of channels—some of them manmade and fake, others self-arisen—that snaked across the land of metaphysics. Samten told me once that when he'd first seen me in class, at the beginning of the school year, I had looked like someone who'd stumbled upon a spontaneous performance by the village idiot. Perhaps what Samten liked about me was that I was very much like him: I was a hopeless heretic.

Samten often joked that he was hoping to be reborn as an Indian cow—because Indian cows were naturally vegetarian, free to go wherever they pleased, and gave people milk. "Cows," he claimed, "are actually useful. Unlike monks." He spent his free time either lying in his bed or staring out his window at the dreary enclosed courtyard where the monks played Ping-Pong and hung their laundry. Occasionally, while out walking, Samten experienced seizures that left him paralyzed and unresponsive for five to ten minutes. He told me that he'd first started having seizures after he'd been released from an Indian prison where he'd spent two years and had been regularly beaten on the head and the feet with metal clubs. He'd entered the prison at age twelve. His crime had been crossing illegally from China into India, like so many others here.

I went to Om Restaurant hoping to find Vinnie and Tsar sipping lemon tea in the far corner, but the waitress told me that she hadn't seen either of them all day. I circled McLeod Ganj twice, peeking into every restaurant and chai shop, and finally decided to sit down at Smiley's and order a plate of soupy dal. Smiley's hole-in-the-wall chai shop was an ideal place for spotting people because the entrance looked out at the juncture of Post Road and Baksunat Road, while the small window in the back offered a view of the bus station and the path that lead down to Om Restaurant. In less than an hour I saw Damien ("What's up bro, yeah, I just got back from Bodhgaya, that place is rad, man, a three-day train ride and everyone throws up the whole time, you've got to see it, the Tree of Enlightenment and the whole shit, they've excavated a temple, dug it out of the ground, you know what I'm saying, and it just stands there, with lots of ornate little stuff on top, and you've got monks from every Asian country, the Burmese monks killed me, man, they all smoke two packs a day, the crazy bastards, but the food is crap, honest to God, I got hepatitis the second day I got there and my shit turned completely white, you know what I mean, whiter than fucking chalk, it's like I was shitting these huge sticks of chalk, and I'd wake up in the morning and I'd go, shit, man, I can't lift my fucking hand, that's how tired I was, down with hepatitis fatigue") and then Purba, who informed me that his mother was dying and he was planning to cross the Indian-Chinese border on foot in a few days (he didn't have any documents). Then Ani Dawa strolled by, pretending not to see me, followed by Ani Lamo, the Buddhist nun from Brooklyn, who really didn't see me, and then Merry Anne, wearing a gray raincoat, camouflage pants, and holding a purple umbrella. I waved at him to join me, and in response, he pulled out a pipe from his rucksack and performed an affirmative Indian-style head wobble. He sat on the curb, filled his pipe with hash, and took a drag. When he'd gotten sufficiently stoned, he walked into Smiley's and ordered the house special. Smiley was in the swing of things. He looked like a 1950s jazz drummer—deadpan and extremely focused, disentangling the dense fabric of time with a jerk of his wrist, anticipating a beat, and then skipping it, making it disappear like a magician. He opened the low cupboard with his foot, took the bag of chapati flour, poured it into a wok, kicked the cupboard shut, repositioned his penis, pumped the kerosene stove three times, let some air out of the fuse, took five rupees from a customer standing in the rain, put a new batch of samosas in the frying pan, made a surprise pirouette—to pour an extra ladle of dal over my rice—checked on his penis, yelled at his seven-year-old slave worker, who was rinsing the dirty dishes over the street sewer (using the rainwater gushing out of the drainpipe), lit a *biddie*, shook the hand of the police chief who had the power to bulldoze any business he didn't like, flipped the samosas, sliced a chili in half and tossed it my way, rolled a paper-thin chapati, added some cumin and lemon juice to his samosa mix, greeted the bus driver who'd poked his head through the window at the back, started the third kerosene stove, put a pot of water to boil, and nodded at Merry Anne who was trying to figure out how many kids he'd fathered.

"Two sons?" Merry Anne asked.

"Three," Smiley answered. "One in the army, other in Puna."

"And third son?"

"Two daughters, one married, other very difficult."

Merry Anne and I walked around McLeod Ganj looking for Tsar and Vinnie, hung out for an hour at the Last Cow Chai Shop, bought some vegetables for dinner, and returned home. I was very perplexed by the fact that I wasn't able to find Tsar all afternoon. One of the special things about living in Dharamsala was that you never had to arrange to meet your friends at a particular time and place. All you had to do was sit in one spot, and eventually everyone turned up.

The sun went down, and the rain was replaced by a violent wind that carried traces of rotten wood, wet grass, and blooming rhododendrons. As it whizzed through the cracks between the slate roof tiles and shook the tarpaulin sheet, it turned our house into a free-reed instrument, a badly tuned harmonica that talked to the leopards and vultures lurking on the outskirts of the human village. I must've fallen asleep while reading because when I woke up to the sound of many things collapsing on the floor, I still had my robes on and I was hugging Tsongkapa's ten-pound commentary on the *Abhisamayalamkara*. My first thought was that I was being attacked by snakes. The room was pitch-black and I couldn't find my flashlight, even though I remembered clearly placing it next to my bed. There was a sound of a large creature kicking and tossing on the ground and the table by the window hit the floor, bringing down a portable tape player, a dozen tapes, two porcelain teacups, books, a metal ashtray, and a jar of Indian coins. *This is no snake*, I thought. *It's probably a thief.* I crawled onto Merry Anne's bed (he was asleep and snoring) and groped around the night table in the hope of finding a lighter or a box of matches. Snatching what I presumed was Tsar's flashlight (*Weird*, I thought. *Why would Tsar leave the house without his flashlight?*), I jumped back on my bed and made a blind leap toward the door—in case I had to run for my life. Squatting in the corner, I turned the flashlight on and scanned the room, starting from the pile of toothbrushes, shaving brushes, razors, towels, and bars of soap, moving to the knocked-over table and the remains of the tape player, and ending at Tsar's bed, where the intruder lay prostrate. I flicked the light switch on and off, then went outside the house and stared into the night: there wasn't a single light on in the entire village. Power outages were a frequent occurrence, especially when there was a strong wind and lightning. I went back inside and shook Tsar by the shoulder. "Get up," I said. "What the hell is going on with you?"

I turned him over on his back and pointed the flashlight at his face. His left eye was swollen and there was dried blood around his nose and eyebrows. "Open your eyes and tell me if you're all right!" I ordered. I shook him again, then grabbed him under the shoulders and forced him to sit up. He smelled of booze. I propped his back against the wall and went into the kitchen to get a pitcher of water. When I got back, Tsar was awake and smiling. Thinking I must be mistaken, I leaned over him and pointed the light at his mouth to double-check: all of his front teeth were missing. Not even stubs remained.

"What the fuck is going on, Tsar!" I shouted at him. "Where are your teeth? Where have you been?"

Tsar giggled and gave me the middle finger. "*Ausweis!*" he yelled with theatrical bombast. "*Hände hoch!*"

This is certainly new, I thought. A toothless, beat-up, drunken Bosnian ex-Buddhist monk screaming in German in the middle of the night. Yanki, the little girl next door, awoke with a cry and started coughing. Merry Anne, for his part, was still sound asleep. The guy could easily sleep through Armageddon.

"Tsar," I said, "can you tell me how you lost your teeth? Did someone try to rob you? Do you know where you are?"

"Who are you?" he asked back, sucking on an imaginary cigarette.

"I'm your roommate," I replied.

Tsar searched his shirt pockets, found a box of matches, and lit a match. "*Ausweis! Hände hoch!*" he shouted again and burst out laughing. I removed the burning match from his pants, took away his matches, and covered him with his blanket. There wasn't much I could do to help the situation, so I picked up the mess off the floor and lit a candle—to keep an eye on Tsar in case he decided to set himself on fire again. "Good night," I told Tsar after I had bolted the door and wrapped myself in three blankets. It wasn't even September and the nights were already freezing. "*Auf Weidersehen*, dumb motherfuckers!" Tsar yelled from his bed. "Suck my dick!"

I somehow managed to fall asleep, but an hour later I woke up again and saw Tsar crawling on the floor with a pillow on his head. "Psst! Get down!" he whispered to me. "Get down, *choveche*, they're shooting at us!"

"Who's shooting?" I asked him.

"Everyone. I don't know who's who anymore. We're surrounded on all sides. Do you have a cookie?"

"Why?"

"If you throw them a cookie, they'll stop. Trust me. Do it now."

I tossed them a cookie and turned around.

"They launched a grenade," Tsar informed me. "We're going to blow up in three seconds. Two. One."

"Tsar," I said without looking at him, "we're in Dharamsala, India, and are surrounded by wild cows who eat plastic bags and read the *Hindustani Times*. Go to sleep."

Someone shouted outside, a rooster shrieked, and our landlord's tofu-making machine announced the beginning of the new day with a series of loud bangs. It was five o'clock in the morning and the electricity had finally been restored.

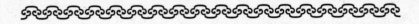

Twenty-one

Out of the corner of my eye I watched as Merry Anne slipped into his khakis, plucked a handful of ganja leaves from the herbarium under his mattress, knocked down the thermos, tripped on the carpet, and examined bloodied, black-eyed Tsar lying crosswise on his bed before he exited the room, closing the door as slowly as possible to ensure maximum squeaking. I got up and made tea with eight spoonfuls of Darjeeling instead of the usual three. "Wake up," I told Tsar, holding a cup of tea an inch from his nose. Tsar opened his eyes and looked around the room. His face was pale, his lips chapped, and his hair, clotted with blood and mud, formed an eccentric, here-comes-the-tsunami hairdo. "*Chove . . .*" he began, but was immediately interrupted by a violent outburst of coughing. Teary-eyed, he took a sip of tea and rummaged through the pens, pencils, erasers, sharpeners, empty ink cartridges, and *rudraksha* beads cluttering his night table. "Mmmmmm!" he exclaimed, excavating a *biddie* broken in half. He lit up, coughed some more, and stuck his tongue in the space vacated by his front teeth. Grinning, he raised a finger, as if to say *hold on one second*, slipped his hand in the front pocket of his corduroys, and took out a small pink-and-white object, the significance of which became apparent only after Tsar had attached it with a snap to his palate. I was stunned. I had known Tsar for two years and never found out he wore dentures.

"Love," he announced, lighting the second half of his *biddie*, "is the total absence of trying. Most people try to exist. Buddhists try not to exist. In the end, everyone's trying. By the way, trying is the most basic reaction of our defense mechanism, which also includes our immune system. We are and we aren't. We are here and not here. We are alive and we've already died. We float in a sphere of interchangeable opposites. What do we do about it? We try to hold on to something. We try one end, then we try the other. It makes no difference. Even on the level of direct perception—we don't let objects float. We try to shape them into something that has never been. Do you know why there are wars, Nikola? Because people are constantly trying to produce solid opposites. Here and there makes people happy. It makes the world almost real. So here is a guy strapped with explosives—by blowing himself up, he's just trying to prove that he exists. It's been like that even before the first people in Africa invented the modern cow for domestic purposes. My advice would be, stop trying. And give up. *I exist! Me, too, me, too! I exist more than you!* Just give up. By the way, people tell you that giving up sex, food, money, and comfort and putting on a monastic skirt will bring you closer to Enlightenment. Giving up things, giving up habits—that's considered a big deal. *From now on I'll never eat apples again!* How is that going to change anything? No one talks about giving up the struggle—the struggle to exist, the struggle not to exist. There is a poster hanging in a chai shop in McLeod Ganj—it has a photograph of the Dalai Lama, and underneath it says 'Never, never, never give up!' I don't understand it, I don't get it. How can you ever be free if you're holding with both hands onto the phallus of reality? Very strange. The biggest problem is that you can't give up by trying. That's why people end up taking sleeping pills. Because trying to fall asleep doesn't work."

I laughed hysterically. Tsar was a perfect example of two opposites that have merged into one: he was absolutely serious, and he was full of shit; he was earnest and ironic; he was a tsar and a pauper; he was a mystic and a crook; he had the biggest ego in the world, and at the same time he was selfless—because it was all a pose.

"Why haven't you told me all this time that you wear fake teeth?" I asked him.

"Why should I? Do you go up to someone and say, 'By the way, I have large hemorrhoids, here, feel them'? You don't."

"So what happened last night? And where were you? I spent three hours looking for you and Vinnie."

"*Choveche*, I don't want to hear about Vinnie ever again. The guy doesn't know how to lose. Every time we play, it's the same thing—he starts shouting and pounding on the table, and when I try to make a joke, he gets really offended. Yesterday we're sitting at Ramesh . . ."

"At Ramesh?" I repeated astonished. "I walked past Ramesh thirty times."

"We're there all day, there were some Australian girls sitting at one end of the table, and I started to imitate Vinnie—you know how he speaks, with a turbo whisper—and he flipped the chessboard in my face and walked out, knocking glasses and plates, it was really embarrassing. Then Ramesh and I split a bottle of brandy, then I drank one by myself—I don't know, there were girls there, I can't remember what happened—then I got into a fight with someone—I don't remember who—and that's it. Nothing special. I must've walked home."

"Nothing special!" I shouted. "You should've seen yourself last night—toothless and smeared with blood. I thought you'd been kidnapped and tortured by Kashmiri separatists."

Tsar got up and examined his face in the mirror, pressing the swelling under his left eye and pinching his nose. "You know, I may be drunk as a pig, but I always remember to take my teeth out before I get into a fight."

He winked at himself in the mirror, smiled smugly, grabbed a towel and a box of soap, and walked out to take a cold, Antarctic shower at the communal spout. When he returned—naked, with the towel wrapped around his waist—all the smugness had disappeared from his face and in his eyes I recognized the flicker of something very unusual for Tsar: panic. He threw his blankets on the floor, then kneeled down and looked under his bed. "Have you seen my bag?" he asked me, walking back and forth in a state of frenzy. "The leather bag, the beige leather bag that I carry every day, did you see it last night? Was I carrying it when I walked through the door? Did you put it somewhere?"

I explained to him the circumstances of his late-night entrance—the wind, the blackout, the tables on the floor, the busted tape player—and concluded with a reasonable degree of certainty that he'd either left the bag in McLeod Ganj or dropped it somewhere on his way back home.

Tsar stood in the middle of the room, his hands buried in his wet, gray hair. I found it hard to believe that he'd get so upset about his bag. Granted, it was a nice bag but it wasn't irreplaceable. "The letters," he said with a dry, defeatist tone. "The letters were in the bag. I forgot to send them."

I told him not to worry: what was the worst thing that could happen? Someone would open his bag and read his letter to his Israeli mistress. White horses jumping in the night, tigers roaring: no one would understand anything. Or they would open the other letter and read a short treatise on metaphysics and plate tectonics. It wasn't a big deal.

"This is bad," he announced, staring at the open door. "If the police got a hold of the letters, I'd be in a lot of trouble. All my personal information is in there, including the date of issue and serial number of my expired passport."

I had to admit that his calculating skills were much better than mine. He was, after all, the second best chess player in Dharamsala, after Erick.

"You have to skip debate today," he said and placed his hand on my shoulder. "Come on, Nikola, just today! I can't show my face in town after what happened last night. You have to go and find my bag. I need your help. Please."

Even though I made it clear to Tsar that I wasn't happy to be wasting my day with his new problems (*Tsar, you know that I came here to study, I can't skip classes all the time!*), I was secretly thrilled with the fact that Tsar's predicament was taking on a new, more dangerous dimension. Ever since Tsar had first told me about his problems with the local authorities two years before, I'd become addicted to the drama that seemed to accompany Tsar wherever he went. In some strange way, I had come to accept Tsar's relentless, almost metaphysical battle with the bureaucracy of human existence as an external manifestation of my own struggle to understand who I was and what I was hoping to find in India. I saw Tsar as a catalyst, as someone who took all of my hopes, fears, internal contradictions, and suspicions, gave them names and identities, and put them in a farcical play, which he then performed himself. While I spent countless nights trying to figure out why sex and the quest to understand reality were considered incompatible, Tsar slept with an Israeli girl, broke his monastic vows, and locked his robes in a metal trunk. *See, Nikola, fucking is very simple. By the way, it's an old ritual, and you don't even need to think about what you're doing. I don't know why people make such a big deal out of it.* While I struggled to find my identity—was I Bulgarian, American, or Tibetan? Was I a musician or a monk?—Tsar threw his passport away and declared life an event that began and ended simultaneously. While I grappled with the hallucinations of empirical materialism, the failure of existentialism, and the one-sidedness of emptiness, Tsar advanced his own version of Buddhism, wherein Enlightenment was as meaningful as ignorance and any earnest attempt to achieve a higher state only made things worse. *Stop putting things in perspective, Nikola! Existence is a perspective, nonexistence is a perspective. You need to see without looking.*

Consequently, I had started believing that the end of Tsar's external struggles would signal the end of my confusion. His catharsis was going to be my catharsis; his fall, my fall.

I tied my *shanthab* and rushed out the door. Walking past the Institute of Buddhist Dialectics, I ran into one of my classmates, who'd just stepped out of the classroom to bring Lobsang Dawa a *pecha* from the monastery library.

"Why aren't you in class?" the monk asked me, scrunching his eyebrows and staring disapprovingly at my unevenly folded *shanthab*. "My friend is sick," I lied. "I'm going to the hospital to get him some medicine." The monk nodded, smiled resentfully, and watched me walk away, as if it were he who had given me permission to leave class. Though he was just an entry-level student, he'd already managed to appropriate all the facial expressions and authoritative posturing from his superiors, the *Geshes*. It was truly amazing, I thought, how quickly people could get so thoroughly warped by a system.

I poked briefly into the post office to check for letters, then ran to the end of the street, took a right, and stopped, panting, at Ramesh's chai shop, a tiny, rectangular shanty with an entrance obstructed by hanging frying pans and walls decorated with straw mats and postcards from grateful backpackers. A sign on the front wall read "The best chia in Asia." Ramesh was an Indian man with long hair, a thin mustache, and a gigolo look about him. He sported a leather bracelet and a silver chain around his neck, and wore an oversized red button-down shirt and linen pants. I watched him make a banana samosa topped with honey (his dessert specialty), then went into the chai shop and sat beside a Western girl with smelly dreadlocks and fingernails whose deposits, if ever extracted, could easily fill a Ping-Pong ball. "*Tashi Delek, Kushu-la*," Ramesh greeted me in Tibetan. "*Chai?*" I responded with a positive head jerk and looked around the bench and under the table. If there had been a violent brawl the previous night, all the signs had been carefully cleaned up. "My friend Tsar left his bag here last night," I said. "Have you seen it?" Ramesh scanned the street, then turned around and looked at the girl with the dreadlocks. "I don't know your friend," he said, opening his eyes as wide as possible. "Do you understand?"

I understood. I sipped my chai and studied the unfinished game of chess at the end of the long table. Ramesh's wife, wearing a gray *salwar-kameez* and a head scarf, walked into the chai shop and placed a milk jug on the counter. She nodded at me and turned to her husband with a worried face. Ramesh raised his hands, as in *It's not my problem*, and covered the milk jug with a cheesecloth. "Last night," he said to me, pointing at the bench outside the chai shop, "people drinking, then some fighting. Two people on the ground, very bad—broken head, cannot go home. Police come, look everywhere. Sometimes bag, sometimes no bag."

Ramesh's wife looked at me, gauging my reaction. "Sometimes police take bag?" I asked. Ramesh raised an eyebrow and did a *maybe* head wobble. "Sometimes I don't know your friend," he elaborated. "Sometimes your friend stay home for a long time. *Acha?*"

Acha. I paid for the chai and thanked Ramesh for the information. "Be careful," he said and winked at me.

When I returned home, I found Tsar sitting cross-legged on his bed, a lit *biddie* in the corner of his mouth, and drawing a map that started with India in the south, went north to Tajikistan, and then stretched west all the way to Bosnia. I told him about my conversation with Ramesh, and he concluded that it would be best for him to go for a week to Norbulingka, just as he'd done the previous year when a golden-toothed STD owner had tipped the police about his visa situation. I noticed that he'd already packed his clothes in a small sack that had once belonged to his American love and now estranged wife, Samantha. There was an immense sense of determination in the way he held his *biddie* and outlined the mountainous region between Samarqand and Dushanbe with quick, precise strokes. (Tsar had a photographic memory: he could sketch out the borders of all fifty U.S. states without having to look at a map, or reconstruct all the chess games that he'd played with Vinnie or Erick.) I had seen him like that—secretive, single-minded—twice before: once when he got his idea to start baking bread, and once on the day he married Samantha.

"I'm going to go into hiding for a few days, and then I'm leaving this place," Tsar announced. "I'm done with India."

At that moment the entrance door swung open, hitting the wall, and in came Vinnie, dressed in his usual apparel: a tattered short-sleeve shirt, checked pants, and moccasins, a rucksack hanging from his shoulder.

"This was a test," he explained, pointing at the door. "We have to be prepared."

He sat on the floor, took his shoes off, and asked for a glass of water. Tsar and I didn't move.

"How could you do this to us?" Tsar asked him, covering his nose with one end of his blanket. "You haven't taken a shower in, what, three months?"

"Not three," Vinnie objected. He looked somber. He looked commanding. He knew things that Tsar and I didn't. He was a problem-solving expert who'd come to volunteer his help, and he expected to be treated with respect. He took his socks off and repeated his request for water, noting that his throat was extremely dry. Tsar and I breathed through our mouths; we didn't move.

"I have good news and bad news," Vinnie announced, nodding slowly.

"I can guess the bad news," Tsar said. "Let's hear the good news."

"Do you remember the American woman who used to live down by the river? The one that had hired an Indian man to cook for her? She was rich."

Tsar removed the blanket from his nose and smiled. He liked good news that involved women. He got up, searched the pockets of his pants, pulled out a torn one-rupee bill, collected the change lying on the table, and exited the room. Vinnie grunted: he hated when people interrupted him. In less than a minute Tsar returned. He was wet and held a pack of *biddies*.

"Go on," he said to Vinnie as he repositioned himself on his bed and began untying the string holding all the *biddies* together.

Vinnie stroked his mustache, unperturbed by Tsar's excitement. "I heard that after you broke up with her, she got very upset."

Tsar giggled and exhaled smoke through his nostrils. "And?"

"Well," Vinnie said, "I guess she sent a letter to the Hague tribunal claiming that you are a war criminal."

Tsar turned pale. He looked at Vinnie with disbelief, reached for the matches to relight his *biddie*, paused to reflect one more time on what Vinnie had just said, and threw both the matches and the *biddie* in the leaf-shaped copper ashtray. "Vinnie, you really need to check your head," Tsar said exasperated. "How could you possibly think that this is good news? By the way, I'm stuck in India with no papers or money, the closest Bosnian embassy is in Pakistan, I can't show my face in a police station because I'll be arrested and thrown in jail, my mother sends me letters telling me she'll see me in the next life, and you come here and inform me that the good news is that now the Hague tribunal for crimes against humanity committed in former Yugoslavia has my name and address and probably is going to send a team to investigate my case—all because some crazy woman got mad at me for God knows what. And I haven't even been in the stupid war!"

"But you can't prove it," Vinnie observed matter-of-factly. "You don't have a passport with arrival and departure stamps that can show your movements."

"You are a sick old man," Tsar concluded. "Unbelievable, coming in here with *good news*. What did you think? *Oh, by the way, Tsar is in a lot of trouble. He needs some good news, too.* There is something wrong with your head, Vinnie. Really wrong."

Vinnie nodded with understanding and said yes. He wasn't about to get offended. "Are you ready to hear the bad news?" he asked politely.

"Go home and find something else to do," Tsar exploded. "What is it?"

"I was in Green Hotel Restaurant this morning," Vinnie confided. "And then they came—three police officers with bamboo sticks. One was a senior officer; I could tell from his badges. I wasn't paying attention to what they were saying until I heard one of them mention your name. Your real name." Vinnie paused to allow the information to sink in. "They said, 'We are looking for a man named Djordje Berkich, also known as Tsar.' That's when I noticed that they had your leather bag. I thought, *scheisse*, this is worse than the October revolution."

"The October revolution happened in November," Tsar observed.

"You're right," Vinnie agreed. "Then the senior officer asked the receptionist to open the register and see if a man by the name of Djordje Berkich had ever rented a room in the hotel. The senior officer knew everything about you: passport number, country of origin, date of birth, face description."

"This is bad," Tsar concluded, scratching his thick three-day beard. With his swollen eye and the bruises on his head, he looked like a failed revolutionary.

"Why the hell did you have to get drunk and beat people up?" I asked Tsar angrily. "I knew I shouldn't have helped you with those letters. It was a dumb idea from the start."

"It gets much worse," Vinnie assured us. "I got up to go to the bathroom, and at that moment Rosenkrantz, the Dutch taxi driver, showed up and asked me if I had seen you. The senior officer heard him say 'Tsar' and immediately jumped on me. 'You know Tsar? You are Tsar's friend?' I told him that Rosenkrantz was asking me about a chess piece that I'd lost. *Tsar* is another name for a chess king—that's how I put it. And I showed him the chess pieces in my bag. The officer wasn't very convinced but he let me go."

Tsar jumped on his feet, grabbed his sack of clothes, and walked to the door. "I knew it," he said, looking through a crack in the door. "They have followed you and now I'll have to fight them."

Vinnie stood up and looked through the crack. "This is not a spy," he said. "I know this man—he is the son of the carpenter who sells tables and bookshelves on Post Road."

"Then why is he standing in the rain, in front of my house?" Tsar asked, examining the man one more time.

"Because he's retarded," Vinnie explained and sat back on the floor. "Besides, I made sure that nobody followed me. I used an old trick: I followed *them*."

Vinnie looked at me and Tsar to see if this new information had earned him some extra points for tactical skill and maneuvering and went on to tell us how he'd followed the police officers to Om, Kailash, Tsonka Restaurant, Ramesh, the post office, the bakery, and then back to the Green Hotel. "When I saw them ordering samosas, I headed down Jogibara Road. I knew that there was no one following me, but I wanted to be absolutely sure and so I went into the chai shop that belongs to your landlord's brother, waited for five minutes, and exited through the window. Just an extra precaution."

I imagined Vinnie lurking behind lampposts, jumping elegantly over puddles, and leaning against a wall, his face and part of his flaming mustache hidden behind the cover of Raymond Chandler's *The Big Sleep*. (Vinnie was addicted to crime novels.) I imagined him sitting at the chai shop up the road without ordering anything and then, to the dismay and anger of the owner, climbing out the tiny back window and plummeting onto the stone-tiled patio two stories below.

Tsar was impressed. He set his sack on the ground and brought Vinnie a glass of water. "Nikola, how can you laugh right now?" he scolded me. "The situation is serious. If they come to arrest me, they will probably take you as well."

"But I'm not laughing!" I lied.

Next on the agenda was an analysis of Tsar's options for escape from India. Sipping from his water and massaging his bluish callused feet, Vinnie presented what he called "the most logical exit strategy" under the present circumstances. During his presentation, Tsar and I frequently jumped in to introduce new ideas or to improve the ones that Vinnie had already discussed. Here is a summary of our joint effort.

The Trans-Siberian Railway Scenario (A Collaboration)

Escaping India can be done in any of the following ways: by air, by land, by sea, and by tunneling underground. Tunneling, first introduced by Alexandre Dumas in his novel *The Count of Monte Cristo* and later implemented by East Germans fleeing into West Berlin, is a lengthy process that requires years of intense labor and poses some risks, such as puncturing an underground water channel and deviating from the intended target, the consequences of which can often be fatal. Swimming across the Arabian Sea and flying a handmade aircraft over Pakistan, Iran, Turkey, Bulgaria, and Serbia are two options that, while worth considering, have only about a five percent chance of success and therefore should not be examined for the time being. The last option, an escape by land, has an enormous advantage over the other three in that it is cheap, requires no labor, and utilizes the routes and techniques used by recent escapees. Testimonies by hundreds of Tibetans—some of them fresh from kindergarten—crossing illegally from China into India every year present a body of evidence that establishes the following beyond a reasonable doubt: one, there are high mountain passes free of border guards; two, despite the high altitude, crossing from China into India or from India into China takes less than a day and can be accomplished even by a six-year-old; three, reports of deaths caused by sniper fire or starving Himalayan bears are scarce and unalarming; and four, losing your toes because of freezing is a relatively painless process, which only rarely results in full limb amputation or impairment of one's reproductive organs.

Having considered the facts, it is natural to ask how going to China will help Tsar get back to the Balkans, which happen to be in the opposite direction. The answer is simple: by hopping on the Trans-Siberian express, traversing the Gobi Desert, the Central Siberian Plateau, the Western Siberian Lowlands, and the Ural Mountains, and arriving in Moscow, where concerned government officials, in a gesture of pan-Slavic solidarity, will put him on a different train and send him back to his hometown, Sarajevo. In light of these calculations, it can be concluded that Tsar's trip across Asia will take anywhere between two weeks and a month.

· In the best-case scenario, the trip will unfold in the following way:

Day one: Start at the bus station in Lower Dharamsala and travel to Sikkim.

Day two: Arrive at Gangtok, the capital of Sikkim, visit Tibetan temple, talk to locals about the safest routes for crossing into China, eat a lot of *momos.*

Day three: Get close to the border by car, then continue on foot until the town of Yadong is in sight: welcome to China. Sleep in a yak barn.

Days four and five: Hitchhike to Lhasa and then Yushu (900 kilometers).

Days six and seven: Hitchhike to Xi'an (1,100 kilometers), visit the tomb of Emperor Qin Shi Huang, locate the train station.

Days eight to fourteen: Sneak onto the Trans-Siberian express, travel to Moscow.

Question: What happens if Tsar is apprehended by a Chinese border patrol near Yadong?

Answer: Having been instructed by Vinnie, who is fluent in Chinese, holds a Ph.D. in Chinese studies, and was married to a Chinese woman and her mother for seven years, Tsar will greet all representatives of the Chinese government with a polite smile and explain the purpose of his visit using the four key Chinese phrases he had committed to memory prior to his arrival in China: *Your country offers many joys; I am traveling on the Trans-Siberian express; I just stepped off the train; Someone stole my passport.* Being 2,000 kilometers away from the nearest train station on the path of the Trans-Siberian express is bound to arouse suspicion. This, however, will only speed up Tsar's arrival in Beijing. Confused about Tsar's legal status, the authorities in Beijing will contact the Russian embassy and arrange for Tsar to be deported to Moscow.

Overall chance of success: seventy percent. Pros: See the terracotta warriors in Xi'an; cross the Gobi Desert; drink horse milk in Ulan Bator; spend a romantic night in Buryatia. Cons: Get shot; encounter bears; lose some or all toes and part of a leg; spend time in

a Chinese prison; ride for seven days on a train full of old Russian
ladies who eat bread and garlic and insist on placing their feet in
your lap.

When we were done drafting the Trans-Siberian express scenario (I
transcribed the most important points in a notebook that was filled with map
drawings and diagrams titled *How to Get from India to Bulgaria by Bus* or
Dharamsala to Istanbul on Foot) Tsar and Vinnie turned to chess. I sat at the
edge of my bed and kept an eye on the courtyard and the stairway leading to
Jogibara Road. Vinnie had left the door ajar so that we could hear if plainclothes officers unloaded from a government jeep and began questioning our
neighbors about Tsar. It was getting dark and the fog, which had hung over
the village throughout the day, was finally starting to disperse. The nunnery
gong sounded eight times—a simple but insightful riff set against a rhythm
section of throbbing kerosene stoves and a choir of mooing cows and screaming toddlers. The young Indian woman living next to Ani Dawa's old room
was sitting out on the steps, holding a copper wok with rice between her
knees. She was making dinner for her husband—a fierce and perpetually inebriated taxi driver. Mr. Chandradas, my old landlord, walked out of his room
and sauntered across the courtyard to pay his evening homage to the clay
statues of Shiva, Wife, and Son. He stood at the gates of the sanctuary, hands
folded behind his back. He had an antagonistic relationship with the local
gods: he acknowledged their privileged position in existence, but didn't necessarily approve of what they were up to. "This is your only chance to win a
game against me," Tsar told Vinnie. "Tomorrow I'm leaving for China and
you'll never see me again. I'll give you a hint—you could checkmate me in
three moves. Forced checkmate, nothing I can do about it." Vinnie grunted
and wiped the sweat from his forehead. "Put out your cigarette, Tsar! Jesus
Christ!" he shouted. "You're making me sick and I can't think!"

    Vinnie went into the kitchen, lifted the large bucket of water, and
poured its contents over his head. Soaked and spilling water left and right, he

returned to the chessboard and examined the position, refreshed. For a moment it looked as if he'd found the key: he raised his hand over his king's rook and ran the calculation again, scanning the open diagonals and nodding with confidence.

"Years from now," Tsar said dreamily, leaning against Merry Anne's bed frame, "you're going to tell people how you checkmated the best chess player ever to visit the Himalayas, a day before he fled to China and was shot to death by a retarded border guard. His last words were, 'Your country offers many joys!' spoken in perfect Mandarin dialect. His body was later eaten by leopards."

Vinnie held his head in his hands and mumbled something in German. He had lost the thread again.

"Tsar was a remarkable man," Tsar went on, imagining how Vinnie was going to talk about him years after his untimely death. "He spoke five languages and made all women around him tremble with excitement. He was born in a working-class Bosnian family, and from an early age developed an interest in stealing. His childhood dream was to rob a bank. His passionate personality was shaped by his grandmother, who had been a chain-smoker and had spent her life drinking coffee and Bosnian grappa and cursing God and his children. She lived to be ninety. By the way, Tsar led a turbulent life. He worked as an electrician, as a conductor on the Yugoslav Railways, as a high-rise construction worker in Germany, and as an entrepreneur, selling tax-free cigarettes in the Netherlands. One night, after a wild tête-à-tête with two Ethiopian girls in Amsterdam's red light district, Tsar discovered that life is an optical illusion and that everything has already happened. Waking up to a world of zombies living on autopilot, Tsar jumped on the first plane to India and a week later became the first Bosnian to be ordained a Buddhist monk. By the way, life still held many surprises. Once in India, Tsar quickly realized that Tibetan monasteries were filled with zombies as well. After a few years of chai-drinking and shitting in the woods, he finally decided to change continents and was shot to death while crossing into

China. He was awarded the Nobel Peace Prize posthumously. On his grave, situated on a hill overlooking Sarajevo, is written *Tsar: an Opel Kadet. Model 1987. Color gray.*"

"Why Opel Kadet?" I wondered.

"It's a type of car," Tsar explained. "I had one when I was living in Germany."

"Guys, I'm trying to think!" Vinnie exploded.

Tsar giggled and poured himself another cup of tea. The swelling under his left eye had gotten smaller and bluer, and in the faint light streaming through the small roof window, he looked almost saintly. This was Tsar's last supper.

"What type of car would you be?" he asked me. "You know the personality test, where you're asked to identify yourself with a car make."

"I don't know," I said. "I've never thought about it."

"Well, I'm officially an Opel Kadet," Tsar announced. "It's on paper. You should've seen the German immigration officers. *Choveche*, they kept me in their office for ten hours. Unbelievable. When I first arrived in Germany, they put me in an immigration camp near Frankfurt. I was there for three months before they called me into the Foreigners' Office to file a petition for an asylum. By the way, living in the camp was great. You got the feeling the Germans were really excited about your decision to immigrate to their country. It was just like you've seen it in the movies: at two o'clock in the morning, the police would storm the barracks where we slept, kicking the doors open and shouting '*Ausweis! Hände hoch!*' You couldn't see anything, just their flashlights pointed in your face, and then they'd line us up in the courtyard and inspect our documents, and then they'd yell our names and we'd take a step forward, and there was barbed wire and powerful projectors, and we'd march back and forth—the whole thing was very well organized. We did that every night. Then on Sunday we got to go to the nearest town and buy toothpaste and cigarettes and other essential things from the supermarket. As soon as you entered the supermarket, the cashier would turn off the music

and announce '*Auslander! Auslander!*' over the speakers, to let all the shop-
pers know that there's a foreigner in the store—in case someone forgot to
smile. Germans are very polite people. Then one day I was called into the
Foreigners' Office to file a petition for an asylum. I thought, *dobro*, I'm getting
out of here. By the way, I get there, and there's a woman officer sitting behind
the desk—she looks nice, a blond frau, and she hands me a set of documents
to fill out. I write my name, date and place of birth, and when I get to nationality, I write *Yugoslavian*. The woman almost had a heart attack. *What are you
doing? There's no country called Yugoslavia anymore! There is Serbia, Bosnia, and
Croatia. Choose one and write it down.* She gave me a new set of documents
and I started again: name, birthdate, place of birth, and when I got to nationality, I wrote *Yugoslavian*. *Choveche*, you've never seen anyone that upset.
There were cogwheels and springs coming out of her ears. She called four
other officers and they all sat around me, instructing me what to write. One
of them said, *Put down that you're Bosnian, you were born in Bosnia.* I told him
I can't. I was born in Bosnia to a Serbian father and Croatian mother. Therefore I can't call myself Bosnian, Serbian, or Croatian. I am a Yugoslavian. *But
such a country doesn't exist!* Well, I told them, put me down as an Opel Kadet.
They all went nuts: *But that's a car model! You're not a car.* I said, put me down
as Opel Kadet. You could take me to court, you could put me in prison, you
could deport me, but I'm not changing my mind. If other people can make up
countries and nationalities, then I can make up my own nationality: *Opel
Kadet*. It sounds good. By the way, everything is made up: Germany is made
up, Europe is made up, the earth is made up, life is made up, time is made up.
There are no facts, only stories. So put me down as Opel Kadet. And they did.
We fought for nine hours. In the end, they gave up. They typed all the documents, signed them, and stamped them. I was officially a car. Color gray.
Model 1987. Four doors plus a hatchback. No power steering."

I looked at Tsar, unable to say anything. I knew he made things up—it
was part of his personality, a way of showing his contempt for the amalgam of
tedious conventions that most people accepted as reality. But whether real or

exaggerated, the idea of someone being officially recognized by a government as a car model was absolutely profound. I couldn't even begin to think of all the implications that resulted from such an act—if we could call ourselves cars, or dogs, or trees, what did that say about the rest of the conventions? What did that say about the substance of names and identities? What did that do to the widely held belief that time goes forward, that one travels from here to there, that there is a plurality of things, that there are opposites, that people come from somewhere, that things arise and cease? Somehow, through the unfathomable workings of the cosmic switchboard, I had come to India to study the writings of Nagarjuna and his disciples on the nature of reality and had ended up sharing a room with someone who, in a way, was larger than the absolute truth, larger than countries, and wars, and names, and borders, Nirvana and hell—a modern-day Zeno jumping borders, breaking laws, and defying conventions, driven by the conviction that people are stuck in an unsolvable paradox, a paradox that needs to be discarded.

Tsar reached for the sack of clothes he'd packed earlier in the day, pulled the zipper, took out a sweater, a pair of pants, and a button-down shirt, and produced a frayed green folder tied on all sides with a long string.

"Here it is," he said with pride. "I've saved it to show it to my kids one day—I must have fathered a few by now, I just don't know where."

He handed me the folder and watched me untie the string with the pleasure and eagerness of someone who'd given their best friend a birthday present. I opened the folder and skimmed through some old photographs, a set of documents written in Serbian, a duplicate of Tsar's birth certificate, and a photocopy of his old passport. And then there it was, Tsar's application for asylum: *name* Djordje Berkich; *date of birth* August 21, 1960; *birthplace* Sarajevo; *nationality* Opel Kadet. The papers were stamped, dated, and signed.

"There's another one," Tsar said, taking out a smaller form. "It's my temporary residence permit. Whenever I was pulled over or stopped on the street, I'd show this to the police officers and they'd just stand there, reading it over and over again, turning it around, checking the stamp—to make sure it's real."

"So they couldn't stomach the thought of someone calling themselves Yugoslavian, but they were fine with Opel Kadet," I said.

"It's a German car, after all," Tsar replied laughing. "If they shoot me while crossing the border tomorrow, make sure you tell my kids that their father was a car."

"I will," I promised.

Tsar showed me a photograph of himself, his mother, his brother, and his sister-in-law standing over an open coffin where Tsar's deceased father lay dressed in a beige suit, his hands folded over his stomach, a lit candle stuck between his fingers. Tsar's brother and his wife stood at the lower end of the coffin. Tsar's mother, wearing a black head scarf and a black dress, stood in the center, staring at the lit candle. Tsar—in jeans, button-down shirt, and leather jacket—was bent over his father's face and was looking into his eyes with the intensity of someone trying to make out a word spoken in a very low, nearly imperceptible whisper.

"He drank a lot," Tsar said by way of explanation.

Vinnie put on his socks and shoes and stood up. "I can't see it, and I have a headache. Forced checkmate in three moves! Nonsense. You didn't let me think for one second—talking and talking and talking."

At the door, Vinnie turned around and looked at the chessboard for the very last time. Then he walked out without saying good-bye.

Twenty-two

I was dreaming that I was riding on an Indian government bus with fogged-up windows and a low roof painted blue and goats sitting in the front seats. There were beggars whose iodine-soaked bandages had gotten wrapped up around the handrails and the seats and the goats and the steering wheel and the standing passengers, and I was sitting all the way in the back, in the worst seat, breathing kerosene exhaust spouting through a hole in the floor. Every five minutes, the bus stopped and a mob of jubilant travelers stormed the front door, pushed their way past the goats, and got entangled in the bandages. Everything smelled of goat piss and vomited *chana masala*. At some point the driver made a sharp turn, lifting both left wheels off the ground, and suddenly I found myself squished beneath an old woman, her husband, and two college students who were discussing the upcoming cricket match between India and Pakistan. They talked simultaneously, repeating all of the fifty words that I knew in Hindi in random order, and when I tried to bring their attention to the fact that I was being suffocated, they just shook their heads and kept on talking. They didn't mind that our bus was rolling on two wheels.

I opened my eyes and saw two strangers—a man and a woman, both

wearing *shalwar kameez* outfits—sitting on my bed (the man was actually sitting on my foot) and speaking animatedly in Hindi as if they were in their
own home and wanted to show me that it was time for me to go. I retracted
my feet and sat up. What was going on? Who were these people? I could tell
from their clothes and gear (earrings, plastic bracelets, head scarf, umbrella,
large hemp bag, rubber shoes) that they were locals and probably owned a
house somewhere in the village. For a whole minute I just stared at them,
unable to put things in order. I felt as if I had spaced out while someone had
told a joke, and now everybody was laughing and I was standing in a corner, blinking and looking perplexed. *Because I don't like bananas with sugar!*
Ha-ha, very funny, but I have no idea what that means. Maybe I was missing
something, some essential piece of information that could explain why there
were local villagers sitting on my bed and having a chat at eight o'clock in
the morning. Maybe after all the things that had happened to Tsar and me,
we had entered a new sphere of reality where irrational occurrences passed as
normal. It was too confusing: Tsar without teeth, Tsar with teeth, Tsar as an
Opel Kadet, Tsar sneaking onto the Trans-Siberian express; me as a monk *trying* to understand the nature of reality and writing letters on Tsar's behalf: *the
tiger sleeps in the forest bereft of valediction.* Drinking horse milk in Ulan Bator.
I looked at Merry Anne's bed: it was empty. Another strange occurrence—he
hadn't come home all night. Tsar opened his eyes and sat up.

"Who are they?" he asked, nodding at the villagers occupying my bed.

"I don't know," I replied.

"Did you bolt the door last night?"

"I did."

It was Tsar's turn to be confused: he stared at the strangers, waved his
hands, shouted, "Hello!" and tossed a ball of scrunched-up paper at them,
but the man and the woman kept on talking, completely unaware of our
presence.

"Nikola, kick them out!" Tsar ordered. "Just push them off your bed.
That they will understand."

"I can't," I said.

Exasperated, Tsar lit a *biddie* and shook his head. "I'm giving up. India is like this giant octopus that attaches its tentacles onto your brain and doesn't let go until every aspect of reality crumbles and you start speaking to pink elephants in foreign tongues. I can't fight it anymore. I don't understand it. I can't figure it out. Would this ever happen anywhere else? Say you're renting an apartment in Berlin—the door is locked, you go to sleep and when you wake up the next morning there are Germans hanging out in your bed. By the way, if this happened to someone in Germany, or anywhere else in the world, people would start screaming and call the police. They might even run into the kitchen and get a knife. They might pull out a gun. And look at us: we're not screaming, we're not calling the police, we're not even trying to kick them out."

"But this is India," I reminded him. "Things happen again and again for absolutely no reason."

Tsar wasn't convinced. "There must be a reason, Nikola. These people didn't just materialize from nowhere. They snuck in somehow while we're sleeping. Maybe they got in through the window, or they unbolted the door from the outside with a knife. Maybe they unscrewed the hinges and then screwed them back on."

"And maybe they aren't humans," I suggested. "Maybe they are the spirits that live in the well on the other side of Jogibara laundry."

It was a truly strange morning. The only thing that I could discern with a great degree of certainty was that I was still in the Himalayas. If I were blindfolded and flown here from Antarctica, I'd know the place by the way that the all-encompassing echo in this part of the world slowed down and stretched every sound—the pulse of the river, the hammer banging in the distance, the shouting of crows. Even in the dead of the night, the uniquely tuned Himalayan echo was always present, an amplified silence carrying memories of past sounds.

A dark cloud veiled the skylight and heavy raindrops started drumming on the tin sheet that covered part of our roof. The man and the woman kept on talking. The man—thin, unshaven, over forty—seemed nervous. His voice wavered and every time he posed a question, he twisted his wrist and quickly wiped his hand on his pants. The woman, for her part, played with her head scarf and exhibited a variety of different moods: one minute she was shouting, the next she was saying "*Acha*" and "*tikke*" and looking utterly docile. Still later, she was chattering at a speed of five words per second with a deadpan expression and the telegraphic voice of a train station clerk relaying urgent messages through a loudspeaker.

"Unbelievable!" Tsar cried and stood in the middle of the room, wearing only underwear. Arms akimbo, he watched the intruders for a minute or two, trying to look scary, then he tapped the man on the shoulder and showed him the door. The man acknowledged the existence of the door, glanced at Tsar's black boxer shorts, said "*Acha!*" and resumed his conversation with the woman. Tsar raised his hands in the air, as if pleading for a quick and devastating demiurgic intervention, and ventured into the kitchen to start the kerosene stove.

"When will this end?" I heard him saying to himself while he pumped the stove.

"You should be happy," I told him. "Today you're leaving for China."

Tsar returned and put on a T-shirt and a pair of corduroys. Then he opened the sack that he'd packed the night before and dumped its contents on his bed.

"I'm not going anywhere," he declared, folding his clothes and putting all of his prized possessions where they belonged—the flashlight on the night table, the folder with documents under his bed, the sign that read "Bosnian bread! Try it! Only five rupees!" on the wall next to the world atlas, the Serbian-English dictionary on the bookshelf, and an English translation of Nagarjuna's *Wisdom: A Treatise on the Middle Way* (which he'd wrestled out of my hands, claiming that it was my farewell gift to him) under his pillow.

"How could I leave when there are people in my room!" he shouted, apparently addressing an invisible entity dwelling in the wooden box where we burned incense. "On the morning that I'm supposed to go to Gangtok, I wake up and . . . look! You show them the door and they just sit there. *Yebem li ti pichku materinu.*"

"You're acting irrational," I told him, as I got up and started folding my *shanthab* around my waist. "Not to mention that you're talking to a box filled with pulverized incense. Put all your stuff back in your bag, and let's go to the bus station. I'm coming with you. I'll take the bus to Gangtok. I'll walk you to the border. If you absolutely have to leave India, we'll find a way for you. Let's go."

Tsar sat on his bed, crossed his legs, and gestured manically at the intruders.

"Nikola, I've been around for a while—how old are you, nineteen? Okay, twenty-four—and I have to say, this is weird. I write a letter to the Secretary of the Indian Ministry of Home Affairs . . . by the way, I get into a fight with a group of idiots, and the letter ends up in the hands of the local authorities, who start going house to house asking people if they have any information about me. *Dobro,* now I'm under self-imposed house arrest, and what's better, the Hague tribunal for crimes against humanity knows my whereabouts and is reviewing my case because some insane woman sent them a letter telling them I'm a war criminal? How is that? Then Vinnie and I devise a plan to escape via Beijing, and then Moscow—a genius plan, by the way, absolutely brilliant—and look! Look who shows up! This is India saying, ah, Tsar, I know what you're up to and you won't succeed. Not in your present body. Maybe it's true what they say: maybe India is a demiurgic intelligence that appears in a way that mirrors people's internal worlds. Many people come here, see the Taj Mahal, go camel riding in Rajasthan, smoke weed in the Himalayas, drink *bhang lassies* in Varanasi, and when they go home, they just resume their little zombie existence and everything's fine: the sky is up, the earth is down, and the compass points north. By the way, if you're already fucked up on metaphysics, things start collapsing one by one—up, down, left, right, past, present—everything melts and turns into pink elephants."

Tsar got up and offered the Indian man a *biddie*. The man took it and pointed at the box of matches on the night table. Bowing down with exaggerated reverence, Tsar took the matches, kneeled before the man, and lit his *biddie*.

"I don't think they get it," I observed.

Outside, someone tripped on the stairs and fell in a puddle. I expected to see Merry Anne. It was Vinnie.

"Good," he said looking around the room. "It could've been much worse."

He took his shoes off and sat cross-legged on the floor. Suddenly the man and the woman fell silent and exited the room.

"Who were they?" Vinnie inquired.

"They were in the room when we woke up," Tsar explained.

Vinnie nodded. "It happens all the time. Once I woke up and found a donkey in my room. It could've been a goat—it's hard to say."

Tsar pointed out that the intruders had left only after Vinnie had taken his shoes off ("You really need to bathe," he added. "The soap is right there. Just walk down to the river, it takes five minutes—I'll give you a towel, too") but Vinnie pretended not to hear. He wiped his face with his shirt, then chipped off a piece of the mud wall and examined the newly emerged hole, as if he were searching for a nest of bedbugs.

"I was worried that you had taken the six o'clock bus to Sikkim and had left town," Vinnie acknowledged. "I'm here to announce that we're abandoning the plan in progress. I'm calling a conference."

After a brief scuffle over the two available teacups (Vinnie: "Do I not get to drink tea?" Tsar: "Not until you bathe." Vinnie: "I demand to have some tea!" Tsar: "You could drink from the ashtray.") the conference began. In his opening statement, Vinnie expressed regret for the fact that Tsar was under self-imposed house arrest and was no longer able to chase women, and then went on to reveal that the Trans-Siberian express scenario had a fundamental flaw and was doomed to fail. Vinnie described the flaw as geopolitical. When pressed to elaborate on the subject, Vinnie explained that China and Russia were de facto at war and that if Tsar were apprehended by the Chinese authorities, he would be charged with espionage (incriminatory factors: connection with the Trans-Siberian express, missing documents) and sentenced to death by firing squad. To support his claim that Russia and China were at war, Vinnie cited a 1969 border incident in which the Russians had supposedly obliterated an entire Chinese battalion with a laser. Tsar wasn't convinced but he gave Vinnie the benefit of the doubt. Next on the agenda were two new plans for escape, which Vinnie claimed to have conceived in his sleep. I was advised to get a pen and paper and take notes. (I was skipping class again.) Here are the plans:

1. *The Hong Kong Scenario.*

Facts: Every week an Indian freighter loaded with hundreds of prostitutes sails from Bombay to Hong Kong. The men in charge of the transportation have an office in New Delhi where they manufacture fake passports and visas for the prostitutes. Vinnie knows where the office is located. *Preparation:* Tsar dresses up as a woman (wig, makeup, fake breasts, skirt) and practices speaking in a high-pitched voice and walking without a swagger. *Implementation:* Tsar travels to New Delhi, shows up at the office of the men in charge of hiring prostitutes, and offers to work for them in return for a fake Russian passport. A week later, Tsar is hired as a Russian transvestite prostitute and shipped to Hong Kong. Upon disembarking, Tsar beats up his pimp captors, frees the rest of the prostitutes traveling with him, and plunges into the vast Hong Kong underworld: there are neon lights and pretty women and guns and Buddhist temples and everything is possible. At first Tsar works odd jobs, such as pushing carts and chopping vegetables in cheap restaurants, but when his Chinese improves, he is hired to work as a bodyguard for a respected local gangster and is soon awash in money. He buys himself a German passport and flies back to Europe.

2. *The Dutch Sailor Scenario.*

Facts: There are many insane people. Some travel around the world in a hot-air balloon. Some travel by bicycle. (Just a week before Tsar was forced into seclusion, an old Western man on a bicycle appeared in Dharamsala. He claimed to have started his trip in Finland. He looked pretty tired.) Some sail across the Atlantic in a handmade boat. *Preparation:* Rosenkrantz, who has just returned to the Netherlands and is driving a cab again, runs an article in a local Dutch newspaper titled "Brave Man from Amsterdam Plans to Sail Around the World in a Handmade Boat." The article features a photograph of Tsar from the time when he was living in the Netherlands and discusses the most likely trajectory of his naval expedition (North Sea, Tangier, Suez Canal, Horn of Africa, Arabian Sea, Indonesia, Australia). Tsar's real name is not mentioned. Instead, he's referred to as the Dutch Sailor: "... *an Amsterdam native, known to everyone in the community as the Dutch Sailor.*" When the article is published, Rosenkrantz sends a copy to Tsar in India. *Implementation:* Tsar travels to Bombay, waits for night, and swims out to sea, pushing a discarded wooden board. He wears nothing but a swimsuit and a money belt. The money belt contains the article from the Dutch paper, including the photograph of Tsar posing in front of a bar in Amsterdam's red light district. In the morning, Indian fishermen find Tsar flapping in the water, apparently drowning. The fishermen bring Tsar to the shore and hand him over to the local authorities. After a brief medical examination, Tsar is brought to the central police station, where the police chief demonstrates his incredible interrogation techniques. Tsar, however, is unresponsive: he doesn't understand English and he can't speak because he's emotionally traumatized and has suffered a concussion. The police chief opens Tsar's money belt and finds the article. He contacts the Dutch embassy and requests a translator. A Dutch government official flies to Bombay to conduct an interview with Tsar. Tsar answers all questions by blinking: *Are you Dutch?* One blink. *Can you speak?* Two blinks. *Do you have family in the Netherlands?* Tsar doesn't blink. He starts to cry. The Dutch government official takes Tsar in his custody and puts him on a plane to Amsterdam.

VINNIE PICKED UP a fist-size spider crawling on his foot and tossed it over his shoulder. "The main question is, what happens when you get to Amsterdam and no one comes to greet you? Your story is going to be in the news. Millions of Dutch people will see your photograph on the TV. What are you going to tell the police when your relatives don't show up?"

"I'll tell them that I don't remember anything," Tsar offered. "I have amnesia and my parents are dead. It could happen to anyone. Besides, we could have Rosenkrantz and a group of stoners stand outside my room and shout 'Welcome back, sailor!' or something like that."

"It won't work," Vinnie said with a tragic expression. "People will be interrogated. There will be court orders and written statements. Rosenkrantz will contradict himself a thousand times and the police will find out that he'd organized the whole thing. He will be arrested. More arrests will follow."

"But what are they going to do with me?" Tsar asked. "Send me back to India?"

"They will never send you back," I said. "Once you get to the Netherlands, you'd be free."

"That's a good point," Vinnie agreed. "A judge will pronounce you incontinent and they will put you in a mental sanatorium. It might be nice."

It was settled: Tsar was going to swim a mile into the Arabian Sea and wait to be rescued by Indian fishermen. Tsar was so excited about the prospect of playing a drowning, mute Dutch sailor suffering from amnesia that he let Vinnie win two chess games in a row by sacrificing both of his knights right in the beginning of each game. Vinnie took full credit for his victory and decided to give Tsar some advice: "Your calculations are strong," he told Tsar, "but they are strategically flawed."

I had missed my morning class at the institute but still had time to visit Geshe Yama Tseten and attend the afternoon courtyard debate, which started at two. I made a list of things that Tsar wanted me to buy from the market (he was hiding from the Indian Secret Service and couldn't even buy himself cig-arettes) and went out. When I returned later that evening, the house looked completely transformed: the floor was swept, a butter lamp in the wall cavity next to Tsar's bed illuminated a postcard-size painting of Nagarjuna, the air smelled of dal and *aloo gobi masala,* Tsar was in the kitchen kneading a ball of dough, and Merry Anne was sitting on his bed, reading the *I Ching.* I asked Merry Anne why he hadn't come home the previous night and he said— blinking slowly and exhibiting signs of intense pain—that he had experi-enced the most amazing two days of his life: he had fallen in love with a stunningly beautiful Irishwoman of Indian descent who had shown him things that he had never known existed. I tried hard to keep a serious face and even contemplated asking him to give me some details, but when I saw Tsar stumble out of the kitchen—bent in half, squealing, a dal-dripping ladle in his hand—I burst out laughing and collapsed on the floor. Tsar followed suit. We were bad friends and Merry Anne informed us that he would never tell us what had happened between him and the woman, and that he was going—alone—on a trip to visit Khajuraho and the Taj Mahal, and then he was leaving India for good. He'd made reservations to fly in two weeks. Tsar regained his composure and asked Merry Anne for forgiveness. "Come on, *choveche,*" he pleaded, "tell us what she did to you!" Merry Anne shook his head and said no. We were doomed.

I joined Tsar in the kitchen and started making chapati. We cooked kneeling on the damp, earthen floor using slate tiles as chopping boards. The walls of the kitchen were splattered with food—a result of leaving the pressure cooker unattended for too long. The air smelled of urine and dead rats (we suspected that the kitchen was built on top of a cesspit) and despite our efforts to seal the brick-size hole, originally intended as a drain, the shallow square pit in the left corner of the room was constantly filled with a greenish, mucus-like liquid. I flattened the balls of dough that Tsar handed to me and examined all the objects and substances that had been stamped into the earthen floor, forming a mosaic of our life on Jogibara Road. There were Indian coins, a discarded razor, rat shit, lychee seeds, beans, lentils, severed spider legs, and newspaper clippings that had become inseparable from the earth.

"We have a new neighbor," Tsar informed me. "Some Western girl. She moved into Ani Dawa's old room this afternoon. I think she's coming over for dinner."

"Did you invite her?" I asked.

"No. You're going to invite her."

"No way," I said. "It's getting dark and I'm a monk—I'm not going to go and introduce myself just like that! What is she going to think? There's no way."

Ten minutes later, I was standing outside Ani Dawa's old room in full monastic attire, smiling piously—just as I'd been instructed. The door opened to a blond, twenty-something girl wearing a long hippie skirt, a T-shirt, and a handmade Tibetan vest. She seemed excited to meet me and said that she'd love to join me and my friends for dinner. I peeked into her room, curious to see how it had been arranged. The floor was covered with straw mats, and there was a mattress in one corner. She either didn't know about the snakes or was incredibly brave.

We ate dinner (the girl's name was Beatrix and she was from Belgium) and played Battleship. Merry Anne won all the games, sinking everyone's fleet in seconds. In a spurt of creativity, Tsar took the broken tape player apart, tinkered with the cogwheels for a few minutes, and got it to work. We listened to

John Lennon's greatest hits—the only tape in our collection that wasn't chewed up and still produced intelligible sound, albeit with an unremitting half-tone modulation. At midnight, Beatrix got up to go, and Tsar offered to escort her to her room, saying that he needed to inspect the wall cavities for hazardous animals. His inspection must've produced some unexpected results, because soon Beatrix started to giggle like a little kid who's being tickled, and a little later Merry Anne and I felt the pulse of a distant beat that made the roof tiles rattle and agitated the rats scurrying on the tarpaulin sheet above our heads. "They do it like animals," Merry Anne noted with revulsion. "And how do you do it?" I asked him, hoping that he'd disclose some details about his affair with the Irish-Indian woman. Merry Anne opened his mouth and was about to say something, but then he changed his mind and shrugged his shoulders instead.

Tsar returned in the middle of the night and went into the kitchen to start the kerosene stove. I flicked my flashlight on and pointed it at the alarm clock sitting on the windowsill. It was three a.m. The little Tibetan girl living next door woke up and her grandmother told her to go back to sleep. Merry Anne kicked his covers off and sat up, grunting. Holding a lit candle, Tsar entered the bedroom, placed the candle on his night table, and lit a *biddie*. "What?" he asked, looking at us. "You should be thanking me, really, you should say, *choveche*, thank you for waking us up from these boring dreams. Sleeping is useless and makes people stupid. Look at this!" Tsar pointed at the tarpaulin sheet, the walls, and the door. "It's super. Call it life. Listen to the mountains!" Merry Anne and I listened; we heard nothing but the pounding of the kerosene stove. "This is the Himalayas, *choveche*. This is where the universe is created, second after second. The whole illusion, from beginning to end. The stars and the earth and the sky and man and all the rest of the creatures who are all human beings in disguise. Illusion comes out like smoke; you could see it coming out from the top of the mountain—it's like a volcano that shoots illusion and we're sitting right on top of it, on the illusion reactor, and you should be excited about it—so what if it's three a.m.?

You're alive, the sky is turning, the leopards are out hunting dogs, it's super. Enjoy it."

After three hours of laborious lovemaking, Tsar looked like he'd wrestled a bear—his lips were cracked, his hair was sticking out in every direction, there was a bruise on his neck, and his eyes were on fire.

"The little girl next door!" Merry Anne protested. "She has tuberculosis. You woke her up: the kerosene stove is louder than an airplane."

Tsar giggled and gave me a look that said, *Your friend, I don't know where you found him, but he's a complete square.*

The tea was ready. Tsar brought three clean cups from the kitchen and sat on his bed, rubbing his hands and jerking his shoulders to warm up. Reluctantly, Merry Anne poured himself a cup of tea and took a sip. "Jesus, Tsar!" he cried out. "How much sugar did you dump in?"

"Only six spoons," Tsar replied. "It's nothing."

For a few minutes we sipped our tea in silence, listening to the wind, the dogs howling by the river, and the propeller-like sound of a huge kamikaze beetle flying around the room. Then, without any introduction, Tsar ventured into a dramatic monologue that, judging by his gesticulations and his poignant glances toward the different corners of the room, seemed to have been directed at a large gathering of invisible spectators—karmic arbiters, gods of death, doorkeepers of primordial reality, etc. It should be noted that Tsar's after-midnight monologues were a recurrent theme in our life on Jogibara Road. They lasted anywhere from twenty minutes to two hours and sparked mixed reactions in the audience. (I giggled; Merry Anne shook his head, clicked his tongue, and cried, "*E-e-eh, Tsar, you really think we're idiots!*")

Here's an account of Tsar's monologue on the meaning of life:

"I don't know why people get so excited about dying. What's the big deal? All this medicine, all the propaganda—as if staying alive is the most important thing in the world. By the way, we're already dead. We've already been reborn. We've walked past the gates, smoked a cigarette with the guards, drunk a cup of Turkish espresso with Yama. People say, *now, now, here and now*—it's like they've been programmed. *Now* is a memory, and *here* is the opposite of *there*. That covers the subject. So what's so special about this life? Everywhere you look, there are people dragging or pushing something. Where are they going? What's the rush? All this excitement! Studying, passing exams, learning skills, saving money for retirement. The bureaucracy of life—go here, do this, get up, sit down, choose a nationality, show your passport, roll over, dance, be happy, be sad. It's too much work. And then they ask: but what's the meaning of this? Why is now *this* now, and why do we know it? By the way, life is very simple. All you have to do is make an appearance: hello. Oh, that's where we're at. Someone invented the radio. I remember that. It already happened. Bye now—and you go. Some people are lucky. They go quick and don't think about it too much. For most people, however, dying is a major ordeal. You have to talk to other people and pretend that you're enjoying the whole bureaucracy of existence. And then there's all this worry: what happens next, and *when* does it happen? By the way, dying is just another magic trick: now you're here, now you're not. Tap the magic wand. Put the rabbits back into the hat: as simple as that. You can never see the rabbits disappear. You could sit with your eyes wide open and count every second, and you're still going to miss it. And then you have all these people who want to live to be a hundred. When I lived in Germany, everyone wanted to live for at least one hundred years. That's why Germans fart so much: because it's scientifically proven that farting prolongs life. By the way, Germans have a constitutional right to fart in public. You get on a bus and it's like watching a conference: one by one, people get up, fart, say 'Guten tag,' and sit back down. Some passengers get so carried away, they just stand in the middle of the bus and fart until it's time for them to get off." (Here, Merry Anne interrupted Tsar's monologue, shouting, "E-e-eh, Tsar, *we've also been to Germany. You can't possibly think that we're going to believe you!*") "*Choveche*, I'm absolutely serious. You go to a restaurant or an opera, and every two or three seconds someone will get up and fart really loud. When I lived in Frankfurt, I worked for a construction company that built high-rises. It was a really dangerous job: we'd be standing on a fifty-story-high skeleton, bare metal beams all the way down, and you'd see a construction worker walking across a twenty-meter-long beam—no ropes, nothing—and just when you'd think he's going to slip and fall, he'd stop, stand on one leg, and fart for a whole minute. If Germans had to choose—miss an opportunity to fart, or die farting—seventy percent would choose to die farting."

Tsar's monologue lasted a lot longer. He talked in circles, he raised rhetorical questions and covered the advance of human civilization from the Miocene epoch to the construction of the pyramids. When he was done it was five o'clock in the morning and our skylight was starting to change colors. Tsar got up, stuck a pack of *biddies* and a box of matches in the pocket of his pants, and walked to the door. "I don't know what your plans are for today," he said with a smug smile, "but I'm going to go over to Beatrix and get some more."

Merry Anne and I remained in bed and listened to the kamikaze beetle take off, roar over our beds with great determination, hit the wall head-on, and fall on the floor or on our blankets, unleashing a fierce barrage of electric sparks. Himalayan mornings are strange, especially when your heart is charged with caffeine and you've spent your entire night stuffing real rabbits into magic hats. Half-awake, half-asleep, I watched the skylight turn paler and paler as my thoughts grew heavier and heavier, a train loaded with unfamiliar things. The tarpaulin sheet seemed unfamiliar, and so did the room and the mud walls and my bed. The shadows from the dark rainclouds passing overhead created the illusion that we were moving: the entire Shiva sanctuary, together with all the mud houses stacked up around it, was afloat. The clay statues of Shiva, Wife, and Son were actually aeronauts, and our landlord's tofu-making machine was a space-erasing turbine, and even though Tsar and Beatrix were making love, the cows were mooing, and the kamikaze beetle was trying to knock everything down, we knew that we'd reached the end and there wasn't anything we could do to bring about a new beginning. Even Shiva, in his clay manifestation, seemed cynical about it, and some of us remembered time, and some others remembered that they'd never been born and had never had parents, and everything was made out of memories, but we couldn't remember who had given them to us and when. Everyone spoke many languages simultaneously, and we remembered all the questions and all the answers, but we couldn't remember what they were meant for, except for the question about consciousness. There were always exceptions, because if the present was remembered, and consciousness was nothing but memory, then no one could ever claim that they were conscious, say, of the strange volcanic stone standing behind the clay statue of Shiva's wife. And if no one was conscious of anything, consciousness couldn't be called "consciousness," memories would exist without an agent, being alive and not being would be one thing, and as a consequence of all this, Merry Anne, Tsar, and I could never know for sure if our memories were our own or borrowed from somebody else. There was also a possibility that all memories were invented, in much the same way that the Egyptians had invented the camel, and the Chinese, the moon. Perhaps one day our landlord had walked across the Shiva sanctuary courtyard, pulling his donkey by a rope, and had thought, *I remember that strange volcanic rock!*—and from that point on everyone had remembered the rock, even though no one had seen it. Similarly, it could be suggested that when our landlord had turned on the space-erasing turbine and the Shiva sanctuary had taken off, everything that had taken place prior to the takeoff had been forgotten and everyone had invented new memories to fill in the gaps. Of course, different people had remembered different things but eventually we had all agreed to remember *something else* instead. Then someone had remembered that the difference between us and the Buddha was that we first remember and then see, whereas the Buddha first sees and then sees again—he cannot remember—and when people had remembered that, they'd gotten very happy, because remembering was a very satisfying business. And Merry Anne and I remained in our beds for at least a thousand years, and Tsar and Beatrix went on fucking until all the slate tiles covering the roof of Ani Dawa's old house collapsed to the ground and the room filled up with rain water, at which point they briefly thought about other things, but then remembered that fucking was nice and decided to keep going indefinitely. And when the kamikaze beetle finally succeeded in puncturing a hole in the wall and was free to go wherever it pleased, it suddenly died (because of karma) and was reborn as a powerful Mexican farting beetle that could kill its prey from three feet away. In the end, Shiva and his wife crashed the floating sanctuary into a snow-capped Himalayan pinnacle, which was okay because the pinnacle turned out to be a volcano, a volcano spouting illusion, and soon everything was recreated backwards, and we still remembered, even though everything had already happened twice. And Merry Anne and I continued to lie very still because we didn't know what else there was to do and we weren't brave enough to get up and ask someone for advice.

Himalayan mornings are strange. Watching the shadows of the clouds passing overhead change the color of the blankets from burgundy to orange to brown. Watching the dark green table turn beige and then gray.

Twenty-three

anz gut! Ganz gut!" Vinnie shouted heroically and put the long *kusha*-grass broom under his arm. "We're going to do this again. Tsar, I need more from you. Everything is about acting. Everything. I need passion. You will never make it across if you keep that silly grin on your face. Life is a serious matter. You've been misinformed: you have to look misinformed. Lodro, remember that you're carrying a huge and very heavy rifle. You can't just jump out of your booth and start running like a . . . grasshopper. Let's start from the place where Tsar enters the room."

It was the beginning of November, and Tsar, Vinnie, and I were rehearsing Vinnie's latest border-crossing plan, which involved a checkpoint on the Indian-Pakistani border near Amritsar, two border guards, and five hundred meters of neutral territory that had to be crossed on foot. The plan was based on the assumption that the checkpoint in question was closed during the night, and if Tsar showed up early in the morning—somewhere around four or five a.m.—the border guards would be either asleep or not present, and he would be able to walk across the border without having to show a passport or talk to anyone. Not too long ago, Vinnie claimed, he'd taken a trip to Pakistan, and when he'd arrived at the checkpoint near Amritsar, he'd just walked halfway across the neutral territory and no one had tried to stop him. The guards, apparently, had gone on a chai break and abandoned their posts. Vinnie could easily have entered Pakistan illegally, if that had been his goal. Vinnie's new plan—just like all his other plans—had a central problem that needed to be addressed at the outset. The problem was that, at any point during the operation, the guards could wake up or suspend their chai break and see Tsar crossing the five-hundred meters of neutral territory. They'd fire warning shots and rush toward Tsar to apprehend him. Tsar's disadvantages in this situation were clear: he was exposed, he couldn't run, and he had to follow orders or get shot. For most people, a plan whose success is determined entirely by luck is not worth considering. What were the odds that Tsar could walk for eight minutes (the amount of time it took to cross the neutral territory, according to Vinnie) without being spotted by any of the guards on either side of the border? Ten percent? Twenty? Tsar and I thought that the plan was absurd. We ridiculed Vinnie and told him to take a cold bath in the river. We did that because we failed to realize that we were dealing with a master tactician, a man whose calculating power could transform a losing position into an attack that brought inevitable victory. Vinnie had, in fact, solved the central problem in his plan, and he'd done so with brilliance. The solution was simple: Tsar would walk backwards. It's five o'clock in the morning, the guards on the Indian side of the border have gone missing, and Tsar enters the neutral territory, walking backwards. Halfway through, an Indian guard wakes up, sees Tsar, and runs after him, firing his rifle indiscriminately. When the Indian guard orders Tsar to go back, pointing his rifle at Tsar's chest, Tsar smiles politely and says, "But sir, I *am* going back—see? I came from Pakistan, then I realized I had taken the wrong road and started retreating. I had been misinformed." Or: Tsar has traversed two-thirds of the neutral territory when he is intercepted by a Pakistani guard and ordered to go back to India. "I can't go to India illegally!" Tsar protests. "I came from Pakistan and now I'm going back. I didn't know this was the border—I've been misinformed."

Here is a reconstruction of the rehearsal that Vinnie directed with the aim of helping Tsar learn more about the *psychology* of border crossing.

Tsar Walks Backwards Across the Border
(Stage Directions and Suggested Dialogue: Take 2)

"Good! Good!" Vinnie said thoughtfully and pretended to load the *kusha*-grass broom with ammunition. "Tsar enters through the kitchen. Tsar?"

"What?" Tsar said from his bed.

"This is the day that fate decides if you live or die!" Vinnie exploded. "What do you do?"

"I stay in bed," Tsar replied, giggling.

Vinnie started pacing around the room, broom in hand, then stopped suddenly in front of the mirror and examined his mustache. "Lodro!" he called, looking at me in the mirror. "Keep your rifle upright. You don't want to shoot anyone by accident."

I sighed and pointed the rolling pin at the ceiling. Vinnie was an experienced director. He cared about the details.

"Tsar appears into view," Vinnie announced, still facing the mirror. "He is walking backwards. Tsar, take a position in the kitchen and walk slowly into the bedroom."

"All right, Vinnie, we get it," Tsar said, exasperated. "I've spent the entire morning pretending to get shot and arguing with imaginary entities."

Vinnie turned around, propped the broom against the wall, and stretched his arms as if he'd just woken up from a nap. "Ah, the sun!" he exclaimed with a Pakistani border guard expression (raised eyebrows, pouting lips, nervous blinking). "The sun is killing me. Every day the same routine—clean my rifle, drink chai, smoke *biddies*. When will this come to an end? I see heat rising in the desert. There are camels dancing in the distance. It must be a mirage."

Tsar and I looked at each other and shook our heads. "What sun are you talking about?" Tsar asked. "It's supposed to be five o'clock in the morning."

Vinnie looked at his watch, tapped it, brought it close to his ear. "I must've slept through breakfast. I dreamed about the accident again. My best friend was sitting next to me. Hassan. There was a truck in front of us, loaded with metal rods. I didn't hit the brakes in time. One of the metal rods went through Hassan's eyeball. Horrible death. We talked a bit before the end. He didn't mind."

"Vinnie, you need to see a psychiatrist," Tsar said, looking worried. "I've no idea what you're talking about. And neither does Lodro. We've discussed all the scenarios. I'm leaving for Amritsar tomorrow."

"Lodro, look through your binoculars and tell me what you see," Vinnie ordered.

I shaped my hands into binoculars and scanned the room. "I see an intruder."

"Then do something about it!" Vinnie shouted, clenching his fists. "Show some passion—you guys are totally dead."

"Mister," I said gravely, and aimed one end of the rolling pin at Tsar's head. "I'm afraid I'll have to shoot you."

"Shoot if you have to," Tsar said agreeably. "Make sure you shoot the Pakistani guard as well. He's getting on my nerves."

I cocked the rolling pin and shot Vinnie in the chest. He instantly dropped dead on the floor. "This is not in the script," Vinnie confided from the Afterworld. He attempted to move his hands, kicked his legs for a few seconds, and expired for the second time.

"I'm a Buddhist monk and I just shot a man with a rolling pin," I shouted, trying to sound angry. "Why did you ask me to do such an awful thing?"

Tsar lit a *biddie* and added the last card to his solitaire. "My luck is just shit," he said with disappointment. He wiped a raindrop from his forehead and looked up at the ceiling. It had been raining for the third straight day, and the tarpaulin sheet had started to collect water, forming two large, perspiring balloons: one above Tsar's bed and one above mine.

Vinnie got up from the floor and stretched his hands. "The sun!" he exclaimed, shielding his eyes with his hand. "Scorching heat. Every day it's the same—drink chai, clean my rifle."

"It's November, it's cold, and you're dead," Tsar informed him. "Lodro just shot you with his rifle."

"And who are you?" Vinnie asked, threatening Tsar with the broom.

"I'm an Opel Kadet. Gray. With no luck."

"Turn around and go back to India!" Vinnie ordered him, putting his finger on the trigger.

"If I turn around, I'll enter Pakistan," Tsar reminded him.

Vinnie lowered the broom and nodded. "That's right. You're walking backwards. If you turn around, you'd enter Pakistan. Brilliant. A genius plan."

He pondered the complexity of the situation a while longer and stepped into the kitchen. "Brilliant!" he kept saying to himself. There was a sound of water being poured on the floor and I tried to imagine what Vinnie was doing in the kitchen. Was he washing his hands with the drinking water from the bucket, or was he doing something to the roof? I got up from my bed and peeked into the kitchen: Vinnie was standing in a corner, peeing on the wall. The stream passed between his legs and snaked to the middle of the kitchen, where it formed a large puddle. "Goddamn it, Vinnie," I shouted. "We cook on this floor. Why couldn't you go and pee outside?"

I stood in front of Tsar's bed and gestured in the direction of the kitchen.

"What?" Tsar asked, picking up a card from the pile facing down. He'd started a new game of solitaire.

"What do you mean, what?" I said, working myself up. "Vinnie just peed all over the kitchen floor. Aren't you a little concerned? How are we going to cook dinner now?"

"Nikola, you're going to have a nervous breakdown," Tsar warned me. "Relax. It's an earthen floor. It absorbs water. And pee."

"I feel like I'm in an asylum for the mentally insane," I said. "What is this—Vinnie walking around with a broom, pretending to be a Pakistani border guard. We're not kids."

"Then why did you shoot me with the rolling pin?" Vinnie inquired, emerging from the kitchen. His fly was open, his hands wet.

"Because this is what I do these days," I replied. "I sit around all day and play games with two people who are completely nuts. Vinnie, you're almost seventy years old! What are you doing dropping on the floor, kicking your legs, and chasing Tsar and me with a broom? I can't do this anymore. I don't know how I ended up stuck in this room, rehearsing Tsar's escape from India, day and night, week after week—it's been almost three months since Tsar barricaded himself here. All I wanted to do was to live a simple life and study the Buddhist classics in Tibetan. It's not too much to ask for."

"He came to India for the Enlightenment," Vinnie confided, nodding at Tsar.

"Then give it to him," Tsar said, studying the combination of cards laid out in front of him. "I don't want anything to do with it. Last time I took it out of the box, it destroyed my *biddies*, wiped the colors from my eyes, and disconnected all my notions—I couldn't smile, couldn't get angry, couldn't move, couldn't remember. It's like I was hospitalized after a stroke. At least now I could die whenever I want. I can get shot crossing the border. I can feel pain. I can go to hell. I'm free to do whatever I want. I can be bad, I can be good. There are so many choices. And I can travel and see new things. That's what life is about, right? Travel. Meet new people. Get laid. Play different roles. Can the Buddha *experience* hell? Can he *experience* illusion? No. He could see it, the way we see Jerusalem on a postcard. So, no. I don't need the Enlightenment. He could have it."

"Take it," Vinnie said to me, pointing at the floor. "It's under the bed. In a box."

"Maybe I should go live somewhere else," I said. "In a meditation hut up the mountain. Somewhere I could focus on my studies."

"Somewhere!" Vinnie grunted. He looked at the door, as if he expected Somewhere to enter the room, coughing and spilling rain water on the carpet. "There's nothing outside. Nowhere to go. Beyond this door, it's a desert!"

I crawled into my bed and opened up the Tibetan text I had been struggling to memorize for the last two days. I stared at the letters but all I could see were snow-tipped Himalayan ridges, goat trails, and lonely mud houses encircled by overlapping green terraces. Even though our tiny window showed only a part of a wall and a few slate tiles, the image of the mountains was always at the back of my mind, like a magnet pulling at my thoughts and distorting my memories. I looked over at the hole-in-the-wall bookshelf where I kept most of my belongings, craving something familiar, something that could remind me of the time before I had gotten stuck in this Indian eternity. Strangely, I had almost nothing from my past—no photographs, no letters, no memorabilia. What I owned were stacks of Tibetan books—looseleaf, hardcover, paperback, hand-crafted books, some printed in South India, some in China—bags of Tibetan medicine to treat my recurring amoebic dysentery (I was certain that the Tibetan medicine didn't work and was absolutely

useless, but I kept on chewing the bitter pills, perhaps out of superstition), notebooks, seeds blessed by the Nechung oracle (given to
me by Geshe Yama Tseten, who believed that the seeds had the
magical power to keep thieves away), a flashlight, and a tape of John
Coltrane's *Giant Steps*. I cherished the tape as a relic and often
caught myself staring at the cover photograph of Coltrane—shown
from below, against the backdrop of an extremely depressing gray
curtain—blowing his horn, with his eyes closed. I had bought the
tape during one of my trips to New Delhi. It was manufactured in
Bombay and cost 175 rupees, which was half of what I paid for a
month's rent. Unfortunately, the tape never worked—when I
played it, it sounded as if it had been recorded at slow speed, under-
water. Unable to listen to the tunes, I tried to play them in my head.
I remembered the first time I had actually *heard* what Coltrane was
doing—in a dingy Huntington Avenue apartment, not far from
Berklee College of Music, where a friend of mine lived—a long-
haired bass player named George. George was in the kitchen,
stoned, watching porn and practicing his scales. I don't know why
he was watching porn—it was noon, and both of us had a class at
one. I was in the living room, looking out the window: yellow-red
leaves covered the sidewalk; a sign across the street invited college
students to sign up for a free AIDS test. I wasn't aware that the tape
deck was on until I heard the familiar sound of the auto reverse
mechanism turning around. There was a powerful tremor in the
hundred-watt speakers, and suddenly Coltrane was on, gliding
down the fast changes of "Giant Steps," at first innocuously and
then with increasing intensity, rushing through the first bars of the
solo as if he'd caught fire, building up a giant mass of tension and
exploding on bar seventeen with a high D, a high D over a B major
seventh chord, turning the whole world upside down and inside
out—and that's when I heard the effect of Coltrane's famous major

thirds cycle, an elliptical chord progression that made everything around you spin: it made time blurry. Stunned, I sat on the hardwood floor and listened to the rest of the album, unable to move, unable to think.

"Does anyone want chai?" Tsar asked, getting up. "I'm starting the stove."

I raised my hand. Vinnie thought about it, grabbed the broom, and walked to the middle of the room. "Guys, we're out of time," he said with the air of someone who'd just stumbled upon a large-scale conspiracy. "Let's rehearse this again. Lodro, pick up your rifle."

The train station in Pathankot was dusty and deserted. A beggar girl no older than nine was crawling on the floor, pushing herself with her hands; her twisted, crippled feet dragged behind, as if they had been attached to her body by mistake. Tsar and I sat on a bench and watched a station clerk spray himself with a thick hose that was usually used to flush the toilets on the passing trains. Tsar was eating his third omelet. "*Choveche*, we are like vampires," he said, chasing the flies with his free hand. "It's not normal to live without sun. No wonder everyone goes insane in Dharamsala. The rain, the fog, everywhere you look, walls of mountains—like a prison. By the way, you go fifty kilometers to the south or to the west, and it's summer all year round. Feel the sun! My skin tingles like I've been pricked by a million tiny needles. Incredible."

The train was two hours late, but we didn't mind waiting. It felt great to be traveling after sitting in our room for so many months. We talked about Beatrix, who'd survived the living conditions on Jogibara Road for only two weeks, and we remembered the day when Merry Anne had returned from his trip to Agra and Khajuraho and had told us, in all seriousness, that he'd met the Devil and that his days were numbered. "The Devil sells carpets in Agra," Merry Anne had announced, standing in the door frame frail and scared, a rucksack slung over his shoulder. Goggle-eyed, Tsar and I had begged him to continue. "I go to see the Taj Mahal, and . . . and I go back to my hotel, it's night, and . . . and he says—he was an Indian man selling carpets—he says, 'Come, see my shop.' He spoke Russian! And Japanese! And German! And his left eye was green and the right one was black: do you get it? The Devil speaks every language and his eyes are different colors! And . . . and first I saw him in front of his shop. Then I walked back, and he's standing in front of my room. He'd teleported himself! I stayed in all night, and he was outside, speaking to someone in Russian and . . . and the next day, I ran, and he was outside, limping with his left leg, and then I saw him near the train station, limping with his right leg . . . and . . . and . . . he was the Devil and I met him."

Tsar got up and spat on the ground. "I'm telling, you, *choveche*, India does this to people. Take Merry Anne. He came here to finish his thesis and look what happened to him. He fell madly in love with an Indian woman, and when the woman told him she's married, he went to Agra and met the Devil. And he was lucky: he had a passport and a return ticket, and managed to escape before it was too late. You, and me, and Vinnie—we are fucked. We'll never get out of here alive."

Tsar sauntered down the platform, to see if there were any trains coming. The girl with the crippled legs crawled after him and pulled at his pants. Tsar rooted in his pocket and gave her a coin. The girl wasn't happy: she rubbed his shoes and asked him for more coins. "See that guy there?" Tsar asked her and pointed at me. The girl turned around and began crawling my way.

It had taken me a long time to understand what Tsar meant when he said that we'd never get out of India alive. At first, when Vinnie and Tsar had started devising various plans for crossing the border illegally, I had tried to persuade Tsar to accept his predicament and stay in India. I thought that it was stupid for someone to risk his life for the privilege of setting foot in another country. Tsar didn't even believe that countries existed—why was he so obsessed with escaping from India, then? Why get killed when he could live a good, simple life, and have plenty of time to think about reality? Tsar loved India—he'd told me so many times. He'd also told me that he'd never been happier than when he'd lived in the small hut by the river and had baked and sold bread. Why then was he in such a rush to get himself killed? It was totally irrational. For three months Tsar had lived in a self-imposed solitary confinement—to avoid getting arrested—and every day Vinnie had come to our room, convinced that he'd thought of the perfect scenario for jumping the border. The Trans-Siberian express scenario had been replaced by the Hong Kong scenario, which, in turn, had been replaced by the Dutch Sailor scenario. More plans had followed, each one crazier, more impossible, than the one before. At one point we had even discussed a plan in which Tsar would get himself kidnapped by Kashmiri separatists and then either run away or wait to be rescued by the Indian army—the idea being that once Tsar was free and the story of his kidnapping was in the news, he would be flown back to Europe without charge and he wouldn't have to show a passport or a valid visa. Day after day, I had rehearsed imaginary border-crossing situations, taken notes, and made suggestions—all the while trying to figure out what was happening in Tsar's head. Why was he afraid of being detained by the local Indian police but didn't mind getting shot by a border guard? Why was he so eager to jump the border just to be illegal and on the run somewhere else? How was being without a passport in Pakistan, China, or Iran better than being illegal in India? And even if Tsar miraculously managed to get to the Balkans, what then? His house had been destroyed during the war. What was he going to do?

One day, as I was thinking about all this, it suddenly occurred to me that perhaps Tsar's predicament had very little to do with countries, passports, visas, and border guards. Perhaps what appeared to me as irrational and contradictory made perfect sense on a different level, on a higher plane of logic, where India, its border, and the world beyond were only stand-ins for larger, metaphysical symbols. It was very possible that in Tsar's mind, India represented the ultimate source of illusion, a primordial apparatus that transformed fears, desires, and ideas into rocks, stars, galaxies, carbon, trees, and then divided everything into halves, so that whatever appeared to exist actually didn't, and whatever seemed to have arisen had already disappeared. Perhaps, then, for Tsar the act of leaving India was really about reaching the limits of illusion and enacting the ultimate feat of emancipation—crossing to the other shore. And it didn't matter whether he got killed in the process. Could he really die while stuck in an apparatus that spouted illusion day and night, like a volcano? Could anyone? What mattered was the act of defiance. By walking backwards across the Indian-Pakistani border, he was showing the world that he'd figured out what everything was about—he'd seen the hoax and the hoax beyond the hoax, he'd seen through Samsara and Nirvana, and now he was free to do whatever he wanted. He could get shot and start over from the beginning. He could cross into the Dharmadhatu, the sphere of Enlightenment, smoke a pack of *biddies* with the disenchanted Buddhas, and then come back. He wasn't just another victim of the bureaucracy of existence who had ended up stuck in a mud cell high in the Himalayas—he had free will and he was going to use it.

Our train finally arrived and Tsar and I went in, trailed by the crippled girl. By the time we left Pathankot, the sun was setting and the half-dozen Indian army guards had all fallen asleep, hugging their rifles. Some slept coiled on a bench, others slept sitting, and still others dozed off leaning against a wall or a pillar. In the distance, beyond the squat houses and the cone-shaped temples, a vast patch of smoldering farmland dissolved into a wall of thick black smoke. I watched the world rush past—a man coming home from work, a half-naked child shitting in the middle of a field, a giant scorched tree surrounded by cows eating newspapers, mud houses plastered with round cow dung patties, brick houses with stained-glass windows, a woman hanging laundry on the roof of her house, an old saddhu tending a miniature road shrine. All of the images juxtaposed with Tsar's reflection in the window, and suddenly everything felt wrong and I got really angry about the fact that I had agreed to help Tsar carry out a plan that was nothing but pure suicide. What was I doing on that train? Escorting Tsar to the scaffold?

"I'm not going to write to your mother informing her how and why you died," I told Tsar.

"Do whatever you want," he replied.

We avoided looking at each other. I was angry with him, and he was angry with me. An hour went past and the train stopped in the middle of a field, perhaps to wait for another train to arrive. Tsar purchased a pack of *biddies* from a man selling chai and told me that he was going to walk to the last car to smoke. I followed him reluctantly. We stepped out onto an open platform and stared into the quiet night. The train started moving again, and Tsar remembered the time when he used to work on the Yugoslav railways and would spend weeks and sometimes months sleeping on different trains and traveling from one end of the country to the other. I told him that when I was nine, my dad and I had traveled to Italy by train, and on the way back, right before Belgrade, someone had broken into our compartment during the night and stolen my dad's passport and money. "Did your dad find his passport in the toilet, behind the sink?" Tsar inquired. "Yes, he did," I replied. "The ticket collector told him that when someone gets robbed during the night, they usually find their passport in the toilet, either behind the sink or on top of the water tank."

Tsar did some calculations and concluded that, given our age difference, it was highly possible that it had been he who had stolen my dad's passport and money. He'd been twenty-two at the time and he'd been assigned to work the Ljubljana-Belgrade route. I looked at Tsar, trying to process what he'd just said. The possibility that I was riding on a train, in India, with the person who'd nearly given my dad a heart attack sixteen years before was so utterly absurd that I just started laughing. "Fucking karma," Tsar said, sucking on his *biddie* and giggling. "Fucking karma," I repeated and thought how strange it was that now it was Tsar who'd found himself stuck in a foreign country without money or passport.

Tsar explained that he'd done many stupid things in his twenties. He'd even spent time in prison, for masterminding a string of pay-phone robberies along the Croatian coast. I told him that I felt like I was part of an endless Latin American soap opera where every character eventually turned out to be someone other than the person they've claimed to be. What else was I going to learn about Tsar? That he was my brother and that we'd actually been born in Papua New Guinea? Or that his left hand was fake and he was six hundred years old?

The train came to a stop and Tsar and I jumped off. There were no motor rickshaws outside the train station and we had to settle for a bicycle carriage whose owner—a drunk old man wearing a tattered dhoti—demanded that we pay him outright. "I don't know about this," Tsar said as we left the main road and entered the slums. Sure enough, the man on the bicycle pulled next to a single-room shanty and explained—using a combination of hand gestures and head wobbles—that he was going home because he needed to go to sleep. Tsar and I continued on foot.

First we heard the music. It was a slow Sikh hymn sung to the accompaniment of a tabla and a harmonium. We followed the singer's voice blindly and soon came out onto a large square swarming with pilgrims, rickshaws, bicycles, juice vendors, omelet makers, corn poppers, and chai dealers, barricaded on all sides with shops selling gifts, Sikh paraphernalia, religious books, and sweets. Tsar immediately picked up a pamphlet from a nearby bookstall and began reading out loud: "The number-one enemy of mankind is the car. There are more people killed by cars than by war or disease." Tsar put the pamphlet in his bag and picked up a different one, which claimed that the number-one enemy of mankind was tobacco. "I guess the Sikhs aren't very friendly to smokers," he observed, looking around to see if there was anyone holding a cigarette. There wasn't. A metal sign nailed to a tree informed all visitors that smoking in the area surrounding the Golden Temple was forbidden.

We entered the temple compound and were greeted by a Sikh man who told us that we could sleep for free in the dormitory. The food—rice and dal—was free as well, and the showers were at the end of the corridor, to the left. Tsar and I were shocked. Free food? Showers? We didn't have to go wash in the river like cows? "*Choveche*, this is unbelievable," Tsar exclaimed as we hurried toward the showers. "We should stay here for a month and rest."

After we bathed and ate dinner, we sat on the banks of the lake surrounding the Golden Temple and listened as the voice of the singer, the drone of the harmonium, and the offbeat tapping of the tabla man streamed through at least a dozen loudspeakers, glided across the water, and bounced off against the walls of the temple compound, creating the impression that the musicians who were playing live inside the Golden Temple were bound by a time signature that defied the gravity of the present and looped back and forward, repeating moments that had already ceased to exist and borrowing extra beats from a plane that had yet to be conceived. I wanted to say to Tsar that I would miss him and that without him India would be a very different place—but I didn't. What was the use of talking about the future?

We left the temple compound and approached a group of rickshaw drivers gathered around a burning barrel. Tsar took one of the drivers aside and proposed to give him a hundred rupees if he took him to the border crossing at four o'clock in the morning. "Are you going to be here?" Tsar asked, extending his hand. "Yes," the driver confirmed. "Hundred percent?" "Hundred."

With the pilgrims gone and the shops closed, the town square looked like a vast dumping ground, with cows and beggars rooting for scraps of food. Tsar spotted a mobile chai stand in the distance and hurried toward it, convinced that he'd seen the tiny cinder of a lit cigarette. He was right: the owner of the chai stall was smoking and was proud of it. "I am not Sikh," he explained. "I believe in Shiva."

"I like Shiva," Tsar told him. "Shiva the smoker."

When we returned to the temple compound it was after midnight and all the tourists staying in the dormitory were already asleep, cocooned in their sleeping bags. Tsar and I had no blankets or sleeping bags. We found an empty spot near the entrance of the room and lay down on the cement floor. I set the alarm clock for four o'clock.

When I woke up, Tsar was gone and the clock showed ten minutes after four. The alarm had never gone off. I sat up and tinkered with the little red button on the back of the clock. How did Tsar wake up? And when did he leave? A minute went past and I heard someone walking down the corridor. It was Tsar, returning from the showers. His faced was shaved; his wet hair was combed back.

I got up and gave him a hug. "Send me a fax when you get across," I said.

"I'll send one to the STD near the hospital," Tsar replied and, shrugging his shoulders as if to say, *Well, that was that,* he turned around and walked out.

I tried to go back to sleep but the image of Tsar dashing across the border pumped adrenaline into my veins. Soon I was wide awake and cursing myself for not accompanying Tsar to the border crossing. Perhaps I could've helped him by keeping the guards distracted.

I left the temple compound and headed toward the train station. I was going to sleep on the train.

Twenty-four

Holding my breath, I extended my hand slowly, so as not to stir up the air, and trapped the giant brown-red moth clinging to the ceiling inside the porcelain bowl. Then I slipped a piece of paper between the bowl and the ceiling, ran across the room, and tossed the moth out the window. Disoriented, the moth spiraled down like a paper plane and disappeared between the branches of a tall pine tree.

Geshe Yama Tseten grimaced. "You killed it. Why did you do that?"

"You told me to get it off the ceiling," I said. "And I didn't kill it. It was flying just fine."

"Just fine!" Geshe-la exploded. "Moths can't fly around during the day! They go blind. How would you feel if I threw you out the window and you instantly went blind, like that animal, *ka re sa*"—what is it called—"the one that digs underground and has a face like this . . ."

Geshe Yama Tseten crossed his eyes, scrunched his face, and, with his hands shaped like paws, began digging a hole in his bed.

"I don't know the name in Tibetan," I admitted.

"It has a tail," Geshe-la hinted. "And moves very fast."

"I know that," I told him, "but I can't remember the name."

"I know," he says. "You don't know anything—throwing blind animals out the window. *Kun chog sum.*"

I squatted next to the plastic tub filled with dirty cups, bowls, and silverware, and picked up the soapy metal sponge, which was so old, it looked like a ball of human hair. Washing Geshe Yama Tseten's dishes wasn't necessarily something that was expected of me as Geshe-la's student, but I did it anyway, whenever I went to him for a lesson. It was the only thing I could do right, incidentally.

I rinsed the bowls and the dishes with clean water and arranged them on a towel, spread on the floor. I did everything slowly and meticulously, as if I were performing some sort of religious ritual. When I was done, I dumped the dirty water in the toilet out in the corridor and returned to my seat, three feet away from Geshe Yama Tseten's bed. I closed my eyes and took a deep breath. The warm, gentle wind coming from the open window moved through the room, ruffling the pages of Geshe-la's looseleaf text and playing with the door curtain. A group of monks, shouting definitions and debate formulas, descended the staircase below the window and dashed across the monastery courtyard, their sandals clapping like castanets. I looked at Geshe Yama Tseten. He was either asleep or meditating—I couldn't ever tell which. I sat quietly, watching a flock of crows trying to intimidate an enormous vulture perched on the top branch of a cedar tree. For a while the vulture remained in its spot, ignoring the shrill cries of the crows and their hysterical pirouettes, but in the end it gave in and flew off, beating its wings slowly and with great force. Stirred by a series of loud noises out in the corridor, Geshe Yama Tseten opened his eyes and looked at me with displeasure.

"What are you still doing here?" he asked, wiping his glasses on his *zen.*

"I thought we were going to read some more," I said.

Geshe-la clicked his tongue, expressing dismay, and put on his glasses. "Why don't you ever pay attention? I'm leaving for Bodhgaya the day after tomorrow. We're done with the text. It took us a whole year to get through it. Every day you came here to torture me: *Geshe-la, what is this? Geshe-la, what is that?* And in the end—nothing. Really, it was a total waste of time for me, and certainly a meaningless endeavor for you, being a monk of mediocre intelligence. A person of high intelligence would take this text"—here, Geshe-la transformed into a smug, highly intelligent person walking down the street with the swagger of Robert De Niro in *Taxi Driver*—"glance through the first few pages, and say, I get it, I need something harder."

Geshe-la gave me the thumbs up, meaning to say that highly intelligent people made the best students. (Tibetans often use their fingers to rate things: a good restaurant, for example, gets a thumbs up; a bad restaurant gets a pinkie, usually administered with a twist of the wrist.)

"Then there are people with low intelligence," he went on, showing me his pinkie. "Taxi drivers, butchers, scientists, and *Engie* professors that come here, learn two or three Sanskrit and Tibetan words, and then go back home and tell everyone they are scholars. Very arrogant. Writing big books." Geshe-la demonstrated how *Engie* professors write books—with a mean face, typing haphazardly with their forefingers on a typewriter the size of a coffee table. "Thieves, liars, monkeys, and cows are usually of middling intelligence. Your mind is this."

Geshe-la showed me his middle finger and looked at me intently, gauging my reaction. Though it wasn't uncommon for an older-generation Tibetan to use his middle finger when describing something as *so-so*, or *not so bad*, I found it hard to believe that Geshe Yama Tseten wasn't aware of what that gesture meant to an *Engie*. Nevertheless, I was flattered. To be ranked on the same level as thieves and cows, one notch above scientists and *Engie* professors, was certainly a remarkable achievement.

"Thank you, Geshe-la," I said with a humble bow. "You've done a lot for me."

Geshe-la made a sour face and pushed Chankya Rolpei Dorje's text on the Buddhist and non-Buddhist philosophies of ancient India toward me. "You can keep that copy. Now you can go back to the West and pretend that you're a scholar, just like the rest of the *Engies*. When you don't understand even the most basic things!"

"I memorized fifty pages of definitions," I countered, fully aware that this would trigger a violent outburst.

"Fifty pages! A donkey can memorize fifty pages. What arrogance! I memorized, he says. Who are *you*? Let's hear those definitions. Who are *you*?"

"I am the same as a rabbit with horns," I replied confidently. I'd found that this was a relatively safe answer. The self, just like the notion of a rabbit with horns, was a pure fabrication—a fantasy of a permanent center from which the spokes of duality shot out to form the grand, subject-object wheel of existence, which had little to do with the way the self actually existed: as a mere thought projection arisen from the confluence of time, space, and the flickering of ephemeral mental images.

Geshe Yama Tseten appeared amused. "A rabbit with horns! And who am I?"

"A rabbit with horns," I said automatically.

"And what's this?" Geshe-la pointed at his porcelain teacup.

"A rabbit with horns."

Snickering, Geshe-la scanned the room, looking for a good object for his test. When you were playing the game of nonexistence, you often found yourself looking at things as if they were part of a large-scale hoax to cover up the truth about the nature of reality; as if they'd been *placed* there, labeled, and artificially blown up to three dimensions by some strange, unexplained force—like gravity.

Geshe-la pointed at his nose, then at the small copper statue of the Buddha, placed on top of his bookshelf. I responded accordingly. The earth? A rabbit with horns. Space? A rabbit with horns. Geshe-la adjusted his glasses and put on his fierce going-into-battle expression.

"Really?"

"Really," I confirmed.

"You really believe that? You are absolutely convinced that everything around you is a big lie? A big, fat rabbit with horns which is not even remotely real?"

I nodded. I expected Geshe Yama Tseten to switch to debate mode, clapping his hands and sending a barrage of cunningly threaded sentences, where each conjunction was a booby trap and each clause a death sentence. Instead, he took a sip of butter tea and leaned back onto his pillow. "Give me the *pecha* that's wrapped in a yellow cloth, right there, on the top shelf."

I got up and started removing the twenty or so looseleaf books stacked on top of the book that he was pointing at. When I finally handed the book to him, he unwrapped the yellow cloth and, licking his thumb and forefinger, began paging through it, reading out loud all the notes that he'd written to himself on scraps of paper.

"It's not here," he announced irritated. "Give me another *pecha*; that one."

Geshe Yama Tseten flipped through the pages of the second book and quickly demanded that I give him another one. When he'd scanned all the *pechas* that I had brought down from the top shelf, he pointed at the middle shelf. I took down the painting of Manjushri, the portable radio with a broken antenna, and the ornate copper fruit bowl that I'd given him as a present at the end of my first year as his student, and unloaded the next batch of books. I didn't ask Geshe-la what he was looking for because I was afraid that he'd get upset and kick me out before he'd hit upon what appeared to be the most important quote or passage in the entire Buddhist canon. The amount of effort that Geshe-la was putting into finding the passage—undoubtedly his final lesson before he embarked on his annual journey to Bodhgaya—was absolutely unprecedented. Geshe-la, it should be noted, was the kind of person who would skip lunch and even dinner because he didn't feel like getting off his bed. His lunch and dinner—soup, rice, and a meal (dal, potatoes), transported in three round metal containers, stacked upon each other—was brought to his door by a young monk every day of the year.

We moved to the lowest shelf and Geshe-la began paging through his enormous encyclopedia of marine life. What exactly was he looking for? I began to wonder. A scrap of paper? A loose page from an old Tibetan text?

"It's not here, either," Geshe-la concluded, adding the encyclopedia to the mountain of books piled on the foot of his bed. He seemed angry and tired. His neck was sweaty. Assuming that the search was over, I started wrapping the looseleaf books in their orange and yellow garments and putting them back on the bookshelves. Hands folded over his chest, Geshe-la stared out the window, breathing slowly. I poured more tea in his cup and crammed the last dozen books wherever I found extra space. Then I propped up the painting of Manjushri and placed the radio and the fruit bowl in their original spots. It was time for me to go. I grabbed my bag and headed for the door.

"Sit down," Geshe-la said gently, as if he were speaking to a little kid. "Sit."

He lifted the cloth covering the table in front of his bed and pulled out a thin booklet, the kind that usually contained a short sutra or a summary of the monastic vows. Geshe-la opened the booklet in the middle and took out a postcard. "Here," he said, and bent forward to hand me the postcard. I expected to see a snapshot of Tibet, perhaps Mount Kailash or Blue Lake. What I saw was a photograph of an animal. That wasn't unusual. Geshe Yama Tseten had a collection of albums and photographs of marine animals— dolphins, sea turtles, whales, and sharks. What was I supposed to make of this? For one, the desert-like scenery depicted on the postcard—dunes, shrubs, cactuses—was a clear deviation from the nautical setting that Geshe-la was so fond of. And the animal? At first I thought that I was looking at a deer. A weird-looking deer. A deer standing on his butt and hind legs, like a kangaroo. I stared closely at the animal's face. It was actually a rabbit. A rabbit dwarfed under the weight of a pair of massive asymmetrical antlers. A rabbit with horns. Suddenly, I couldn't think anymore. All of my ongoing internal arguments ceased, every learned definition evaporated. Existence was nonexistence was existence was nonexistence. Right was wrong was right was wrong. The past was the present was the future was the past. Here was there was here and there. One was many was everything was nothing, and being alive was being dead was living was dying. Out there was in here was nowhere was everywhere was everyone was never, and everything was moving was still was spinning and all the buildings and the streets and the temples and Gamru village and the vegetable market in Lower Dharamsala and Norbulingka and the Tibetan Library and the tofu-making apparatus on Jogibara Road and the post office and the river and the Shiva temple on top of the mountain were all crammed in Geshe-la's room, together with the music, and Geshe-la's room was in Boston and Boston was in New York and New York was in Europe and Europe was in India and India was in my head and my head was smaller than Geshe-la's room, which was smaller than me and I was inside it, and everyone I had known had already died was born was older was still young and I was my father was my mother was Tsar was Geshe Yama Tseten was Merry Anne was Vinnie was the prettiest Tibetan prostitute in town, and everyone was unfamiliar and I had known them since the beginning of Existence.

"Rabbits with horns exist," Geshe Yama Tseten observed with a smile.

And just like that, he erased absolutely everything that he'd taught me since the first day I'd met him. It was as if Geshe-la had spent two years proving to me that pink elephants didn't exist, and just when he'd seen that I had finally been convinced, he'd clapped his hands and from under his bed had emerged a tiny pink elephant named George. *Lodro, meet George. George, meet Lodro.* This wasn't the famous Buddhist formula demonstrating the inseparability of appearances and their illusory nature (form is emptiness, emptiness is form). The Buddhist view held that because things arise in dependence on other factors (ultimately, on the mind that perceives them), they appear; because they lack independence and an intrinsic source, they are empty and illusory. Geshe Yama Tseten was saying something entirely different—independent-looking things are no less real and true than dependent-looking things; misconceptions are as erroneous as valid perceptions;

pink elephants are as profound as emptiness; everything is right; everything is wrong; it's all a huge mess and there's no solving it on a rational level. Geshe Yama Tseten had attempted to show me that underneath all the clinging and the illusory projections of being and nonbeing there was something else, something that couldn't be named and couldn't be entered through the catacombs of thought and memory; an ever-present pedal point drowned in the cacophonous psychobabble of existence. This wasn't Buddhism and Geshe-la wasn't a Buddhist. This wasn't a philosophy or a religious view. This had nothing to do with the fluffy clouds of spirituality or the utopian idea of Enlightenment.

I WISHED THAT TSAR HAD SEEN Geshe Yama Tseten's feat of destroying the mandala. In a strange way, what Geshe-la had said to me was identical to what Tsar had proclaimed the day after he'd gotten drunk, beaten a bunch of people, and lost his bag.

I handed the postcard to Geshe-la and stood up. There was a giant moth crawling on the ceiling—perhaps the same one that I'd thrown out at the beginning of our lesson.

"You're a good monk," Geshe-la said paternally when I opened the door. "You've done a lot of work."

If Geshe Yama Tseten had said that to me a year ago, I would have felt like crying. But I was smarter now. I wasn't tricked that easily.

"Too bad you're going to disrobe," Geshe-la continued, making a sour face. "You're going to go back to the West, lead a meaningless life, and die a fool. Really, you've wasted my time. Go live with the fools. Now get out."

I thanked him for the lesson with a modest bow and left his room. Was I upset with him? No. That was his way of showing affection. It was the best he could do—after spending forty years in a monastic institution filled with cantankerous, love-starved males whose only means of communication was debate.

. . .

I WALKED INTO THE STD and stared at the owner, a balding, middle-aged Indian man who was relaxing in his chair, cleaning his teeth with a tooth-pick. "Fax for me?" I asked him. "No fax," he replied, and spat on the floor. It was the second time I had visited him that day. Feeling a bit brazen, I grabbed the folders piled on the counter and started going through all the recent faxes. The owner got up and demanded that I hand him the folders but I stepped back and continued flipping through the pages. It didn't take me long to hit upon Tsar's fax. I scanned the remaining folders, making sure there weren't any other faxes for me. Here's what the fax from Tsar said: "Nikola, Vinnie is an idiot. I'll try to cross again tonight, but this time I'll do it the old-fashioned way. I'll send you another fax tomorrow. Tsar."

The fax had been sent the previous day, which meant that by now Tsar was in Pakistan, dead, or in prison. I couldn't imagine what else could happen to someone who tried to jump one of the most strictly guarded borders in the world.

I returned home and made dinner. It felt weird to cook and eat by myself. At least the rats were there keeping me company. At ten o'clock—as if fol-lowing orders—Thomas Edison descended through a hole in the tarpaulin and landed on the table, next to the tape player. "Tsar's gone," I informed him and was startled by the sound of my voice. I had lost a lot of friends. Purba and Lobsang had gone back to Tibet, crossing the Himalayas on foot. I didn't know if they'd made it alive. They could've been shot by Chinese snipers. Merry Anne had gone back to Bulgaria. He'd written to me that he was severely depressed and was planning to go pick oranges in Greece. Damien had returned to the States to get married. Ani Dawa avoided me as if I were her greatest enemy. I had to accept that Tsar was gone as well. Whatever had happened to him, he wasn't coming back.

It was past midnight, and I was sitting in bed reading a book when I heard footsteps and someone tried to push the door open. I got up and looked through a crack in the wooden frame. It was very dark and I couldn't see anything but I could hear heavy breathing. "*Choveche*, let me in," Tsar whispered.

I unbolted the door and Tsar walked past me and collapsed on his bed. He was wearing black pants and a black sweater, his head was covered with a black scarf and his shoes were wrapped in black cloth. His face was soiled with mud and his lips were bloodied and swollen.

"What on earth is going on?" I cried out, looking at Tsar in horror.

"You are not too excited to see me," he said, offended.

He was right. I was pissed and it showed. It's not that I wasn't happy to see him again. I just couldn't stand the fact that nothing ever changed, that everything repeated itself, that the record kept on skipping and we always found ourselves back at the very beginning with no other option but to go around again.

I apologized to Tsar for acting hostile—blaming it on his late and unexpected appearance—and offered him tea. He inquired after Mona Lisa and Geshe Yama Tseten and soon we were laughing again and everything was sucked back into the Jogibara time warp, where each object and event acquired a mythological, near-eternal quality. The mountains became the living and breathing Himalayas responsible for the diffusion of the most essential particle in the universe—the particle of illusion; our house became the secret abode of karmic arbiters and free-floating spirits; Vinnie became the third most important Western philosopher after Kant and Schopenhauer; Tsar became the avatar of Zeno and Nagarjuna, simultaneously; I morphed into a younger and slightly less cynical Emil Cioran, and our life on Jogibara Road became the most important event in the history of metaphysical ideas.

"*Choveche*, the whole plan was absurd. I got to the border crossing at four-thirty in the morning; *dobro*, there weren't guards in sight and so I started walking. I made three steps—no more—and, suddenly, they were all upon me, pointing their rifles and everything. *Yebem li te*, I don't know why I ever listen to Vinnie. Good thing they let me go." Tsar took a drag from his *biddie* and felt the deep, unhealed cuts on his lips with his fingers. "So I thought, *dobro*, I'll do it the old-fashioned way. I took a rickshaw to the nearest border town, waited until midnight, and started walking. Do you like my camouflage? They taught me how to do this in the army. You cover everything with black cloth, slap some mud on your face, and you're ready to go. By the way, you always have to look down or the enemy will see the whites of your eyes and shoot you."

Tsar got up and demonstrated how you're supposed to walk so as not to let your enemies see the whites of your eyes. He tiptoed, hunched and with a conspiratorial expression, from the entrance door to the kitchen and back, and then hopped on his bed.

"You're insane," I told him. "If they'd seen you, they would've shot you for sure. You look like a terrorist!"

"But how could they see me, Nikola?" he shouted. "I was invisible!"

He was, indeed. He'd walked in the dark for an hour, stopping only occasionally to listen for suspicious sounds (the sound of a twig creaking indicated an animal; the sound of a twig breaking indicated human presence). He'd calculated that it would take him no more than forty minutes to get to the border, and so when he'd come upon a small stream, he'd begun walking faster, certain that he'd already crossed into Pakistani territory and was out of danger.

"I was thinking about getting a hotel room and waking up early the next day to get some breakfast. *Choveche*, I was absolutely sure I was in Pakistan. I'd look at the trees and think, oh, that's what Pakistani trees look like; I would've never guessed. And then, suddenly, my heart stopped. I had absolutely no blood circulation. Zero. None."

"How could you possibly have no blood circulation?" I asked.

"How do you think I could have blood circulation when there's a soldier standing right in front of me! He was that close; get up, I'll show you."

Tsar met me in the middle of the room and pushed his face so close to mine, our noses almost touched.

"I felt his breath on my face," Tsar went on, returning to his bed. "It was the scariest thing I've ever experienced. By the way, I had two choices: to head-butt him at the base of his nose, or wrestle him down and take away his gun."

I looked at Tsar in astonishment. How did he manage to put himself in such impossible situations, again and again? How did he manage to stay alive? Where did he get his boldness and the perpetual smirk on his face?

"And what did you do?" I asked, cringing.

"Nothing! What do you think? I'm a pacifist. I stared at him for a minute, making sure that he wasn't aware of my presence, and then started retreating: I took a step back and waited. I took another step and waited some more. I walked backwards for about fifty meters and then I turned around and made a long arch, so that I could get back to the border and try my luck again."

Indeed, the second time around his luck had worked. He'd walked over a roll of barbed wire and crossed unhindered into Pakistani territory. He'd proceeded cautiously for about an hour and then had broken into a run, determined to get as far away from the border line as humanly possible. At five o'clock in the morning, right before dawn, he'd entered some kind of thicket and, realizing that he was too exhausted to wrestle with the dense foliage, had collapsed on the ground. By that point he'd gotten so dehydrated from all the running that he'd started shaking uncontrollably. Without thinking, he'd uprooted a nearby shoot and sank his teeth into it. To his surprise, it had tasted sweet. By some miracle, he'd ended up in a sugar cane plantation.

"*Choveche*, it's like I turned into an animal. I had never acted like that before. I kept pulling sugar cane shoots out of the ground and chewing them from one end to the other, even though I had splinters wedged between my teeth and my tongue and lips were cut up and bleeding. I felt nothing. When I woke up the next day, I couldn't believe my eyes. It was like a flying saucer had landed and had cut a circle in the middle of the plantation. I had chewed up everything in a fifteen-meter radius. By the way, I was in a great mood. I walked for half an hour and arrived at a small village. There was a chai shop and I thought, *dobro*, I can finally relax. The owner brought me chai and a paratha, and I asked him if I could pay with Indian rupees. I told him that I had no Pakistani rupees and apologized. We don't take Pakistani rupees, he said to me. This is India. If you want Pakistani money, go to Pakistan."

"How is that possible?" I cried. "You were back in India?"

"Of course, Nikola!" Tsar replied indignantly. "No one can leave India. Everybody knows that. It's a fact."

FOR A WEEK OR SO, no one said a word about borders and escape strategies. Even Vinnie restrained himself and talked mostly about chess and European soccer tournaments. In the morning I went to debate and at night, after we'd eaten dinner, Tsar and I walked down toward Delek Hospital and played carrom at the chai shop next door with a spectacular view of the Kangra Valley. I thought that Tsar had finally given up and resigned himself to his fate, and that made me happy. I would've been perfectly content to spend the rest of my days studying texts, debating, and hanging out with Tsar and Vinnie. I had two good friends and something to do. What else was there to want from life?

It so happened that at around that time in Dharamsala, there had appeared a few Westerners who'd come to the Himalayas in search of a perfect spot for paragliding. There was, for example, a Swiss man who'd jump from the highest peak above Dharamsala, fly over McLeod Ganj, and invariably crash into an apple tree, right below our house on Jogibara Road. Naturally, Tsar became interested. He befriended him and began taking paragliding lessons. Soon after, Vinnie came up with an escape plan that involved jumping from a high peak in Indian-controlled Kashmir and flying into Pakistani-controlled Kashmir. He provided a copy of a military map, which he claimed to have stolen from the local police office. Rehearsals followed.

One day, Tsar announced that he was going to attempt to fly into Pakistan. "I'm going to borrow a paraglider and we're going to head toward Kashmir."

"No way," I told him. "Not again. I'm not doing this anymore. Really."

Twenty-five

Dear Kaila,
It has been a long time. My white horses have become quiet like heavy stones buried underground. The tiger sleeps at night and for most of the day. Nikola—you probably remember him—has stopped giving me money for cigarettes and these days I spend my mornings sitting by the road and begging passersby to spare a biddie. How can I wake up? A man needs to smoke.

It was the middle of December, and Tsar was composing a new letter to his former Israeli girlfriend. As usual, I was employed in the role of the scribe. We'd already done two drafts but Tsar felt that something was missing.

"Nikola, start a new paragraph. *By the way, I tried to fly into Pakistan with a paraglider. It didn't work. First of all, the map was wrong. It turned out I was just outside Dharamsala. Second of all, the hill was too small. A three-year-old could jump from a hill like that. I later calculated that in order to make it across the border, I'd need to carry a 600-horsepower propeller strapped to my back. Have you seen the cartoon Road Runner? When I was living in Germany I wrote a letter to Walt Disney, asking them to make an episode where the coyote catches the Road Runner— for once.*

"*It's probably going to snow soon. Are you thinking of coming back to India? It* would be great to see you. You could try our new dish: rice with fried chilies. We ran out of money and haven't had dal in a long time."

Tsar got up and opened the door. It was after seven o'clock in the evening and the descending sun had colored the rocky pinnacles dark pink. It was a strange setting: the valley glowing like a ball of fire and the mountain villages enveloped in shadows, the cold, granite sky bearing down on trees and houses and cows and weary goatherds returning home. Tsar grabbed his stick (for chasing dogs away) and motioned at me to follow him. Every evening at dusk we took a long walk. It was our ritual. We walked slowly, in the direction of the setting sun, kicked stones, and every once in a while, summed up the existential predicament with a somber "*Da*"—meaning, *Yes, so it is, it will never change.*

We had reached the outskirts of Lower Dharamsala when Tsar asked me to recite the opening stanza of the second chapter of Nagarjuna's *Wisdom: A Treatise on the Middle Way.* I did, in Tibetan, and then translated it roughly into English. Tsar stopped and, gesturing at an invisible entity standing on his right side, repeated everything I'd said, only slower, and with a cunning expression on his face: "Once you make a step, you're not moving; before you make a step you're not moving; we can only know before or after; then where is the moving?"

Tsar scrunched his eyebrows and thought about it. I thought about it. The invisible entity thought about it.

"*Da*," Tsar concluded in the end.

"*Da*," I agreed. Then we resumed our walk.

THE NEXT DAY WE WERE AWAKENED by the sound of someone stomping his feet and spitting loudly outside our room. I stumbled out of my bed and opened the door: it was Vinnie. Grunting and twisting his fingers like he was about to have an epileptic seizure, he squeezed past me and walked into the room.

"How many times, Vinnie!" Tsar exploded and kicked his blankets on the floor. "How many times do we have to ask you to let us sleep in the morning!"

Vinnie opened his rucksack and pulled out a white envelope. "I don't know what it is, but I think it's urgent. You should thank me. I wrestled it out of the postman's hands. He would've stolen it for sure."

Tsar took the envelope and examined it on both sides. "It's from my mother."

He ripped the envelope and dumped its contents on his bed: there was a letter, a photograph, and a brand-new passport. "It's a Bosnian passport. And it's blank," he announced with a smile. "Absolutely fucking blank. My mother must've bribed some high-ranking official."

"Which can only mean one thing," Vinnie offered.

"What?" I wondered.

"We are going to print Tsar an Indian visa using a computer."

"That's like saying that we're going to manufacture a dinosaur using a time machine," I observed. "We don't even know what a computer looks like, let alone how to get it to work."

"Someone does," Vinnie said mysteriously. "Someone who lives next door."

I pictured Gamru village and tried to imagine where a computer was most likely to fit. In the cow shed? In the room next to the tofu-making machine? By the river? On the second floor of our landlord's mud-plastered house? Tsar was having a hard time as well. He was staring at the door with a pained expression, shaking his head.

"We give up," I said. "Who is it?"

"The Japanese architect," Vinnie confided. "He must have a computer. He's rich."

Tsar and I immediately realized that Vinnie was right. The Japanese architect lived in a house with solar panels and water tanks and large windows. It was probably the most luxurious house in the whole of Dharamsala.

"He might have a computer, but he's never going to forge a visa for Tsar," I argued. "I've been in this village for three years, and he's never even said hello to me. He'll never do it."

"Which can only mean one thing," Vinnie concluded.

Tsar and I stared at him intently. What were our options? Kidnap the Japanese architect and force him to print an Indian visa and entry stamps on Tsar's passport? Sneak into his house at night and steal his computer? Being a man of knowledge, Vinnie didn't disclose his plan right away. He waited for us to get exasperated and then announced, clenching his fists, that we had to be strong and that we had only one shot.

"Lodro," he said with the expression of a military commander sending his troops on a suicide mission, "you must go over to Hiroshi's house and seduce his girlfriend!"

"Me?" I cried. "Why should I seduce his girlfriend? If anyone should be doing any seducing, that should be Tsar. It's his passport and he likes doing it."

"But you're the only one who has a chance to succeed," Vinnie argued.

Tsar nodded in agreement. "She likes you," he said. "Remember when our landlord invited everyone to his house for Diwali dinner? She was looking at you."

"You're just saying that because you don't want to do it," I countered.

Vinnie sat next to Tsar and examined the new passport. "We have a problem, guys," he announced. "You can't run a passport through a printer, and it doesn't seem that there's a way to take one page out without ripping the whole thing apart."

The three of us studied the stitches in the middle of the passport, trying to find a solution to the puzzle. We could cut the string holding the pages, but we couldn't possibly sew them back together without also sewing through the dark blue plastic cover. Frustrated, Tsar threw his passport against the wall and lay down, squeezing his head with his hands. Vinnie sat quietly for a few minutes, then suddenly remembered that he had a meeting and left the room.

Later that day, Samten, my classmate from the institute, stopped by our place. When I explained to him why Tsar couldn't do anything with his passport, he laughed and slapped Tsar's feet. "Get up, old man," he told him. "I know how to fix this."

Ten minutes later, Tsar was standing over a pot of boiling water and peeling the dark blue skin of his passport with a huge grin on his face. The steam was melting the glue, just as Samten had predicted. Samten—who'd never been given a passport or any other form of identification. Once the skin was off, Tsar cut the outside stitches with a razor and spread the pages across his bed. "What's my lucky number?" he wondered.

We spent the next morning listening to Vinnie talk about the wonders of modern computers. He revealed to us that a computer aficionado armed with a scanner and photo-editing software could turn donkeys into humans or make the Dalai Lama look like Princess Diana. Tsar and I were impressed. While we had been busy chasing snakes and rats in the Himalayas, someone somewhere in the world had invented something called Photoshop. Around noon, Samten, who was out on a reconnaissance mission, rushed in and announced that Michiko, the Japanese architect's girlfriend, had just left her house and was walking in the direction of the tofu-making machine. I straightened my *shanthab*, threw my *zen* casually over my shoulders, and went out to intercept her.

Picking up girls isn't the easiest thing if you're wearing a long skirt and your head is shaved. I looked down at my bare feet, squeezed into a pair of tiny blue flip-flops. *Good God!* I thought. *When was the last time I clipped my toenails?* I couldn't remember. I didn't even own a nail clipper. Aware of my disadvantages, I decided to focus on what I did best—acting like someone who'd just been hit by a falling brick and now understood the workings of the universe. After all, I was a student of metaphysics. I could muster a pretty profound expression.

And there was Michiko, dressed in jeans and a sweater, carrying a chunk of tofu in a pink plastic bag. She was in her early twenties—half her boyfriend's age—and was very attractive. *I have to say something smart, I coached myself. Something that doesn't involve talking about the weather.* I looked at my landlord's emaciated gray cat for help. I looked at the three clay statues at the end of the courtyard. There was absolutely nothing smart that I could think of.

"So," I began, hoping that my brain would surprise me and spout out a brilliant sentence, complete with witty jokes and profound wisdom. There was an awkward silence, and in a moment of desperation I pointed at the sky with both hands. "It stopped raining!"

She examined the sky and nodded. It hadn't rained in two weeks.

"Do you like tofu?" I asked. More nodding followed. I was out of things to say. Michiko smiled politely and started up the slate-tiled stairs that lead to the street. Suddenly, she turned around and gestured at my room. "Your friend, gone?"

"Tsar?" I offered. She shook her head. "Merry Anne? Yes, he's gone. He went back to Bulgaria."

"Oh!" Michiko exclaimed, genuinely surprised. "You know Bulgarian music?"

There you go, I thought. That should make things easier.

"I know Bulgarian music quite well," I confessed. "I studied it in school."

"I like Bulgarian music very much. You have some?"

As a matter of fact, I did. I had a tape of three bearded Bulgarian grandmothers performing ear-splitting screeches to the deafening accompaniment of bagpipes and pigskin drums. I carried it around with me because I'd found that, for some strange reason, people really liked that stuff. I told Michiko to wait, and ran to my room to get the tape. Tsar and Vinnie stared at me, expecting that I would fill them in on the latest developments, but I said nothing. I took the tape, my passport, and one of the loose passport pages lying on Tsar's bed, and rushed out.

"Oh!" Michiko cried as she looked closely at the faces of the Bulgarian singers.

"You could have it," I told her. Michiko thanked me profusely and was about to turn around when I, pretending to have just remembered something very important, asked her if she had a computer and knew anything about photo editing. She nodded positively. "Is it possible," I began, showing her my passport and the blank page from Tsar's passport, "to move this Indian visa from here to here, without copying the background and the things written in pen?"

I explained to her that Tsar was in trouble and that this was the only way he could ever leave India, and she took my passport to study the stamped visa. I was certain she was going to say no. I could see it on her face. I was crazy to think that I could walk up to someone I barely knew and ask them to forge some documents. In fact, it was very rude.

"Okay," she said, and started walking away. "I'll come back in ten minutes."

I was stunned. Maybe she didn't understand what I'd asked her to do. What if she printed the wrong thing or copied the visa with my name on it? I returned home and explained to Tsar and Vinnie what was happening. "All we can do is wait," Vinnie concluded wisely. Tsar was too excited to sit in his bed. He was pacing around the room, smoking and sipping tea from a metal cup.

When I went out again, Michiko was already waiting for me by the side of the road. I couldn't tell from her expression if she had good or bad news for me.

"Is this okay?" she asked, showing me the loose passport page.

It was. I thanked her and ran back to the house. Everyone agreed: it was a masterpiece. Now that he had a visa, Tsar assembled all the loose pages, sewed them together, and glued the blue plastic cover on top. Then he transferred two entry stamps using two hot, peeled, hard-boiled eggs—one for each stamp. "The Road Runner just showed up again," he informed me, taking a bite from one of the eggs, the mirror image of the words "Indira Gandhi International Airport" tattooed across it in purple ink. "And this time I'm going to catch it."

Tsar spent his last week in Dharamsala saying good-bye to his friends and collecting donations for his trip back to Europe. No one believed that he was going to make it across the border and out of Asia. Vinnie predicted that Tsar would be back in less than a month. "There's nothing outside," he told me as we sat for a game of chess at Om Restaurant. "He'll walk around, get bored, and come right back. I've done it many, many times."

In the third week of December, Tsar and I boarded a government bus and left for New Delhi. Tsar's plan was to get a Nepali visa, take a bus to Katmandu, and catch a cheap flight to Europe. On the morning of his departure, we went to Connaught Place and sat near a juice stall, drinking *jal jeera* (lime juice with salt, cumin, and mint), the sweet stench of dried feces and betelnut spit oozing from the pavement. "Here," Tsar said, pulling his former monastic robes from his rucksack. "I can't carry them with me any longer. Take the sign as well."

I took the robes and the sign that read "Bosnian Bread! Try it!" and placed them in my bag. *This is how karmic knots are tied, time and again,* I thought. *I will wear his monastic robes; he will wear my lay clothes and my Indian visa.* I was absolutely sure that he was going to return to Dharamsala in a week.

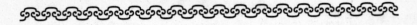

Epilogue

R ed earth, red dust, red spit. Faces of people I've never seen. Gas lamps at the back of chai shops, bicycle rickshaws, their bells ringing, relaying lonely messages in a secret code. Hordes of black pigs trotting up and down the bazaar in search of food. I glance at the muddy remains of the dried-up river and the grove of palm trees on the other shore. I can hear what the palm trees are saying, these temptresses; they're luring me into the wilderness, the enchanted wilderness where the holy ones have walked two thousand and five hundred years before. But I know there is nothing there, nothing except Bihari mobsters with homemade sawed-off guns and an empty well where—if one is to believe the golden-toothed Indian man in charge of the well—the Buddha once spent seven years in uninterrupted meditation. The mosquitoes have decided to follow me everywhere: it's true love. They cover my head and bare feet, kiss my mouth and tongue, get caught under my eyelids. I sit on a bench outside a chai shop to take a rest. Walking still makes me dizzy, yet I keep trying, amazed that after two weeks spent in a state of delirium bordering on unconsciousness I am still alive, moving, and getting better, if only incrementally. Something has changed, something has shattered or perhaps gotten fixed, and I feel, for the first time in years, that I am free to choose what to do with my life. Whatever circumstances have pushed me this way or that have run their course and, in the absence of anything strong enough to propel me forward, I have entered a sphere of intense calm where the thought of tomorrow evaporates as soon as it appears. I've lost my ability to plan or project myself into the future. I've lost my faith in mathematics. The other day my landlord asked me to give him two hundred rupees for rent and I handed him twenty, thinking that it was enough. For a moment I even considered throwing my money belt away—it's just a drag always carrying it around, clinging to its imaginary treasures. I could do without a passport or money. I couldn't possibly have gotten thinner than I already was. When I came down with malaria at the beginning of December, I thought of calling my parents and telling them that I wasn't going to make it. I was in the court-yard in front of the doctor's office—a cow-dung-splattered courtyard and a mud-plastered office—watching as the doctor's assistant, a young Bihari man with the movements of a skilled car mechanic, stuck the long needle of his syringe into the naked butts of one- and two-year-old babies. There was a huge line of young mothers with screaming toddlers and just one syringe and needle. Before each injection, the doctor-mechanic filled the syringe with water to rinse it off. *Good thing I only have malaria,* I thought, imagining what the babies were getting. There was a Western woman sitting beside me. She'd practically carried me from the dormitory where I'd been staying into the rickshaw, and from the rickshaw into the courtyard, but I was too sick to ask her for her name or even say thank you. I hadn't eaten anything for a week, and even though it was over a hundred and ten degrees, I felt extremely cold, as if I'd been trapped in a glacier. A cow and a family of black pigs had decided to share a plastic bag. The pigs oinked and the cow wagged its tail, swatting flies. Above the brick fence I could see the pyramid-like top of the main temple in Bodhgaya, the spot where the Buddha had attained Enlight-enment. *I'm not going to call my parents,* I thought. *There is no point.* Then it suddenly occurred to me that the connection between children and their par-ents, between people and their countries, between believers and their gods, between humans and their home planet, between me and my body, between the I that perceives and the I that is perceived, is completely illusory, mind-made. All this worry—drawing up boundaries, weaving imaginary strings—when in reality things are neither in harmony nor in conflict, this doesn't belong to that, one plus one doesn't make two, the beginning tastes like the end, and dying, really, is just fine. Dying changes nothing. I must've said something along these lines because I remember that the woman who'd brought me to the doctor had tried to console me—which was kind of absurd because I was laughing.

And now things are different and I have a hard time figuring out what it means to be a monk, a layman, an untouchable. How am I connected to these robes? And how are these robes connected to the guy who spent seven years sitting in a well across the river? How are people tied to their identities? Tsar has been gone for a year and I've learned only two things about him: that he'd made it to Nepal (he'd sent a postcard to Ramesh, the chai shop owner) and that Beatrix, his last girlfriend, had gotten pregnant from him and had decided to have the child. How strange that I would know this, and he wouldn't. After Tsar left, Vinnie and I became very close. We played chess every day, and on the weekends we hiked to Triund and watched the vultures hop around us. He told me that he had a son from his failed marriage who lived in New York and worked as a stockbroker, or something of that sort—Vinnie didn't know very much about him. I asked him why he didn't travel to the U.S. and try to find him, and Vinnie replied that it was up to his son to decide whether he wanted to know his father or not. Then it dawned on me that throughout all these years that he'd spent in the Himalayas—stooped over a chessboard, reading crime novels on the roofs of restaurants, roaming the streets for hours on end, sitting by the bus stand and scanning the faces of the newcomers—Vinnie had been waiting for his son to come and find him; he'd been waiting for someone to take an interest in him and understand how far he'd traveled—not geographically, of course, but spiritually. Vinnie was a man of many mysteries, he was a well-kept secret, and, sooner or later, someone was going to discover who he really was: one of the last great German philosophers; a Chinese scholar; a man without an identity; an eccentric whose single pair of socks covered only his ankle and a part of his heel, whose fits of anger stopped buses and tripped rickshaws, and who was too lazy to go to the bathroom and peed in the empty bottles of *raksi* lying around his room; a comedian who told incomprehensible German jokes about Freud and Jung; a singer who danced and sang World War II German cabaret songs despite the fact that he was missing his voicebox; and finally a playwright whose most famous works included *The Trans-Siberian Express*, *Walking Backwards Across the Border*, *Paragliding into Pakistan*, and *The Hong Kong Affair*.

When I told Vinnie that I'd decided to spend the winter in Bodhgaya and then head south to Karnataka to study at Drepung, one of the biggest Tibetan monasteries in India, he got visibly upset, and in an attempt to hide his anger, told the other people sitting at our table that I was his only son and now I was leaving him to die alone of old age in the Himalayas. Everyone laughed because Vinnie's acting was always overly dramatic and absurd, and I didn't think of what he'd meant to say until weeks later, when I was lying in a bed I didn't recognize, covered in cold sweat, and slipping in and out of consciousness. I remembered that he'd pleaded with me not to go, and that he'd told me that I was too young to understand that one gets to make only two or three good friends over the course of a lifetime; I remembered him lying on the highest hill above Dharamsala and saying, "Turn the light off now, I'm ready to die." Why didn't I notice how much I meant to him, in his lonely existence? That I was his lost son from New York, a son who knew who he was and what he believed in? Weren't we all running away from something, trying to replace the missing pieces with new people and new circumstances?

Erick—Dharamsala's number-one chess player—is here, in Bodhgaya. We meet every day and, well, play chess. We talk about Tsar, too, and the good old days when Dharamsala wasn't overrun by junkies and backpackers, and Hans, the German Buddhist monk, would walk up and down the street telling people that he had a black belt in karate and that he'd acquired special Tantric powers that allowed him to control the weather. Erick and I play for five or six hours at a time and often, when I take my eyes off the board and look at him, I see the shadow of a painful memory passing over his face. I know that he's hiding something but it'll probably take me years to find out exactly what it is. You can't get to know someone overnight.

Geshe Yama Tseten is also here. I ran into him the first day I went for a walk after lying in bed for two weeks. When I told him that I'd nearly died of malaria, or whatever it was that had struck me down, he seemed disappointed. "I wish you'd actually died," he replied, scrunching his face. "At least you would've died in a good place and in your monk robes. Now you're going to go back to the West and die like a fool."

That was Geshe Yama Tseten at his best: kind, understanding, full of encouragement.

It's beginning to get dark and the place where I'm staying is all the way on the other side of town. I pay for my chai, despite the fact that it came with drowned mosquitoes floating on the surface, and start walking unsteadily toward the turnaround by the Main Temple where the bicycle rickshaws usually line up. The first steps are the hardest; then it gets easier. Even though the air is dry, there's a haze that turns the gas lamps and the streetlights into enormous vibrating halos. The rickshaws and bicycles zooming past me make no sound, they bend and melt into the halos like dream images, and all the dust in the air makes me cough, I spit, again and again, and the dust has a pungent smell and for some reason I'm certain that it tastes red. Now I hear voices and someone laughs. Two silhouettes emerge from the haze, and as I look closer, I see Drago and Reena, a Croatian man and his Indian wife whom I've known for a long time. At first they don't recognize me, but when they do, they hug me and start talking and asking me questions simultaneously. I respond in one line: yes, no, Drepung, three weeks ago. They're wonderful people and I'm excited to see them. Drago knows Sanskrit and Tibetan; Reena is a painter.

"You wouldn't believe it!" Drago cries, grabbing my hand. "When Reena and I were in Croatia this fall, I went on TV to talk about Tibetan medicine, and later that night the phone rang and it was Tsar! He'd seen my interview and had called the TV station to get my number. I asked him what he was doing and he said that he was peeling potatoes in some dingy restaurant."

"Peeling potatoes!" I repeat, puzzled. For some reason the words sound really absurd and I fail to grasp their meaning. I imagine Tsar digging for water on Mars. I imagine him operating the Eiffel Tower elevator. I imagine him playing accordion on the streets of Berlin.

"Do you get it?" Drago asks, laughing harder and harder. "Every time Reena and I came to your house on Jogibara Road, Tsar was in the kitchen peeling potatoes. Every time! And now, when he finally made it back to the Balkans, he's doing the same thing!"

Drago and Reena invite me to their room for dinner and I follow them through the empty streets, staring at the halos and listening to the buzz of the crickets grow louder and louder. The room where Drago and Reena are staying is in a one-story compound with a small courtyard in the center. Drago leaves the door ajar and as I sit at the edge of his bed, I watch a night gardener water the flowers in the yard with a hose. We are on the outskirts of town and the cricket noise is so overwhelming, it seems as if it's coming from inside my head. I remember the day I decided to take a walk through the fields and the ground underneath me came alive and thousands of crickets shot straight up, like shrapnel, and then poured on top of me, getting on my neck and under my robes. It was cricket rain.

Drago tells me that he and Reena are looking into buying land in Bodhgaya and asks me to go with them to the courthouse in Patna the next day. I tell them I'll come. Why not?

"Look at this," Drago says, handing me a pamphlet from some local association of Indian Buddhist scholars. The pamphlet is written in nearly indecipherable English, with an abundance of interjections in Sanskrit and Hindi. Drago points at the very bottom of the page and giggles. "Can you believe this?" he asks. "There's not a single Buddhist text that says that the

Buddha was born, got married, had kids, took to the forest, found Enlightenment, taught emptiness, and died simultaneously. Simultaneously! That's
absolutely impossible. It must be a mistake."

"It must be," I say, but I don't really mean it, and when I try to think
about Tsar peeling potatoes and Vinnie sitting in the Last Cow Chai Shop in
Dharamsala, it occurs to me that I remember what is going to happen. I
remember that I will go down south to Drepung Monastery, I will take classes
and attend the debate sessions, and when I'm finally fed up with being constantly surrounded by monks—five thousand chattering males in uniforms—
I will throw away my robes and flee to the West, just as Geshe Yama Tseten
had predicted, and I will do other things, like have kids and play chess and
drink coffee instead of tea, and Tsar will do the same, and one day we'll find
ourselves back in Dharamsala, or someplace that looks exactly like Dharamsala, and Vinnie will be waiting for us, because he would've known that we
can never leave India, no one can just leave India, and Vinnie will be missing
his teeth, Tsar his liver—from drinking—and I a few marbles, and we'll get
stuck again, and we'll have the faint feeling that everything has already happened but we won't be able to know when and to whom, and I will remember
some things and Tsar will remember others, and Vinnie will make us take part
in a play about escaping India and we'll all recite our lines from memory, and
Tsar will remember the cartoon about the coyote and the Road Runner and
exclaim, "*Yebem li ti pichku materinu,*"—*why is it that I always end up in the same
situation with the same people*—and I will remind him that this is India—
things happen again and again for absolutely no reason—and the clay statues
of Shiva, Wife, and Son sitting at the end of the slate-tiled courtyard will nod
in agreement, and then there will be a loud bang, like an explosion, the mud
walls will start vibrating, and we'll realize that it's five o'clock in the morning,
the tofu-making apparatus is on, and we still haven't gone to sleep. We've
been awake for a thousand years.

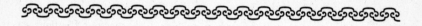

Afterword

I spent my first month as an ex-monk camping at Heracles, a wild, unregulated beach south of Varna, where the Balkan Mountains dissolve into the Black Sea. The conditions were primeval—no toilet, shower, telephone, or convenience store within ten miles—but I still felt extremely privileged. After all those years in India, this seemed to me like a five-star resort. In the morning I swam in the sea and in the afternoon I walked to the nearest road juncture to buy grapes, feta cheese, and bread from the local farmers, who would arrive in ancient Soviet-made vehicles and lie under a propped-up white sheet, smoking and eating sunflower seeds. The farmers, perhaps fed up with my insatiable curiosity, told me that Heracles had once been the place where a famous Greek philosopher had settled after he'd been driven into exile. When I asked them which Greek philosopher that would've been, they weren't sure. One said Heraclitus, another Herodotus. I didn't believe them at all. I desperately wanted to talk to Tsar. Where was he now?

From the entrance of my tent, which I had built at the edge of the forest, I watched the other campers—about a dozen high school and college students—roll in the sand and play volleyball completely naked. Contrary to all the manic assertions of the monastic scholars, women's and men's bodies were beautiful. And clean. I was amazed at how unaware and unashamed they all were of their nakedness. They didn't pretend not to notice each other's sexual attributes; they just didn't care.

I was naked, too, even though I kept my boxer shorts on for the better part of the day. I was naked because my monastic robes were locked up in a metal trunk under Samten's bed, twenty-seven hundred miles away from Heracles.

Taking monastic vows had turned out to be much easier than renouncing them. Freedom is a relative phenomenon: as a monk I felt free of the burdens of the mundane world—work, career, relationships, elaborate plans for the future. Now I felt free of the burden of keeping vows and acting as a noble representative of an organized religion. Still, I missed my robes. It is so easy for us to find something to hide behind. The Buddhist monastic vows are made of an incredibly thick material. They would protect you from many things; they're especially superb in protecting you from knowing yourself.

I disrobed in Dharamsala, a day after I returned from Drepung Monastery in South India, where I had lived and studied for some time. If my past as a musician, my inborn aversion toward authoritarian structures, and the vacuum created by Tsar's departure weren't enough to persuade me to change the course of my life, living in Drepung Monastery—amidst five thousand testosterone-swollen virgins with identical uniforms and haircuts—did it. *This isn't right*, I told myself as I walked every morning to the debating ground. Whose idea was it to divide the binary world—of highs and lows, of East and West, of pleasure and pain, of men and women—and manufacture a group of broken people who were somehow supposed to understand the totality of Existence? It should have been obvious from the start that, left to their own devices, without any supervision by women, men would do the only thing they were really good at—create another army. And I didn't want to be in an army—not in a military one, not in a religious one, either. I didn't want to wear uniforms and answer to honorary titles. I didn't want to parade my spirituality through the streets. I didn't want to be part of any institution. I wanted to search for the truth alone.

The disrobing ceremony was simple: I walked into a dark room in the Institute of Buddhist Dialectics and sat on the floor, across from a senior Tibetan monk, who was a close friend of Gedun, my Tibetan language teacher. "Do you renounce your vows?" the senior monk asked me somberly. "I do," I answered. It was noon and I could hear the monks clamoring outside the monastery kitchen. Raindrops tapped on the windowsill. I felt conflicted. If I really wanted to leave all this, why were my eyes full of tears? The senior monk gestured at me to get up. It was done.

When I walked out of the Institute of Buddhist Dialectics I was still wearing my robes, but I was no longer a monk and my name wasn't Lodro Chosang. Life seemed like a silly game. I said good-bye to Samten and Vinnie, returned to my room to change my clothes and grab my luggage, and boarded the first government bus to Pathankot. At a roadside *dhaba*, where the bus driver had stopped to have chai, I sat on a bench and lit a cigarette. It was nice to be back on the other side. I thought of Tsar and his irreverent way of parting with the robes. I was wearing his pants and sweater now.

Geshe Yama Tseten, of course, was right: Westerners are fickle. He had predicted that I would disrobe, fall in love, write silly books, and live like a fool (drinking wine, playing chess for hours on end), and I had acted accordingly. But he and I always disagreed on one very important point. He believed that there was only one way—his way. I, on the other hand, believe that in order to understand something clearly, one must first give it up.

About the Author

NIKOLAI GROZNI was born in Sofia, Bulgaria, and educated in the United States and India. In previous incarnations, he has been a piano prodigy, jazz musician, Buddhist monk, and, most recently, the author of three novels published in Bulgaria. Grozni holds an MFA from Brown University. *Turtle Feet* is his first book of nonfiction.